Breaking out again

In the early 1980s feminist social science remained highly positivist in its ideas about the research process. Consequently, the original *Breaking Out* had a signal impact on ideas about feminist research. Its authors, Liz Stanley and Sue Wise, were concerned to emphasize that most aspects of positivism were antithetical to feminist principles and practice, and also that most qualitative styles of research tended to be as positivist as more scientistic and quantitative ones.

In the first edition Liz Stanley and Sue Wise argued that academic feminists should be less concerned with the choice of method and techniques and much more concerned with the epistemological bases and claims of different styles of feminist research. In making these arguments they challenged large areas of existing feminist social theory, including ideas about socialization and the hegemony of structural approaches which denied the theoretical and political importance of everyday practice and experience.

This new edition provides an introductory discussion of the sociological, political and academic context in which *Breaking Out* was first written, and reviews its reception among feminist scholars. A new concluding section considers recent development in feminist social thought, including essentialism, deconstructionism and the epistemologies of the oppressed. In this section the authors offer a new thesis for the feminist agenda, based on their notion of fractured foundationalism.

Breaking Out Again thus provides a context to current debates concerning the feminist research process as well as its own new perspective. As a refreshing contribution to feminist social theory, it will be widely read by students in women's studies and sociology.

Liz Stanley is Senior Lecturer in Sociology at the University of Manchester, and **Sue Wise** is Lecturer in Applied Social Science at the University of Lancaster.

Also available from Routledge

Feminist praxis
Research, theory and epistemology in feminist sociology
Edited by Liz Stanley

Doing Feminist Research
Helen Roberts

Partial visions
Feminism and utopianism in the 1970s
Angelika Bammer

Getting smart
Feminist research and pedagogy with/in the postmodern
Patti Lather

Feminism and the contradictions of oppression
Caroline Ramazanoglu

Breaking out again

Feminist ontology and epistemology

Liz Stanley and Sue Wise

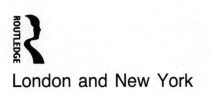

London and New York

First published as *Breaking Out* in 1983 by
Routledge & Kegan Paul plc

This second edition first published in 1993 by
Routledge
11 New Fetter Lane, London EC4P 4EE

Simultaneously published in the USA and Canada by
Routledge
29 West 35th Street, New York, NY 10001

© 1983, 1993 Liz Stanley and Sue Wise

Phototypeset in Bembo by Intype, London
Printed and bound in Great Britain by
T.J. Press (Padstow) Ltd., Padstow, Cornwall

British Library Cataloguing in Publication Data
A catalogue record for this book is available from the British Library.

Library of Congress Cataloging in Publication Data
Stanley, Liz, 1947–
Breaking out again: feminist ontology and epistemology/Liz
Stanley and Sue Wise. – 2nd rev. ed.
p.   cm.
Includes bibliographical references and index.
1. Feminism. 2. Women – Psychology. 3. Women in politics.
4. Women's studies. I. Wise, Sue, 1953– . II. Title.
HQ1154.S642   1993
305.42 – dc20   92–28809
                                                               CIP

ISBN 0–415–07270–0 (hbk)
     0–415–07271–9 (pbk)

This book is dedicated to
Dale Spender and Pippa Brewster,
midwives of the original *Breaking Out*,
and to
Gill Davies,
a central figure in establishing British feminist publishing.

Contents

Acknowledgements
Second edition

Judith Aldridge, Bogusia Temple and Lisa Adkins read an earlier draft of the introduction and afterword to this second edition. We are grateful to them for their comments and criticisms. Celia Lury's review of *Feminist Praxis* nudged us in the direction of writing about postmodernism – many thanks to her. We would also like to thank the participants in the Feminist Thought seminar in the Sociology Department at the University of Manchester – Jo Bird, Tom Cockburn, Heather Elliott, Darlene Emerson, Miriam Fitzsimons, Ruth Jamieson, Liz Jones, Merja Kapanen, Rebecca Key, Rosemary Kidd, Debbie Lowe, Laila Luumi, Brigid Moss, Karen Page, Maarit Ritvanen, Mika Saikkonen, Bogusia Temple and Verena Wilde – for their useful responses to the draft of the afterword and also to the recommended reading which surrounds it.

Furry thank yous all round to St Thomas Aquinas, Precious Mackenzie, Jessye Norman, Mrs Whisky Rochester, Alfred Schutz and Tiny Stray.

Introduction to the second edition

When this book was first published, in 1983, it joined two other Routledge women's studies[1] texts dealing with what were then called the 'methodological' aspects of feminist social science. These were the collections edited by Helen Roberts (1981), *Doing Feminist Research*, and by Gloria Bowles and Renate D. Klein (1983), *Theories of Women's Studies*. All three books were important in Britain for a number of years, providing the basic feminist references on methodological topics and issues. *Breaking Out*, then sub-titled 'Feminist Consciousness and Feminist Research', continues to be widely cited and used, in Australia, Brazil, Canada, Finland, India, New Zealand, the USA and other parts of the world, in books, journal articles and in theses, and in spite of having gone out of print in 1989.

Breaking Out was written for reasons that related closely to the organization and preoccupations of feminist social science of the time. Its origins lay in a journal article, 'Feminist consciousness, feminist research and experiences of sexism' (Stanley and Wise, 1979). This analytically used our experience of receiving hundreds of obscene telephone calls from men while our home phone was the contact number for a lesbian group through the 1970s; it did so in order to discuss the theory, counterposed and challenged by the actuality, of feminist research. It emphasized that, for academic feminists, 'research' and 'life' should be neither compartmentalized nor analytically unpacked using separate intellectual means. It also argued that the precise content of 'women's oppression' varies for different women, for it is decidedly not the same for lesbian women like us as compared with heterosexual women, and also that 'oppression' encompasses a variety of means by which women fight back, for in some times, places and circumstances women have relative power as well as in others having relatively less. In it we argued that: (1) 'feminist research' should become more sophisticated and less naively positivist than it mostly was at the time; (2) models of research are precisely that, and feminist social science needed empirically grounded investigations of the means by which research knowledge is produced, rather than its own version of 'methodological cookbooks' which prescribe rules for how to do research 'correctly'; (3) styles of sociology concerned with 'experience', with everyday life and the means by which people go about analysing and understanding it, were worth closer, more sympathetic consideration by feminist social scientists; and (4) 'women's oppressions' are complexly varied and need equally complex means of analysing and understanding them.

We were then commissioned to write a book exploring similar themes. The result was submitted in 1982 to its intended publisher, Pergamon. Organizational changes and the transfer of our manuscript to New York meant that it was read in relation to very different ideas about what 'academic feminism' should look like, for our original editor had liked the manuscript – but its new editor thought that it was far too accessible, included too many jokes and was exactly the kind of thing that gave academic feminism a bad name (all quotes from a letter the original editor received and passed on to us). A year later than planned, and after much pressure on Pergamon to regain the right to publish the manuscript elsewhere, a shortened version was published by Routledge, whose feminist books editor seemed to find less in it that was frightening and to be suppressed.

Breaking Out is, like any other book, a product of its time as well as of its authors. Its time was a beleaguered one for academic feminism in Britain.[2] Between 1979 when we were asked to write the book and 1983 when it was published, academic feminism was located mainly in the discipline of sociology, in a few tenured lecturers and a couple of professors, but particularly in an increasingly large number of research workers and graduate and undergraduate students. At this time feminist social science in Britain was characterized analytically by a number of key concerns: with producing a powerful critique of mainstream theory and research; with arguing that 'male methods', quantitative methods, were biased whereas 'female' qualitative ones were not; with reforming academic marxist theory and practice, including through debates concerned with the theoretical implications of the 'marriage' of marxism and feminism and its resultant progeny 'capitalist patriarchy'; with theorizing gender as learned through a system of roles inculcated during the processes of childhood socialization; and with carrying out 'gap-filling' substantive research on many areas of social life but particularly on domestic and paid work, class, family, motherhood, education, crime and violence.

A number of things worried us about the methodological basis of this emergent feminist research programme. Predominantly it adopted a 'scientific' stance towards women as the *objects* of its study; it ignored the power dimensions of the research relationship and of writing as perhaps the key means by which academic feminists establish authority and power over 'Women'; it drew a line between the lives of women, to be researched, and the lives of feminist researchers, which remained hidden from analytic scrutiny; it adopted either mainstream positivist methods or equally positivist interpretations of 'qualitative' approaches (erroneously treated by many British feminist social scientists as synonymous with interviewing); and it assumed the existence of a single and unitary 'Women' and ignored – or rather silenced – those who were not white, middle class, heterosexual, first world, able bodied, young (and in Britain also Londoners).

As working class by birth and in academia by the backdoor of adult education, as lesbians by luck and as northerners by choice, we both felt outsiders to the activities, preoccupations and assumptions of most other feminist social scientists. More than this, we wanted to be able to explore the grounds of such difference within academic feminism. We also thought it worthy of comment that a good deal of the energies of marxist feminists were devoted to criticising and discrediting radical feminism. And, as 'out' lesbians since the early 1970s, we also wanted to comment on the implicit heterosexism of much feminist theory and research practice, and to emphasize that important ramifications followed the interrogation of feminist knowledge from the vantage point of (one group of) the dispossessed.

However, it seemed that our sisters in social science – or at least some of those in established positions – saw this as illegitimate. Another book proposal came back with the insistent and anonymous message that not only was the draft manuscript complete rubbish but that its author would never write anything publishable. An article dealing with research issues in relation to obscene telephone calls sent to a feminist journal produced the response that one 'lesbian paper' had already been published that year. Feminist work continued utilizing undigested and determinist versions of socialization theory that were predicated on the assumption that even a feminist theory of gender learning should take heterosexuality as axiomatic. And phenomenological, ethnomethodological and interactionist approaches continued to be ignored or disparaged within feminist social science, in favour of structuralist approaches, predominantly but not exclusively marxist, which not only denied the importance of the events and occurrences of everyday life but also positioned 'theory' as the preserve of experts.

Behind these stood the state of academic publishing in Britain from 1979 to 1983 and the place of feminism within it. There was one feminist imprint, Virago (not then independent), that published academic books; another, The Women's Press, was mainly associated with fiction publishing. There were two journals, the marxist (and London) *Feminist Review*, which started publishing in 1979, and the eclectic and internationally orientated *Women's Studies International Quarterly*, which started publishing in 1978 (and changed its name to *Women's Studies International Forum (WSIF)* in 1982). A few mainstream publishers were beginning to be interested in including feminist material in their lists, although its nature was conditioned by the preferences of the readers who commented on manuscripts and proposals, who appeared to have little interest or competence in methodological topics.

To us, as emergent feminist sociologists who were openly lesbian, interested in the interactional sociologies, who saw theory as something everyone produced out of mindful social action, who treated structure as the product of interaction, and who were predominantly interested in methodological topics, the British academic feminist publishing scene appeared on a spectrum ranging from hostile to irrelevant. However, luckily for us academic feminism and the publishing predicated upon it were in the process of expanding and becoming more diverse. Paradoxically, *Breaking Out* was both a contributor to this increasing diversity and a product of it. Without the existence of *WSIF* and its then-editor, Dale Spender, neither that journal nor the concrete interest of a number of mainstream publishers in feminist academic work, in the form of feminist lists and imprints, including at Routledge, would have existed in the form they did. The progress of *Breaking Out* from a journal article to a manuscript suppressed by one feminist imprint, and finally published in another feminist list, closely follows the beneficent influence of Dale Spender in helping to diversify both British feminist publishing and British academic feminist life more generally; and we are eternally grateful to her.

Breaking Out explores feminist research and feminist consciousness, specifically around the topic of methodology and its relationship to the production of feminist knowledge about the world. In the late 1970s the term 'methodology' was used rather differently from now, in the early 1990s. At the time, for us it stood for two closely related sets of concerns: one located in the interests and ways of working known then as 'the sociology of knowledge', the other focusing upon concrete research processes and the means or methods – by which we meant the intellectual means, rather than particular techniques of data collection and analysis – through which feminist researchers make sense of what is going on and derive 'theory' from a material research process. In other words and using the terminology of the 1990s, *Breaking Out* was a book about *feminist epistemology* – a feminist theory of 'knowledge' – which discussed epistemological topics and questions around the example of one important academic feminist activity that produces knowledge-claims: research (with another being theory).

Both in the paragraph above and in what follows, we provide a particular reading of *Breaking Out*. That is, we emphasize and interpret particular arguments and ideas within it as a means of influencing the way that readers of this second edition will understand and read the book. However, present readers who have come across our earlier reading of *Breaking Out* (Stanley and Wise, 1990) will note that there are differences of emphasis between the two and in particular that the earlier one provides a more detailed guide to and thus interpretation of the book's contents. These differences are occasioned in particular by the fact that this present reading is followed immediately by the original book itself. However, their existence also points to the fact that different but equally plausible and supportable readings of the same text are always possible; and we return to the issue of 'readings' later. At this point it is also worth noting that rather than rewriting our original text to produce a 'second edition' in the more usual sense, we have decided to write around our original, first commenting on it, and then working out from it to the terms of today's feminist debates. The original for us speaks very much to the particular 'moment' in the life of British academic feminism that occasioned it, although with contemporary reverberations and echoes.

Succinctly, *Breaking Out* was written to challenge the knowledge-claims of a large slice of feminist social science of the day, including its claims for authority and special expertise. Our intentions were constructive, thinking that the problematics we raised were among the most interesting, because most challenging, intellectual and political issues there are; and that feminist sociology might become less 'scientific' as a consequence of responding to them, but also more true to feminist principles and better able to grapple with the intellectual issues involved.

One such issue concerns the nature of 'generalization' in feminist quantitative research, another concerns 'description' in feminist qualitative research. Both point up the key role of the feminist researcher in *producing*, not just reflecting, the social reality such research is apparently designed to 'uncover'. Quantitative approaches have foundationalist origins – they rest on an epistemological position which sees a single unseamed reality existing 'out there' which the special expertise of science can investigate and explain as it 'really' is, independent of observer-effects. A foundationalist position also assumes that 'research knowledge' gathered in one set of circumstances can be applied unproblematically in others which are seen as to all intents and purposes 'the same': other classrooms, or families, or workplaces, and so forth. In contrast to these interlinked assumptions, we argued that knowledge is contextually specific and that the reason much research doesn't 'work' when its findings or conclusions are applied is that its users deny its elliptical and indexical properties.[3] Qualitative approaches have their own problematics; in particular, they inscribe the assumption that the researcher first observes and investigates and then describes the setting or group of people or events being researched. In other words, they assume that researchers' descriptions are indeed precisely that, *reflections* or *representations* of a reality captured within them. In contrast, we argued that the researcher is an active presence, an agent, in research, and she constructs what is actually a viewpoint, a point of view that is both a *construction* or version and is consequently and necessarily *partial* in its understandings.

The conventional form that both quantitative and qualitative approaches take situates 'the researcher' as detached, omnipotent: an expert on a different critical plane from those they study. In other words, both approaches position the researcher in a knowledge hierarchy with – or rather *over* – those they research. There is a massive contradiction here for feminist social science, and one that was at that time – and still we think now – largely ignored or denied or argued away. On the one hand feminist social science proclaimed its egalitarian impulse, but on the other it seemingly welcomed a very traditional and élitist notion of 'us', the theorizing researching élite (feminists), and 'them,' the experiencing researched (women). We certainly recognized that there might be no alternative to academic feminism being located within some kind of knowledge hierarchy if it is to continue existing within academia; but at the very least, we thought, feminist social scientists must acknowledge the ethical and political issues involved in what we do, how we do it and the claims we make for it.

Another intellectual issue concerned how the category 'Women' was understood and used in feminist writing. We pointed out that generalizations about 'Women' gloss a multitude of different experiences of sexism and oppression, and that feminist structuralist theories were particular offenders in denying such difference in their moves to colonize all women in their self-appointed theoretical task. Neither sexuality, nor 'race' and ethnicity, nor age, nor disability, nor the relationship between first world and third world (so-called) countries were taken seriously at the level of theory or of methodology/epistemology.

Alongside this, the developmental ideas that underpinned much feminist theorizing appeared to us as not only crude and over-determined versions of learning theory, but also as positing 'the child' as innately heterosexual unless something 'goes wrong'. More than this, such theories failed to explain the existence of feminism itself as anything other than a deviance from an assumed norm. A feminist developmental theory that can explain neither feminism nor difference between groups of women (and men) except as the product of malfunctioning should be anathema to feminists, but it seemed not only to be acceptable but also as effectively *unquestionable* at this time. Certainly our remarks on feminist socialization theories occasioned some of the strongest critical reactions to *Breaking Out*.

Our alternative to these perceived problems and issues was to argue for a *feminist sociology* – not a sociology of gender, nor a sociology of women, but the remaking of the discipline in feminist terms. We saw this as encompassing a distinct epistemological position, which:

1 locates the feminist researcher on the same critical plane as those she researches;
2 sees these 'researched' as including the category 'Men' and men's behaviours, not just the category 'Women' or experiences specific to women;
3 positions feminist research as proceeding from the organizational and intellectual location of the feminist researcher, as the person who makes sense of 'the world' and produces generalized knowledge-claims on the basis of this;
4 treats 'knowledge' as situated, indexical and competing knowledgeS, as versions, as small slices of reality confronting each other in an epistemological frame that systematically adjudicates between them;
5 analyses 'structure', the structured and repetitive regularities and inequalities in social life, particularly how such structures are defined as 'facts' external to and constraining upon people;
6 recognizes that, although the statement 'women are oppressed' is true at one level, it masks not only differences between women but also the ways in which differently located women can gain and exercise power and authority, including in relation to men;
7 it thus necessitates prising apart the category 'Men' and women's experiences of different men in different times, places and circumstances;
8 it therefore recognizes the specificity of material differences between differently located groups of women and rejects using research to colonize such difference within an unchanged feminist social science: it takes seriously the resultant *epistemological* differences between women's knowledges and so changes its organization, assumptions, ways of working;
9 throughout it presents a social constructionist and non-essentialist notion of 'the self', whether female or male, homosexual or heterosexual;

10 and although traditional foundationalist views of 'reality' as single and unseamed, 'out there' and unproblematically available for experts, scientists, to discover the truth about are rejected, none the less it accepts that there *is* a social reality, one which members of society construct as having objective existence above and beyond competing constructions and interpretations of it; and it recognizes that social life is in good part composed of discussions, debates and controversies concerning precisely what this objective reality consists of.

The above points are key elements in our epistemological approach in *Breaking Out*, and later we came to call this approach 'fractured foundationalism' (Stanley and Wise, 1990, pp. 41–2). In arguing it, we felt largely alone in our intellectual concerns as academic feminists. Reactions to the publication of *Breaking Out* ambiguously confirmed such feelings. Most of the negative criticisms appeared in reviews and in discussions in published articles and books, while most of the positive reactions were expressed in letters and other more personal encounters such as at conferences and meetings; and this suggested there was a hierarchy of reactions to the book which paralleled the hierarchy that exists between 'teachers and taught'. Certainly the book spoke to the experiences of many beginning feminist researchers (as it continues to do), for these women – and a few men – are still outsiders and relatively unalienated from their own processes of knowledge-production; and this was and is very pleasing. We also felt gratified that our discussion of the analytic issues involved in unpacking grounded feminist research processes struck so many chords for these readers. However, because these positive responses weren't worked out on paper and embedded within a more complete response to the book, they didn't engage (at least in what was expressed to us) with the epistemological and methodological issues it raised. Also we felt that those more established critics who responded negatively in print seemed to be reacting less to the book itself and more to pre-defined and oppositional positions within British feminism.

The negative reactions made five broad and interrelated criticisms (which we discuss and respond to in Stanley and Wise, 1990). These were that: (1) by invoking 'experience' as the grounds for feminist social science, it was said, our approach condemned us to remain in a phenomenological morass, for 'theory' of the abstract deductivist kind we criticized was the only route out; (2) by criticizing the content of varieties of feminist theory, such as ideas about socialization, it was implied, we were anti-intellectual, modern-day Luddites smashing the intellectual machinery that would help free women; (3) by focusing on 'the feminist researcher' as the constructor of the 'reality' that research purports to describe, it was claimed, we condemned feminist research to investigating the experiences of one person or one kind of person only; (4) by arguing that feminist research was predicated on exploring feminist consciousness of particular material circumstances, it was said, our view that men could not be feminists meant we thereby made essentialist – and indeed separatist – claims about 'feminist research'; (5) and, throughout, our insistence that theory must work at the level of 'the individual' or it doesn't work at all was treated as old-fashioned individualist solipsism, a reduction of everything to an individual trapped in their own mind alone, a denial of the reality and materiality of oppression which over-emphasized the ability of the vast majority of women to wrest any vestige of power or ability to change from their situations.

Powerful criticisms indeed – except that they are unrecognizable to us in terms of the book we wrote, as distinct from what such critics have read into it. Of course it could be argued that the book was written so that these 'misreadings' derive from an unclear and badly-written text, or that, more straightforwardly, these are simply the 'different but equally plausible and supportable' readings of a text that we referred to earlier. Readers of this second edition will of course make up their own minds about this. However, there are a number of examples of such 'misreadings' that support our interpretation that these derive less from the actual text than from prior assumptions built into referencing of the book. For example, *Breaking Out* has been cited as supporting the view that a distinct feminist method exists (e.g. Abu-Lughod, 1990; Game, 1991), whereas the text of the book makes it clear we do not agree with this view, for in it we reject the simple division of methods into 'quantitative/hard/male/sexist' and 'qualitative/soft/female feminist' (pp. 17–23), and emphasize that some feminists find the use of quantitative methods perfectly acceptable (p. 22). Another misreading depicts our argument as saying that only one person, the researcher, should be the subject of research, and that this delving into 'subjectivity' means we remain concerned with 'experience', which in the critic's view is *a priori* untheorized (e.g. Hollway, 1989; Weedon, 1987). A further misreading is that the book argues that feminist research is 'by women, for women, on women' (e.g. Gelsthorpe, 1990 p. 90); however, as readers will see, we outline this (stereo)typical view in order to criticize and reject it, beginning by saying that 'there are dangers in such an approach' (p. 17). And a fourth related misreading concerns the opening paragraph of chapter 1, which begins 'Feminism demonstrates, without any possibility of doubt, that the social sciences are sexist, biased and rotten with patriarchal values' (p. 12), for some critics seem not to have read beyond this decidedly tongue in cheek remark to our deconstruction of it, and mistakenly portray this as our opinion. While we do not object to fair criticism of what we actually wrote, we certainly do object to critics who damn not our book, but a text of their own construction.

A more considerable criticism concerns the charge of 'methodological separatism'. By arguing that feminist research can only be done by feminists, and that men cannot be feminists because they can never share women's experiences of oppression, we have been seen as essentialists and relativists as well as separatists. That is, what we wrote in *Breaking Out* has been responded to as though we were positioning women/feminists as essentially different from men, and also as though the book rejected any and all truth-claims and thus the existence of 'reality' itself. But not so.

In *Breaking Out* we were in fact arguing that 'feminist experience', 'feminist research' and 'feminist analysis' are social constructions, not essential categories, as are the categories that feminism is predicated upon, 'Women' and 'Men'. Within the kind of sociology we align ourselves with, all such categories, including class and 'race'/ethnicity, are treated as constructions and not as essences. Moreover, saying that 'men can't do it' isn't of itself separatist, and the idea that the recognition of difference precludes debate and mutual learning is ridiculous. However, it seems that it is only one kind of difference, 'separatism' (which we see as a gloss for some conjunction of radical feminism/lesbian feminism), is treated so negatively, for difference concerned with 'race'/ethnicity has been welcomed wholeheartedly by the same critics (e.g. Barrett, 1988).

Moreover, 'separatism' at the level of ontology (a theory of being and of reality) is of course a defining aspect of the human condition: none of us can ever convey to other people exactly what is in our minds, nor convey exactly what our feelings consist of and *feel like*. This is not, however, to promote solipsism, because typically people bracket away this knowledge and instead act on the assumption that intersubjectivity *does* characterize everyday interaction: when someone tells us of 'a row' or 'grief at a death' or 'what X really meant', we fill these categories or glosses with our direct knowledge of these feelings and experiences. It is thus mainstream social science with its 'scientistic' (in Habermas' term) generalizing anti-indexical claims that is deeply problematic, for it fails to see, let alone explore, the most fundamental methodological issues of all: those that occur in everyday life as people negotiate intersubjectivity, invoke and use categorical understandings, achieve adequate descriptions of social life and events, competently decide between competing knowledge-claims, piece together which version represents the 'real reality', and so on. It was, and still is, precisely these methodological issues that mainstream feminist social science, as well as male-stream social science, ignores or rejects the importance of.[4]

Breaking Out was also seen by some critics as promoting a radical relativism that denied the existence of any 'real reality': an endless downward and inward spiral of versions that condemned proponents to analytical paralysis. However, we were in fact arguing something very different: that ontological relativism marches hand-in-hand with everyday foundationalist claims and practices – an everyday foundationalism which is both highly sophisticated and astoundingly successful in resolving differences between versions, between competing reality claims. As noted earlier, we came to call this epistemological position 'fractured foundationalism': our recognition of this great complexity and sophistication of everyday theorizing and the correspondingly complex relationship between ontology and epistemology that it encapsulates. Certainly *Breaking Out* rejected feminist or any other 'grand narrative' versions of social science. This is not, however, to reject all truth-claims. It is rather to insist that truth-claims, like all knowledge-claims, have indexical properties and these must be not only recognized but analytically explored and theorized.

Among other things, *Breaking Out* argued that feminist theory of the day ignored or failed to recognize the epistemological issues involved in what it did, how it did it, what claims it made for it. We consider that critical reactions to the book demonstrated this point very clearly.

The positive reactions that *Breaking Out* occasioned, as already noted, were expressed largely in personal, private responses. Overall, these reactions focused on the re-evaluation of subjectivity (when in contrast we had suggested that both objectivity and subjectivity were differently valued and gendered constructions of fairly much the same thing), and a concern with emotional vulnerability (when in contrast we had argued that the paradox of vulnerability was that often it empowered). We still look for an in-depth response to our work from critics who share a similar feminist epistemological position, and hope that with the publication of this second edition such an evaluation will be forthcoming. In addition to these kinds of positive response, our insistence on grounding feminist sociology in researching the everyday and analysing the researcher's constructions of this became incorporated within what we think of as the Barbara Cartland school of feminist thought: a variant of radical feminism largely but not solely American-based, concerned with invoking 'women's dailyness' (said in a breathless and reverential tone) but which persistently fails to subject such 'dailyness' and feminist researchers' part in constructing it to critical analytic scrutiny.

Of course readers of this second edition will make up your own minds about the matters we have discussed here through your reading of the original *Breaking Out*, which follows this new introduction. We continue to find much of interest and value in the book and still enjoy its deliberately provocative style and language, its jokes and its non-reverential attitude towards academia; and we hope that you will too. But built into your reading needs to be the awareness that some things have changed since it was written. Academic feminism is considerably larger, more open and diverse, and more confident than it was; and a scrutiny of its labour process (Eichler, 1980; Stanley, 1990b) no longer seems as way-out as it once did. Feminist publishing is big business, including academic as well as trade publishing; feminist publishers, imprints and lists publish an astonishing range of work, and long may they continue to do so. 'Methodology' has been well and truly placed on the academic feminist agenda in its new guise of 'epistemology'. The hold of feminist structuralisms has loosened; and 'difference' has become the new watchword of feminist theory. And it is certainly easier to be a 'different' kind of feminist and have this taken seriously.

So much has changed, and so much of it for the better. But

there are still questions to be asked of the new developments in academic feminism in general and in feminist sociology in particular – awkward questions on topics and issues many of us would rather were left alone. Many of these new questions are epistemologically grounded and consequential; and we discuss them in the afterword to this second edition. In the afterword we develop the concerns dealt with in the original *Breaking Out*, looking at the activities of academic feminism as a particular kind of 'epistemic community' which constructs its own distinctive theory of knowledge or 'epistemology', lays claims to 'epistemological privilege' for its members, marks out a 'feminist ethic' to guide the research practices and everyday relationships of these members, and disputes interpretations and usages of its fundamental defining terms such as the category of 'Women' and its conceptualization of the relationship between body, mind and emotions. This epistemic community, we argue, should become concerned with constructing a more fundamental feminist challenge to foundationalist and Cartesian[5] epistemology, in particular through insisting upon the necessarily ontological basis of all epistemological positions.

NOTES

1 The term 'women's studies' collects into it an actually highly divergent set of interventions into academic life. Our particular variant is one in which we prefer to call ourselves feminist sociologists. We use this term to indicate that our allegiances (rather different for each of us) to the discipline of sociology have been and remain both strong and constant, but also and particularly because we see the task in hand as one of remaking sociology in its entirety: a bottom to top total revolutionary change.

2 Our discussion focuses throughout on the situation of feminist social science in Britain, and does so for two interlinked reasons. The first is because of the epistemological arguments we develop concerning the contextual specificity of knowledge, its indexical relationship to particular and grounded epistemic communities. The second relates to our objection to the *de facto* colonizing approach of American academic feminism (although we are aware that many American academic feminists scrupulously reject such colonizing activities, too many engage unthinkingly in its practices). Of course the account we provide here and in the afterword may well apply to other academic feminist communities; but this is a matter for investigation rather than assertion or assumption.

3 By 'elliptical' we mean that in interaction people assume a common

and shared stock of knowledge, which does not therefore need to be explained, as, for example, if we had not explained our use of this word: and by 'indexical' we mean that the meaning of language (and thus knowledge itself) is tied to the occasion of its use – it is specific and contextual, as is, for example, the particular use of the word 'epistemology' within recent feminist writings as compared with a philosophy mainstream usage.

4 It is these issues that constitute the defining concerns of the phenomenological and interactional sociologies. These approaches cannot be reduced to the work of particular theorists, but rather represent a number of overlapping kinds of approach. For space reasons, we obviously cannot provide the grounds of a feminist phenomenology here.

5 We discuss the feminist critique of Cartesian ideas in detail in the afterword, which follows the original text of *Breaking Out*. The term derives from the seminal – we use the word advisedly – writing of the philosopher Descartes, who, in particular in his *Meditations*, outlines a mathematically based way of taming rampant (and female) nature by the use of rational (and masculine) scientific methods.

Introduction to the first edition

ONE SUNDAY AFTERNOON . . .

A: What we ought to do is to write down something about how we felt when we decided to write the book.

B: Well, why did we decide to write it?

A: Because I was fed up with being told I wasn't a proper feminist.

B: Yes, and we were both pissed off because we'd been bound up in feminist politics as they affected gay people for a long time, but we'd grown completely alienated from that because we'd come to realize that feminist politics for gay people didn't actually mean anything.

A: Well, feminist politics for gay *men* means absolutely nothing beyond a few liberal words. It involves absolutely nothing that involves them changing their lives or not doing things that they want to. Feminism for them is something to have nice chats about but not something that you *do* . . .

B: . . . that affects your life.

A: And as far as I'm concerned that's something I feel about many feminists too. Feminism is something in your head and then . . .

B: Yeah, well, there's two things going on there. One is the traditional split between political beliefs and how they actually affect your life. And the other is the cop-out. The cop-out of holding political beliefs in such a way that you can wholeheartedly believe it's terribly wrong to live in certain ways and do certain things. But you also hold on to the idea that it's also all right to carry on doing them until the revolution comes, because 'the revolution' doesn't bear any relation to the way that you live your life.

A: Yeah, it's the split between structures and everyday life. Structures are somewhere above and beyond the everyday, and the revolution . . .

B: . . . structures are where it's at. Structures are where the revolution will happen and so there's no point in actually changing.

A: No point in changing your relationship with your husband, or your children, or your anyone else.

B: But there were some other considerations as well, weren't there? Like the feeling we both had that there wasn't any feminism left anymore. That it was all marxism and no feminism. That research was being done in a simple positivist way which was looking for 'the truth'. And this would be, I don't know, presumably enforced in some way on women who didn't recognize it as truth. Or women who didn't recognize it as truth would be labelled as having false consciousness or something like that. And we both objected to that. . . .

A: To all of it . . .

B: But also to the whole idea of doing research and thinking you can find *truth* out of it. Being able to find *the* way.

A: There are two things there which kind of overlap but which aren't synonymous, aren't there? One of them is the thing about marxism. That everytime you read something produced out of the women's movement here it's implicitly marxist in what it says about the reasons for women's oppression and what's going to achieve women's liberation. And then there's the other thing which sort of overlaps, the whole positivist thing where you have these ludicrous pieces of research where the researcher finds out the truth about other people's lives for them.

B: Why do I feel that marxist-feminists are *marxists* who simply want to add women into their theories? One of the reasons I want to write this book is as a rejection of that, in a sense.

A: Well, I'd agree with that, but I'd want to make it more sweeping than that. I'd want to say that I object to more or less everybody! I mean, I particularly object to marxist-feminists because they're often particularly objectionable, because they think they've found the truth and they particularly want you to accept this. And so you spend all your time arguing in *their* terms. But I think that's just an extreme version of something more general. Most feminists, or rather most feminist academics, seem to want to add women into what's already there – add women into courses or set up courses on 'women'. Add women into this theory, add women into that theory. . . .

B: That should be the first sentence of our first chapter: 'feminist academics want to "add women in" . . .'

A: What they seem to want is to take away the sort of ripple of discontent on the surface of academic life called 'women' and incorporate this. And then having done this everything will be all right. We can say 'psychology is *really* a science, anthropology is a *truly* scientific discipline these days.' What no one seems to want anymore is to do something which disturbs the whole thing. . . . If you take women seriously, if you make women's experience the central feature of what you're doing, then you just *can't* leave the rest undisturbed. And once you start saying this about women you have to start saying the same thing about children, about black people, about prostitutes. . . . And you don't get left with anything 'cos you have to start saying the same thing about *men*, ordinary naff heterosexual men. I'm quite prepared to believe there are a lot of women who think like that, but precious few . . . you don't see any written signs of it.

B: Something else that's really quite removed from this but . . . is this idea that . . . whenever I meet feminists that I've never met before, they always ask me 'what are you involved in? what are you *doing*?' And I find myself making excuses and saying 'well, I'm not doing very much at the moment, but for years I've been involved in lesbian groups – I've been involved in this and that and the other.' And I always do that. Whenever they ask I find myself making excuses. But then afterwards I think, well, if I'm not really involved in any 'feminist activity' (because they seem to be saying that you've got to be involved in some campaign or group or something), I think to myself, well, if I'm not involved in feminist activity then how come almost every day of my life I feel *knackered* by the fact that I've been *doing* feminism all day long? Do you know what I mean?

A: Mmmm.

B: That because I'm a feminist it doesn't matter whether I'm involved in a campaign or a group or in writing something or in anything else. Whatever situation I go into, wherever it is, wherever I go and whatever I do involves feminism – because that's *me*. Because that's a part of my everyday interaction with people that I meet each and every day.

A: But most people don't seem to think like that at all. Most people seem to have lives that are chopped up into lots of bits. So that you can say, well, you do feminism in that bit of your life and then, well, this bit of it is when you knock off from feminist work, when you go home or whatever.

B: Yes, I've never been able to understand . . .

A: Well, neither have I. But the thing that totally infuriates me is that I have conversations with people and they say all of this stuff, and you find yourself answering in their terms. Then you go away and think 'shit, it's happened again.' *Again* you find yourself apologizing and explaining, not just that you're not 'involved' but the fact that you *don't think like them*. I mean, when you were saying that I could hear myself apologizing for daring to be interested in the things that I am. I mean, saying 'do you want me to explain why I am?' and them saying yes, and then I *do*. You know, *apologizing* and *explaining* and saying, well, it really is feminism, please accept that it's feminism . . .

A: It's them trying to get you to see that you're wrong or misguided . . .

B: . . . that you're wrong and they're right . . .

A: . . . that you're suffering from some kind of false consciousness . . .

B: . . . and the thing that's really upsetting is that you *join in*. There's no way that you can win or even . . .

A: But you can't win with anybody who works within a sort of framework that's a closed system whereby anything that you do is interpreted in their language, in their theorizing about the world.

B: The other thing I was thinking was this peculiar kind of theorizing that feminists seem to have got into now as much as everyone else. Like taking seriously what they think but not taking seriously what other people think. . . . Like their estimation of their oppression is true and valid, but if someone else's consideration of her situation isn't the same then it's not true and valid because she isn't seeing truly and objectively. And that's another reason I wanted to write this book. I wanted to say something about how feminist academics seem to see a difference between themselves and other women. They seem to be saying 'I can see and conceptualize the truth about things but those poor falsely conscious morons can't.' You'd think all these years of men saying that women can't really understand what's going on

in the world would have had some kind of impact on this idea of false consciousness *and* on how feminists do theory and research.
B: I can only think of a couple of things written by feminist social scientists that actually challenge that way of doing research.
A: You'd think there'd be more wouldn't you. . . . One interesting thing which has been written about a bit, I mean interesting if you're a feminist but commonplace if you're an ethnomethodologist, is that you understand what's going on by virtue of how *you* understand what's going on, and that we should be much more concerned with using that to look at how women construct their lives as, say, housewives who aren't uptight and who aren't oppressed. And take how and why they do seriously. Because the alternative is, basically, to say that they're wrong. . . . Now have we talked about what we were going to talk about?
B: Yes, well, I think we have, but I think we've yet to resolve whether . . . I mean, I think the influence and domination of marxism within feminism has played an important part in my wanting to write this book, and I don't think we've reached a consensus about what emphasis we're going to place on that. Not to anything specific to marxism but to, you know, the way some women use it to produce the one allowable version of truth, which they want to impose on the rest of us.
A: Well, the reason we don't have a consensus is because I don't have any objections to marxism as such. I mean, I'm quite prepared for it to carry on doing what it does so long as it keeps in its place. And its place is *not* to be seen as synonymous with feminism. If there were lots of strong alternatives then I wouldn't care. I just don't see marxism as any more objectionable than positivism. In fact I see most feminist versions of it as a kind of arch-positivism.
B: That's what I think about it too. It isn't anything marxism says, it's in a sense that it symbolizes all of the other bad things about feminist research that's being done.
A: So don't you think we ought to point out our objections to grand theory and to positivism, and in fact to anything which doesn't take seriously what people do in their everyday lives. . . . Don't you think that might be better? Because I'm frightened of it becoming a reaction *against* rather than saying something *positive*. . . .
B: But not *positivistic*!

. . . AND ITS CONSEQUENCES

The invocation of 'we' in many non-fiction books is a device to divorce the writer from the written. The royal 'we' looks less blatant on the page, less like a declaration of personal belief than the naked 'I'. In this book 'we' is used rather differently. 'We' are two people. We use 'we' to signify that what we write absolutely is personal belief. For us 'feminist consciousness', feminism itself, is deeply and irrevocably connected to a re-evaluation of 'the personal', and a consequent refusal to see it as inferior to, or even very different from, 'science'.

But, having said this, it also needs to be emphasized that although there is little or nothing in this book with which either of us (at the time of writing it) disagrees, it also represents some kind of a compromise. Written by either of us individually it would have looked (very? a little?) different. Because of this we felt it would be interesting, and perhaps useful, to use the transcript of a taped conversation we had one rather drunken Sunday afternoon when we were just starting to write 'the book' as the introduction to this introduction. This is what you've just read. This transcript is the only place we appear as separate, and disagreeing, individuals. The transcript you have just read is edited. We decided not to identify which of us said what, so that the rest of the book isn't seen in terms of 'bits' which each of us 'really' produced. It wasn't written like that, and we'd rather it wasn't read like that either. We decided to edit the tape because our purpose in using it is to communicate content and not to provide uncontaminated material for conversational analysts. And now, in the rest of this introduction, we'd like to present some rather disparate thoughts about authorship, and authorship of this book in particular, some of which deal with matters touched on in the transcript.

Books are neat. They have corners, beginnings and ends, first pages and last pages. Because of this the book form itself influences the content, as does the felt-need to write in such a way that what is written is fairly easily read. To write 'the book' as its contents occurred, with all the changes, transitions, revisions and sudden flights of thought that simply putting pen to paper occasioned, might in one sense be interesting. After all, poetic notebooks are objects of interest and study as much as finished, polished, poetic gems themselves. The creative process there is recognized and treated as such. But written science, it would seem, must be seen as simply the direct communication of 'facts', and not as the product of the *act* of writing as much as anything else.

However, our feelings about this are ambiguous, for we also feel that deliberately to construct such a thing as the finished product itself is to place barriers between writers and readers, and to create books as mysteries, as puzzles. We see existing 'difficult' or 'complex' (more often than not read 'badly written') social-science texts as examples which feminists really shouldn't try to emulate. We don't want the act of reading to be an intellectual assault course which only the especially athletic can get through. Too often this has been one of the ways in which women, as non-initiates, have been excluded from what passes for 'knowledge'. We believe that feminists ought now to resist doing the same thing because feminist writings and, particularly, feminist theory and research shouldn't be only for the deserving few. With this in mind we have tried to make this book accessible to non-social scientists, non-sociologists and non-academics, and easily read by everyone. Of course we haven't altogether succeeded, and for this we are regretful.

Much of what we have written insists that feminism, for us, means accepting the essential validity of other people's experiences. Feminists, we say, shouldn't tell other women what to be, how to be, how to behave. But all this in a book which is about what we see as a better, the best, way to construct feminism within life and research. Horror of horrors, is this a contradiction you see before you? Well, we believe it is – and it isn't! It is in an obvious sense. Less obviously, perhaps, we believe that accepting the validity of other people's beliefs, feelings and behaviours doesn't mean that we either have to share them or see them as preferential – just different. The idea that there are many feminisms is welcome to us because it suggests that feminism is alive and well, and not a closed system of belief in which deviation means excommunication. We certainly don't intend to agree with all other feminists, or expect you to agree with us.

But sometimes we feel that contemporary feminism, in its academic guise particularly, is becoming closed, fixed, is developing rigid orthodoxies. And this feeling perhaps more than anything else provided an impetus for writing this book (in so far as we are willing to accept any causal origins for it). As the transcript makes apparent, for one of us marxism-feminism, for the other positivist and structural approaches more generally, has become or is becoming the prevailing orthodoxy within contemporary British feminism. This may be, in the particular form it appears here, a peculiarly British phenomenon. But, even if it is (which we doubt), we still believe that what we write has wider relevancy. Positivism, after all, is no purely British invention.

This 'positivism' crops up many times in the course of the next couple of hundred pages. While we discuss it in more detail later, a brief caricature of it here will provide readers with a taste of what follows. 'Positivism' is a way of interpreting our (people's) experience of social life which insists that material and social 'worlds' are in all essentials the same. In the world 'facts' of various kinds exist. These facts can be discovered, uncovered, by collecting enough evidence. A road accident occurs, a child is seriously injured. What really happened, where responsibility and blame are to be located, is to be found by reference to the evidence. There is one true set of events which occurred, and this is discoverable by reference to witnesses of various kinds, including both people as 'eye witnesses' and 'material evidence' (skid marks, type of injuries and so forth) which 'technical experts' interpret for us.

All very sensible. But imagine another example. A woman goes to see her general practitioner, depressed and suicidal. And the collected evidence amassed by the doctor? no physical ills, no psychoses, no money worries, lovely house, charming husband, wonderful children. Verdict? a case of neuroticism. This 'problem without a name' was given many names by many technical experts, most of them slighting or derogatory. But, later, feminism insisted that the diagnosis should have been sexism, and the prescription should have been personal and societal change and not handfuls of pills. Feminism, in other words, disputed 'the evidence', 'the facts' and 'technical expertise', and by doing so denied the positivist insistence that only one reality exists. All of this can and should be seen quite differently, was one of feminism's messages.

Since then something interesting, and for us rather upsetting, has been happening. For many feminists 'feminism', 'the' feminist way of seeing reality (as though there were only one), is now seen as the *true* way of seeing it. These are what the facts *really* are, this is what is *really* going on, is the message now coming across, certainly within much of academic feminism. The development of feminist orthodoxy and of 'scientific feminism', and the interesting relationship that these bear to earlier feminist arguments and beliefs (such as every woman's experience is valid, the personal is the political, and we shouldn't put down other women as men have put women down) is 'what this book is about.' In essence, we are fed up with being told how we should behave and what we should think and believe as 'right-on feminists'; and we're equally fed up with being told that our kind of feminism and feminist research isn't really feminist at all.

This book is 'about' these things in the social sciences. We haven't written about the natural sciences because our involvement in these is minimal and we've tried to stick to writing about what we know first hand. We haven't written about the arts for different reasons. It will become clear to any reader who gets as far as the end of the book that we don't accept any easy distinction between 'fiction' and 'fact', between 'science' and 'literature', or between 'fantasy' and 'reality'. But we have chosen not to discuss feminist consciousness and feminist research in relation to the arts for two main reasons. By trade we are both social scientists and we wanted to address ourselves to issues of interest to and a part of this trade. And also we wanted to write a fairly short book.

One final introductory remark. In what follows we do something which seems to have become taboo, unless done in secret conversations or in anonymously commenting on work sent to journals or publishers – we criticize other feminists' work. We have already said that we believe that non-agreement among feminists and within feminism is to be welcomed. To this we'd now like to add some further comments about the basis on which we make these criticisms. Traditionally social science 'criticism' has been directed at the 'truth', the 'validity' of one person's work by others who lay claim to the 'real truth'. The critical use of other people's work in the social sciences has been largely destructive, and critics see their accounts as preferential on evidential or interpretive grounds. What we do and how we do it is, we hope, rather different from this.

Our grounds for criticism involve feeling, belief, and experientially based knowledge. In other words, if something is contradicted by our experience then we choose our experience, if something runs counter to our beliefs then we choose our beliefs, and if we feel something is wrong then we choose our feelings. We believe all criticism does this, but dishonestly, presenting it as something else. We do so as honestly as we can and as explicitly as we can: we do not dispute the truth and validity of such work for other people, merely its truth and validity *for us*. To this end we have, in the text, displayed our feelings, beliefs and experiences in a way that is not usual within the social sciences. We make certain claims about power and vulnerability as part of our general argument about what our kind of feminist theory and research is like, and in the context of this to do anything else would be hypocrisy. But, having done so, it must be said that such a process is not at all comfortable, either to write or to contemplate the publication of. Other people's responses are unknown and so rather worrying. But this is another story and, perhaps, another book.

Chapter 1

Feminism and the social sciences

Feminism demonstrates, without any possibility of doubt, that the social sciences are sexist, biased, and rotten with patriarchal values. However, feminist social science can be truly scientific in its approach. Having eradicated sexism, we can see and research the world as it truly is. Feminism encapsulates a distinctive value position, but these are truly *human* values, not just those of a 'women's perspective'. And so these values should be those of all people.

Our response to this view is 'well, perhaps'. We feel that such criticisms of the social sciences are justified – as far as they go. But we also argue that the basic assumptions about social reality which are present within sexist social science are also present within most feminist social science. These criticisms, we say, are not far-reaching enough, not radical enough, not *feminist* enough.

A necessary starting point in examining some of these ideas is what has been called the 'female critique' of the social sciences. Work produced within this critique has been pioneering in what it has said and what it has attempted to do. And because it has been pioneering in this way we, and all other feminist researchers and scholars, are deeply indebted to it. But although we see this work as a necessary starting point, we don't think it should be treated as tablets of stone brought down from the feminist mountain top. We pick out various pieces of work as 'standing for' certain ideas we want to explore within this critique. In doing so we've not attempted to examine whole bodies of work but particular themes and ideas which seem important and interesting.

KEY THEMES IN THE FEMINIST CRITIQUE

'The female critique'

The most simple and in many ways the most powerful criticism made of theory and practice within the social sciences is that, by and large, they omit or distort the experience of women. Perhaps the most fully developed of such criticisms is made in relation to sociology by Ann Oakley (1974), who argues that sociology is sexist because it is solely concerned with the activities and interests of men. The subject-areas sociology is concerned with are artificial constructs which distort human experience. One consequence of this is that women's 'social presence' within these areas of life is high although their 'sociological visibility' is low. In other words, although women are frequently massively present within whatever is studied, we but rarely appear in the end products of this. This may be because women are simply not 'seen' by researchers, are ignored by them or else our experiences are distorted by them. Oakley goes on to examine some possible explanations for sexism in sociology. She argues that there are three main explanations. The first of these lies in the origins of sociology, more specifically in the sexist interests and personalities of its 'founding *fathers*'. Second, it is a 'male profession', because a preponderance of the people within it are men; it is therefore bound to reflect their interests and views of reality. Oakley feels that the third, and the main, reason for sexism within sociology concerns the 'ideology of gender' which leads people to construe the world in sexually stereotyped ways. Such a world view not only focuses attention *on* some areas of social reality (those which concern men), it also focuses attention *away* from others (those which concern women). She hits the nail right on the head when she says that 'a way of seeing is a way of not seeing' (Oakley, 1974, p. 27).

This feminist criticism has cogently argued the point that much social science work quite simply ignores women's presence within vast areas of social reality. But also where women's presence isn't ignored it is viewed and presented in distorted and sexist ways.

In the field of criminology Carol Smart suggests that, although women have been 'a topic' in existing literature, the quality of this work leaves much to be desired (Smart, 1976). She examines the two main forms that sexism takes in it. The first kind of research is based on fundamentally inadequate perceptions of women which rely heavily on a 'determinate model' of female behaviour. This model argues not only that women are fundamentally different from men, but also that female criminality derives primarily from women's role within reproduction and from the physiological differences which it sees as underlying this. The second kind of research classifies female offenders along with juvenile delinquents and mentally abnormal offenders. These groups of people, it argues, behave criminally for quite different reasons than the 'normal criminal', and these reasons are primarily psychological or emotional.

Smart has discussed how theoretical presuppositions and assumptions lead to distortion in both theory and practice. Such an identification, although on a much broader scale, indeed formed one of the starting points for the feminist critique of the social sciences in the early 1960s. This is Betty Friedan's critique of 'functionalism', a major theoretical conceptualization of the relationship between the individual and social structure. Functionalism, both then and now, is for many people a totally accurate and morally correct description of social life. Social stability is all important, people internalize the rules and norms of their society, men work the economy and women's place is in the home rearing children, within functionalist theory.

Betty Friedan attacked functionalism as a 'moral theory' (1963), deeply sexist in its beliefs and assumptions, and primarily concerned to describe the world 'as it should be' rather than how it was or is. She points out that functionalism has accurately described the decline in importance of the housewife role, the serious strains resulting from current definitions of femininity, and the strains discernible within marriage, but sees this as entirely retrograde and 'dysfunctional'. They still advocate a strict division of roles between males and females and the confinement of women to the domestic sphere as absolutely socially necessary.

Oakley, Smart and Friedan point out that not only is women's experience often ignored, but also where it is noted it is distorted. Frequently this distortion occurs in a specific way, and this has been picked up by feminists from various disciplines. Starting out from ideas in the work of Oakley, one of the present authors has looked at sociological research articles in a content analysis of three major British sociology journals (Stanley, 1974). Substantive work reported in these journals is generally focused on men and boys, and that which focuses on women and girls or on mixed groups of people is in a small minority. An extension of sexist thinking leads to most of this research seeing absolutely no problem in generalizing from the experience of these males to 'people' in a way that never occurs with the all-female research populations.

This ready generalization from the experience of males to all people has been noted in psychology by Jane Chetwynd, who similarly bases her observations on an examination of journal articles (1975). Psychology journal articles contain fewer females than males, generalize from male experience to the whole population, and also treat women as 'non-men'. By this Chetwynd means that they take male experience as the norm and assume that female experience falls at the other end of a 'bi-polar scale' from that of males. And so females are characterized as *under*-achievers because males are typified as achievers, are described as *non*-aggressive because males are typified as aggressive, and so on.

Chetwynd argues that the biases of under-representation, and the failure to take sex as a variable into account, 'can all be corrected by simple attention to the fact' (1975, p. 5). She also argues that far more serious and difficult to change than this are stereotypic ideas about women; but these too can be challenged by constantly questioning attitudes, and by being aware that such biases can affect the entire research process. And so she maintains that 'bias' can be removed from theory and practice and that 'we must strive for the neutrality which true scientists exhibit' (1975, p. 5). Chetwynd, as well as many other feminist academics, seems to accept the idea that 'neutrality' and 'true science' can be achieved within the social sciences. Indeed some feminists seem to go further than this by seeing the inclusion of women's experience as the *means* of achieving this. We detect something of this in comments made by Michelle Rosaldo and Louisa Lamphere in relation to anthropology's current 'deficiencies' (Rosaldo and Lamphere, 1974).

The lack of interest about women and women's concerns within conventional anthropology is seen by them as leading to a 'genuine deficiency, that . . . has led to distorted theories and impoverished ethnographic accounts' (Rosaldo and Lamphere, 1974, p. vi). They argue that the concentration on male interests and concerns now necessitates a refocusing of attention on women and a consequent reappraisal of old theories.

This re-evaluation of existing theory and practice occasioned by feminist criticism is, they suggest, necessary for the development of anthropology as a 'science'. To become truly scientific requires the recognition of old biases and the examination of areas of concern previously ignored within it. In other words, they suggest that this incorporation of women's perspective will lead to the development of truly scientific work within anthropology.

The kind of feminist criticisms we have outlined so far are described by Jessie Bernard as 'the female critique' – the concern with the removal of sexist biases from, and the refinement of existing ideas and practices within, the social sciences (Bernard, 1973). She characterizes 'the female critique' as 'normal science'. By this she means that it accepts existing social science assumptions, beliefs, ways of working and ways of viewing the world, and is concerned with removing sexism from these rather than producing any more radical alternative. While Bernard is largely approving of this emphasis in feminist academic work, we find it merely the beginning of a fully developed feminist alternative. We shall discuss this more fully at the end of this chapter, but the substance of our argument concerns our rejection of 'normal science'.

Research on, by and for women

One implication of feminist criticisms of sexism within the social sciences is that future research ought to be *on* and *for* women, and should be carried out *by* women. Such research is, at least in part, 'corrective'. By this we mean it is largely descriptive and concerned with filling in gaps in our knowledge about women. That this is a major concern of feminist social science can be seen in Arlene Kaplan Daniels' review of American feminist sociological research, which demonstrates that most feminist research is focused entirely *on* women (Daniels, 1975).

Women's present marginality within 'male society' means that women know about two different 'worlds', men know about only one. Including women's 'world' in academic work would lead to the concerted reordering of established beliefs and perspectives, and also to a greater understanding of the many different stratifications which exist within society. But such a contribution, she suggests, can come about only through carrying out research on topics in which female interests have not been previously explored. And so the emphasis on feminist research which is concerned to 'fill in the gaps' by focusing on women only.

This emphasis on 'filling in the gaps' about women's interests and experiences is reflected in much of the literature about sexism in the social sciences. The epitome of such an approach can be seen in the foundation and operation of 'women's studies', in which research on and for women has become the focus for feminists and some academics (Tobias, 1978).

The rationale behind the development of women's studies is that so much has been excluded and so much misrepresented about women that, Tobias feels, the particular study of 'women' as a separate topic area is an appropriate corrective to this.

But there are dangers in such an approach. Studying women separately may lead to a 'ghetto effect', because if 'women' are separated-off in this way then feminist work may be seen as having no implication for the rest of the social sciences. We feel that an equal danger is that if such a separation occurs then the social sciences won't influence feminism. If 'academic feminism' becomes 'women's studies' then this separating-off of feminism from particular disciplines may also separate it off from ideas and debates of crucial importance to it. Feminism, we argue, should remain open to, adopt, adapt, modify and use, interesting and useful ideas from any and every source. If it becomes cut-off from research and thinking in specialist fields and particular disciplines, then academic feminism cuts off its life-blood as much as if it cut itself off from feminism itself.

We also have difficulty with the idea that feminist research must be research on women only. If 'sexism' is the name of the problem addressed by feminism then men are importantly involved, to say the least, in its practice. And so we argue that, essential though research specifically on women is, feminist research (as opposed to women's studies) must not become *confined* to this. Feminist research must be concerned with all aspects of social reality and all participants in it. It seems obvious to us that any analysis of women's oppression *must* involve research on the part played by men in this.

Although we find problems with research exclusively 'on women', we see an emphasis on research *by* women as absolutely fundamental to feminist research. We reject the idea that men can be feminists because we argue that what is essential to 'being feminist' is the possession of 'feminist consciousness'. And we see feminist consciousness as rooted in the concrete, practical and everyday experiences of being, and being treated as, *a woman*. Feminist consciousness, as we discuss it in more detail in chapter 5, is a particular kind of interpretation of the experience of being a woman as this is presently constructed in sexist society. No men know what it is to be treated as a woman; and even fewer interpret such treatment in the ways we shall define as central to 'feminist consciousness'.

Closely associated with the interpretation of feminist research as research on women and by women is the notion that it ought also to be research *for* women. The product of feminist research should be directly used by women in order to formulate policies and provisions necessary for feminist activities. Each of these three elements – on, by and for women – is included in Nancy Kleiber and Linda Light's ideas about 'interactive methodology' (Kleiber and Light, 1978). Their work is primarily concerned with formulating a new approach to research practice derived from feminist principles and understandings. In this they are particularly concerned with the part played by 'the researched' as well as 'the researcher', and with breaking down the power differentials that exist between them in the research process.

Their research was carried out on, within, and for, the Vancouver Women's Health Collective and not from the traditional research vantage point outside the group studied. What they describe as their 'interactive methodology' is, as it stands, no more and no less than a traditional battery of research techniques. However, they attempt to use these techniques and methods in a new way, so that 'the researched' become much more a part of the research process. In attempting to do this the people who were the 'objects' of the research helped to choose methods, to decide what should be focused on within the research, and were involved in the interpretation of results and the use of these in changing the operation of the Health Collective. And so Kleiber and Light suggest that this research was truly 'interactive', because the Collective was always in a state of change, to a large extent because of the on-going application of the research findings.

This approach, suggest Kleiber and Light, can be separated out into different but related issues. These concern the sharing out of power, the ownership of information by everyone rather than just the researchers, and the rejection of traditional interpretations of 'objectivity'. However, they insist that this rejection of objectivity, so-defined, doesn't mean that 'basic standards' of research aren't conformed to. The *type* of research methods used in Kleiber and Light's work are very traditional, so for us what is particularly interesting about it is the part played by 'the researched' rather than its 'methodology' as such. A consequence of this new role of the researched was that the research results became interpreted as *for* them. This research insists that the primary recipients and users of feminist research should be the people who are its *subjects* rather than the researchers.

This is one of the most interesting pieces of feminist research that we have seen. Of course 'action research' itself isn't new, although this was one of its first feminist manifestations (Duelli-Klein, 1980; Mies, 1978). But what *is* new here is the conscious and deliberate sharing of skills, the recognition that the researched have power and knowledge which the researchers need, and the acceptance of feminist principles by everyone involved. But we also feel that this research doesn't go far enough along the path it has chosen. The presence of feminist thinking has affected the 'power' aspect of information gathering, but not the *means* by which this information was gathered nor even the *kind* of information collected. Also the research report is presented by the researchers only, not by the researched as well; we see everything from the researchers' point of view. Our own feeling is that its dismantling of power differentials is more apparent than real, at best only partial. If we were 'the researched', we would find a report written by only the researchers a convincing demonstration of this.

And for us a further problem exists. If research of this kind is a model for feminist research (and surely such a concern with the power relationship in research is central to feminist thinking) then what does it say about research which isn't concerned solely with women? If, as we've previously argued, feminist research should be on *all* people, and not only women, then the use of research *for* the researched becomes a problem. We find it difficult to envisage feminist research which changes its interpretations, its ways of proceeding, because of what, for example, rapists might say. We also find it difficult to envisage feminist research which would insist that the primary recipients and users of it should be sexist men.

Sexist methodologies

We have just suggested that Kleiber and Light's 'interactive methodology', interesting though it is, fails to question how the research information is collected and what is seen as 'collectable information'. Both of these issues have been discussed by other writers concerned with similar problems.

Jessie Bernard has argued that specific processes involved within particular kinds of research methods themselves contain an open 'machismo element' (1973, p. 23). She identifies this 'machismo element' as the creation of controlled realities which can be manipulated by social scientists, who at the same time remain at a safe distance from what has happened. Bernard goes on to argue that the particular methods involved in the production of controlled realities are those which yield 'hard' or quantified data. The production of quantified data also has more prestige than the production of qualitative or 'soft' data. This isn't only because of the nature of the data produced, but also because it is primarily men who are involved with the former and women with the latter. In other words, there is a sense in which quantitative methods are identified as 'masculine', and qualitative methods as 'feminine'.

Bernard's arguments about methodology are concerned with the use of particular methods within sociology. Most other social science disciplines appear to remain almost unaware of the philosophical problems underlying the adoption of particular methodological approaches within research. Because of this our discussion of sexism within the research process necessarily relies primarily on the debate occurring within sociology.

In a similar vein to Bernard, Helen Roberts has noted and accepted the distinction between hard and soft, masculine and feminine, methods; and has attempted to go on from this to suggest what a 'non-sexist methodology' might look like (Roberts, 1978). A 'non-sexist methodology' is one which doesn't adopt sexist practices such as the assumptions that all the researched are male, and that women's experiences of the world are just like men's. It would also attempt to 'integrate a feminist theory, methodology and practice', including by avoiding unduly mystificatory language and hierarchical divisions of labour within research teams. However, her discussion of distinctions between 'male' and 'female' methods doesn't stop her from using both.

That is, she seems to be suggesting that intent, practice, rather than any particular method, is the source of sexism or its absence.

We read this as saying that goodness of heart and mind, and purity of feminist intent, is what constitutes the 'feminism' in 'feminist research', and in a sense we agree with this formulation. But while accepting that there are problems with methods yielding so-called 'hard' data, we find many of the objections and proposed solutions to these unsatisfactory. Our own objections to these as basically positivist in nature are discussed in more detail in chapter 4. In addition, we argue that there is something more to feminist research than simply intent and state of mind. To explore this means that we must go back to an exploration of the meaning, for us, of feminism and its implications for the research process; and a discussion of this is indeed the main focus of this book. But, to get back to our previous argument, it should be pointed out that some feminists find the production of quantitative, 'hard', data perfectly acceptable or even preferable. They reject the identification of particular methods with men and masculinity and the labelling of these as necessarily sexist.

One example of such an approach is Alison Kelly's discussion of 'feminist research' (1978). She argues that the research process can be divided into three stages. The first is choosing the topic and formulating the hypotheses. The second is carrying out the research and obtaining the results. And the third is interpreting these results. 'Feminism', she suggests, can legitimately enter into and influence the first and third of these stages, but *not* the second. While emphasizing that she is concerned primarily with 'traditional scientific' research, nevertheless Kelly does make points which are applied more generally. For example, she argues that separating-off 'objectivity' and 'rationality' by feminist researchers as masculine traits, and then rejecting these because of this, is dangerous. This is because these 'can be seen as the fullest development of our intellectual capabilities, and we should not lightly disown them' (Kelly, 1978, p. 229). Of course, one's reactions to this statement depend entirely on how concepts such as 'objectivity' and 'rationality' are defined; but Kelly seems to treat their meaning as unproblematic.

That *all* such concepts are problematic and resound with definitional difficulties is emphasized in David Morgan's discussion of some of the different implications of using the alternative terms 'non-sexist methodology' and 'feminist methodology' (Morgan,

1981). In particular the term 'non-sexist' methodology implies 'some absolute standard of objectivity by which sociological research could be evaluated' (Morgan, 1981, p. 86). But he argues that few sociologists would accept this idea in relation to other aspects of sociological work, therefore there seems little point in introducing it into discussion of sexism within the social sciences.

Morgan assumes that there is nothing inherently sexist in either 'hard' methods or positivism itself, although he suggests there *may* be something sexist about the use of the terms 'hard' and 'soft', and their identification with men and women respectively. Conversely, the idea that qualitative methods are inherently preferable because of their non-sexism is also rejected by him. He suggests that this approach too 'has its own brand of *machismo* with its image of the male sociologist bringing back news from the fringes of society, the lower depths, the mean streets' (Morgan, 1981, p. 87).

In contrast, Morgan himself focuses on what he calls the 'sociological mode of production' and the way in which assumptions about men and masculinity have been reflected in this, particularly in his own work. He sees sociology as a socially constructed phenomenon, with sexism playing an important part in its construction. How this occurs, he insists, isn't of interest only to feminism or to women's studies. It ought to be of crucial concern to *all* scholars within the social sciences, because it raises questions about the nature and origins of 'scholarship' itself.

RIPPING-OFF THE WOMEN'S MOVEMENT?

So far the criticisms that we have outlined have been produced as academic work, and they have been presented in an academic context, whether feminist or other. Another approach to the issue of feminist research has been presented outside the academic arena, and has indeed fundamentally questioned the right of academic women to call either themselves or their work 'truly feminist'. The work we have earlier outlined is, we believe, tentative and uncertain in its ideas, and sees itself as merely opening up a long and complex debate. In contrast to this, the two pieces of work we now go on to discuss both tend to be proscriptive, and to draw very definite conclusions about the nature and process of feminist research.

Carol Ehrlich has produced one of the most fully developed

descriptions of 'feminist research' (1976). By 'fully developed' we do not mean that it focuses on more fundamental problems and issues, nor that it produces more satisfactory 'answers' to these problems, but rather that it is proscriptive and definite in its ideas about *exactly* what constitutes feminist research, and *exactly* how feminist researchers should conduct themselves.

Ehrlich believes that feminists should be able to distinguish between 'good' and 'bad' research. In making this distinction she divides research into 'feminist research' and 'research on women'. 'Research on women' is a new rip-off which benefits academic women 'on the make'. 'Feminist research', on the other hand, benefits women, and it is identifiable because the researchers involved in it have a 'radical perspective' and produce work of a narrowly utilitarian kind.

Ehrlich rejects the idea that particular methods are in themselves exploitative or sexist. Instead she suggests that sexism and exploitation derive more from a set of attitudes that regard people as objects to be manipulated. She describes 'anti-feminist research' as that which maintains the present economic system, uses captive groups as research objects, uses sexist terminology, and values 'male attributes' above 'female attributes'. She then goes on to describe exactly what she sees as the three main kinds of feminist research: muckraking, corrective, and movement-oriented.

'Muckraking' research examines the shortcomings of insti-tutional sexism by simply publicizing them. This kind of research has a definite but limited value. Once the shortcomings have been exposed and examined then research must come to an end because it has fulfilled its purpose. 'Corrective' research, like muckraking research, is largely descriptive and is concerned with filling in gaps in our knowledge about women. The third and 'best' kind of feminist research is 'movement-oriented'. It is designed and conducted 'in the service of' the Women's Liberation Movement (WLM). And it must be designed and carried out by women who are part of that movement or by men who are supporters of it. She then goes on to describe in more detail exactly what she means by this 'best' kind of feminist research.

Investigating the structures, strategies and goals of the WLM 'is the most important kind of feminist research we can do' (Ehrlich, 1976, p. 11). This kind of research demands commit-ment, and so the people who are doing it must either 'come inside' the WLM and work for political change or else 'go away'.

In other words, Ehrlich insists that the only criteria of the 'best' feminist research is that it must be geared towards political change; and she defines this change in a very specific way. Indeed she specifies exactly what kind of research would be involved in the form of an extended list of research topics. These are seen as important because of their direct use-value to women, in setting up nurseries and improving community facilities, for example. The very clear implication is that what is not included within this narrowly utilitarian and action-oriented list of sanctioned topics isn't feminist at all but is instead a rip-off.

While agreeing that there should be much less concern with muckraking and corrective research in feminist social science, we also feel that there are very considerable problems with Ehrlich's account. It is extremely proscriptive and moralizing in nature, and she's concerned to specify exactly what is contained within, and what lies outside of, the notion of 'feminist research', while failing to discuss what she means by 'feminism'. Moreover, for her there are no problems and no confusions, and no uncertainties. Nor does she admit the existence of legitimate differences in style and approach among feminists. There is *one* feminist research, *one* kind of feminist political action, and *one* kind of feminism – hers.

We find it objectionable to be told how to be feminists in this way. The idea that there is only 'one road' to the feminist revolution, and only one type of 'truly feminist' research, is as limiting and as offensive as male-biased accounts of research that have gone before. To suggest that there are simple questions, simple answers, and simple definitions of what constitutes 'feminist research' is misleading. It is also counter to some of the most basic themes and concerns of feminism as we see them, as we attempt to show in the next chapter.

A pamphlet produced out of the Leeds Revolutionary Feminist Group similarly indicts the motives of academic feminists (1979). This paper makes a number of criticisms of academic feminism's propensity to fit itself into existing institutional structures, to use mystificatory and jargon-ridden language, and to be over-deferrent to various male guru figures. On first reading this paper we both found ourselves in agreement with much of what it said. But on later reflection we realized, to our horror, that its strictures were aimed at *us*, as well as at the academic feminists we were applying its criticisms to. *All* of us, it insists, are making careers by ripping-off the WLM. We *all* trade on women's movement ideas and creativity by turning these into sterile academic papers and books published in order to further our progress in male-defined careers.

But the idea that academic careers are to be made by women writing about feminism is extraordinary to us. Our own experience, and that of many other women, is that to be identified as a feminist is to invite overt and covert discrimination. What is safe and career-advancing for most of the men who now turn out similar work is most decidedly not so for most of the women who do. But there is perhaps a contradiction in what we feel about this. There *is* a sense in which it is perfectly possible to use feminism and feminist ideas to get oneself or one's work noticed. But we feel that this is so only in so far as people interpret it as safe, as fitting into their idea of what constitutes 'normal science'. To go beyond this is to threaten and to threaten, in our experience, is to be dismissed as hysterical man-hating cranks. We firmly predict that the response to this book, for instance, will not enhance our careers one jot. Rather, we expect it to be seen as a demonstration of our lack of academic competence.

We also have difficulty with the idea, so clearly implied in this paper, that feminism and the WLM are synonymous. Our experience of living and working as feminists lie outside the structures of the WLM, as we discuss in chapter 3. And so for us, as for many other women, feminism and the WLM remain separate, although to an extent over-lapping. The Leeds Revolutionary Feminist Group also sees certain ideas as property owned solely by the WLM. We cannot accept this. It will become quite apparent to readers of this book that we are overwhelmingly indebted to other people, primarily but not exclusively feminists (including many that we do not mention by name), for our own ideas. And many of these come out of what the authors of this paper appear to despise – published books and papers. In addition, we argue that most of our debt, and allegiance, is to *feminism* and not the WLM as such. The WLM has no monopoly of feminism nor is it the sole owner of all feminist ideas.

A further and connected objection to the arguments in this paper concerns its view of feminist research. Having insisted that all ideas are owned by the WLM, and discarded the products of academic feminism, the logical next step is to tie these two things together. It does this by identifying research as a tool, to be directly owned, controlled and used in a strictly utilitarian fashion by the WLM. Of course there is a need for such research. But we believe it isn't, and shouldn't be seen as, synonymous with 'feminist research' as such. What *we* feel constitutes 'feminist research' is very different from this utilitarian approach. What this is, of course, is the substance of this book and so we discuss it further in later chapters.

FEMINIST CRITICISMS: A BRIEF CRITIQUE

Each of the works that we have discussed are interesting, insightful and necessary. They have opened up discussions about sexism in the social sciences; indeed, some of them have been pioneering works in this respect. Whatever reservations we might have about them, it is undeniable that they have made an important impact on the social sciences (Spender, 1981). The consequences of this 'impact', we believe, have not been entirely positive. Attempts to appropriate 'women' as previously undiscovered research fodder, total dismissal of 'women's libbers', and frantic attempts to include women (usually in brackets) co-exist with, in some disciplines, an almost total failure to notice that anything out of the ordinary has been occurring. But the nature of this impact is not the focus of our discussion, concerned as we are to explain our feelings about these feminist criticisms. For us, there are important and interlinked problems with them as they stand.

These existing feminist criticisms appear to us to be partial and fragmentary in the sense that, as Bernard has suggested, they are mainly a *response* to existing social science theory and practice. And with few exceptions these criticisms are more concerned with fitting 'women' into existing theories and concepts than in critically examining, from a feminist viewpoint or indeed any other, the entire basis of the discipline with which they are concerned. By and large they seem to accept the operation of these disciplines as they stand. Their main concern is to eradicate sexism from them, and to add into them a 'proper' awareness of the interests and activities of women.

This is frequently accompanied by the argument that this inclusion of women and women's interests can lead to the various social sciences becoming 'truly scientific' and 'properly developed'. And so we find Chetwynd suggesting that 'For the sake of psychology and women we must do all we can to correct such imbalances and injustices' (1975, p. 5), and Rosaldo and Lamphere emphasizing that the development of anthropology as 'a science' requires women's inclusion. Similarly Bernard suggests that she is as anxious to see what women can do for sociology as she is to see what sociology can do for women. Even what was for us the most novel of the accounts discussed, Kleiber and Light's 'interactive methodology', still utilizes traditional research techniques and adopts a traditional concern with the 'basic standards' of research practice.

For us, these normal science approaches aren't radical at all. Mildly reforming in their effect, they focus on only the grossest problems to be found in existing work. A consequence of this partial approach is what seems to be their general lack of awareness of current debates and issues within the social sciences. These criticisms are so concerned with 'adding women in' that they have failed to notice that many other people are concerned with attacking fundamental ideas such as 'science', 'basic standards' and 'scientific development'. As many feminists clamour to jump on to the social *science* merry-go-round, they fail to notice the large number of people trying to jump off.

A very different approach to this is to question the terms of reference within which 'normal science' is conducted. The work we have discussed has mostly been concerned to ask questions *within* the frameworks of normal science; what we're interested in is questioning that very framework itself. We now take up and discuss one aspect of this more fundamental questioning which is of particular relevance to the material discussed in this chapter, and of course to the rest of this book – how academic concepts are defined, related to each other and used within normal science.

Dale Spender argues that the feminist perspective should be concerned with developing new criteria for what counts as 'knowledge', rather than knowledge about females being 'tagged on to' existing sexist knowledge (Spender, 1978). Part of this should be a rejection of conventional, and sexist, ways of construing social reality through sets of interlinked dichotomies:

few, it appears, have questioned our polarisation of reason/ emotion, objectivity/subjectivity, reality/phantasy, hard data/ soft data and examined them for links with our polarisation of male/female. Yet within the dogma of science it would seem that reason, objectivity, reality – and male – occupy high status positions (Spender, 1978, p. 4).

Spender insists that the idea that such attributes are discrete and form mutually exclusive categories is both false and unproductive. These artificial divisions are the product of a particular kind of social reality, a sexist and positivist one, and of the particular distribution of power which characterizes this.

An example of such dichotomies, and one which is frequently central to feminist critiques, is that of 'objectivity/subjectivity'. Implicit – and frequently explicit – in this dichotomy is the idea that pure states of both objectivity and subjectivity exist as dimensions of human experience. And pure objectivity is characterized as both a desirable attribute and as a male one.

But Spender argues that the category of 'objectivity' can be criticized for a number of reasons, not least because of its use in the perpetuation and justification of sexist thinking as 'objective truth'. The whole fabric of objectivity is flawed, and its continued use is bolstered by frequently obvious and simple techniques which transform 'the subjective' into 'the objective' by the use of particular forms of speech. For example, 'it is thought' for 'I think', and so on.

The emphasis on 'objectivity' derives from natural science models, concepts and concerns, but without considering whether this model, and its accompanying search for laws and calculable results, is at all appropriately adopted in thinking about social reality. Spender insists that feminist research ought to question *all* established ways of thinking, including the notion of objectivity and the wider use of dichotomous categories.

We absolutely agree with what Spender has argued, but we feel that feminist critiques seem only too anxious to play on traditional concerns with 'objectivity'. This *might* be a deliberate political manoeuvre – appealing to science in its own terms by saying that true objectivity requires the inclusion of women. But we doubt it. The emphasis is exclusively directed at improving traditional research by including women, without the total reconceptualization and reassessment which Spender has argued is a natural consequence of feminist thinking.

We have suggested that most feminist criticisms of the social sciences end up adding women in to what already exists. We call this the 'women and . . .' syndrome. Research has proliferated on 'women and work', 'women and family', women and this, women and that, and women and the other (Stanley, 1981). Some of the consequences of this kind of approach that we haven't mentioned before can be seen particularly clearly in relation to 'women's studies'. Sheila Tobias has pinpointed the essential corrective emphasis of women's studies – that it is concerned with supplementing an established sociology/anthropology/social administration/psychology/criminology etc., by focusing on what has been left out and on what has been overlooked. We feel that its gap-filling emphasis has led to women's studies becoming appropriated as an *area of study* by existing male-dominated social science. This 'area of study' approach enables 'woman' to be separated-off, and for the study of women to have none of the implications that Spender sees resulting from the *centrality* of women within the feminist perspective. Within women's studies so-defined the idea that research *on* women must also be research *by* women is no longer fundamental. Research 'on women' as a separate area of study is no longer the prerogative of feminist academics and researchers, but is increasingly done by men and other non-feminists. Dorothy Smith discusses precisely this problem of appropriation by the existing, and unchanged, social sciences and she argues, in relation to sociology:

> it is not enough to supplement an established sociology by addressing ourselves to what has been left out, overlooked, or by making sociological issues of the relevances of the world of women. That merely extends the authority of existing sociological procedures and makes of a women's sociology an addendum (Smith, 1974, p. 7).

But we feel exactly this, that most existing feminist criticisms make women's experiences into an addendum to existing social science theory and practice.

Our position is that we reject the simple identification of 'feminist research' with particular methods, and sexist research with others. We don't see it as 'women's studies', and nor do we believe that feminist research can ever be done by men. We believe this because we feel that 'feminist research' is fundamentally involved with, and derives from, the nature of feminist consciousness. Because of this it involves 'seeing reality differently' (Stanley and Wise, 1979).

Ann Oakley has described feminism as a distinct value-orientation and not the removal of commitments and values. To paraphrase here her remark about ways of seeing, we suggest that 'a way of seeing' is also 'a way of not seeing' for *feminists* as much as it is for all other people. And while we see 'feminism' as a particular way of seeing reality, we also feel that 'feminist research' can be identified as something more than this. This 'something more' is to be found in the nature of the relationship between the researcher and the researched, as well as in the researcher's own 'feminist consciousness' and her experience of being a woman.

Our discussion of problems with existing feminist criticisms of the social sciences so far has avoided what we feel to be the most fundamental problem. This is that none of them 'go back' to contemporary feminist theory as the basis for what they say. They either fail to discuss what 'feminist research' might look like or, where they do, they do so without examining what they mean by 'feminism'. All of them criticize 'sexism' as a bias, as a perspective, but they do so without formulating in any detailed and coherent fashion what its converse might look like. This is because their own understanding of feminism remains largely implicit. In our discussion of feminist research we shall attempt to make our understanding of it much more explicit, and in the chapter that follows this we shall examine in some detail what we understand by feminism and feminist theory.

We want 'feminist research' to be constructed out of 'feminism'. In order to do this it is necessary to stop merely reacting to existing social science work by using traditional ideas about how 'science' should be conducted. Instead we need to get back to a discussion of what 'feminism' is, and explore what implications this has for how we view social reality and so for how we do research. It is to this which we now turn.

Chapter 2

Feminist theory

Most of us have been brought up to think of 'theory' as something arcane, mysterious and rather forbidding. And, particularly if we are women, we will have been encouraged to think of 'theory' as special, not a part of everyday life; something produced by clever people (who just happen to be men), not by us. But what we've been brought up to think of as synonymous with 'theory' is, in fact, just one particular kind of theory. This is 'grand theory'. 'Grand theory' approaches have traditionally been used to explain the reason for women's oppression.

Most non-feminist 'scientific' explanations of the unequal status of women in society are written in terms of 'grand theory', and are particularly good examples of this approach. 'Grand theories' provide us with abstract, universal explanations, each of which suggests one single 'cause' for the inequality of all women in all places and at all times. This kind of theory is in essence a system of ideas which attempts to explain a phenomenon, based on general principles which are arrived at independently of any detailed examination of the facts or phenomenon to be explained. These kinds of theory are, therefore, essentially speculative and concerned with abstract knowledge, not knowledge grounded in practical lived experience.

Margrit Eichler discusses a number of such grand theories which have attempted to explain the origins of sexual inequality. She argues that these have two fundamental components (Eichler, 1979). First, they identify exactly what sex differences their proponents believe to exist; and second, they attempt to explain the emergence of such differences. Both are of course interlinked, because different ideas about sex differences lead to different explanations of their origin. However, both are the product of 'mind' in exactly the sense we outlined above. None of these theories is based on a detailed examination of the facts of women's experience, nor do they question the stereotyped images of women and men on which the theories are based.

On first sight most people reading such theories would be struck with their neatness, their simplicity, and their elegance. And they are undoubtedly all of these things. The only thing wrong with them is that they don't 'work'. The main point in producing such theories is that by identifying causes they provide recipes for action. However, by and large the 'causes' identified in them no longer exist, but women's oppression remains. The desired 'action' has occurred, but what should have happened as a consequence hasn't. A classic example of this, although not one discussed by Eichler, is the theory that women's inequality derives from the dependence on us of suckling infants, that this dependence prevents women from participating in hunting; and it is from this activity that men's superiority is seen to derive.

Interestingly enough, the 1960s and early 1970s saw the production of a number of powerful grand theory-type explanations of women's oppression by feminists. In a sense these were produced in competition with the non-feminist grand theories we earlier referred to. These too identified 'a cause' for this oppression, but believed that the experience of their originators *as women* made them more realistic and thus preferable. Among these are Kate Millett's *Sexual Politics*, Shulamith Firestone's *The Dialectic of Sex*, Juliet Mitchell's *Women's Estate* and the 'feminized' Engels, and a number of 'socialization theory' explanations of oppression (Millett, 1969; Firestone, 1970; Mitchell, 1971; Engels, 1972; Friedan, 1963; Greer, 1970).

These feminist explanations of women's oppression have a number of things in common. All of them are 'causal' theories, in the sense that they attempt to offer an explanation of *why* women are oppressed. Some of them are not only causal but also mono-causal – they suggest *one* factor has led to the oppression of all women. All of them see women's oppression as systematic, not as *ad hoc* and random and occurring for only particular kinds of women. And all of them see this oppression as structural: it is 'the system' which oppresses us.

They differ in a number of interesting ways too. First, they identify different causes for women's oppression. Second, the basis for this oppression is seen to lie in different kinds of social 'system'. Some see this as capitalism, some as patriarchy, and some as liberal democracy not working 'properly'.

While recognizing the enormous importance, the insightfulness and the courage of such works, we are also struck by just how *traditional* they are. Apart from their content and language, they are little different from the non-feminist theories discussed by Eichler: they adopt the same conventions about what constitutes 'knowledge'. Joan Roberts' comments on such theories is pertinently included here:

> All of these questions and assertions assume a model of linear causation. But what if the masculinist world view, which has depended on a logic of time lines, is also erroneous? What if the most fundamental error is the search for mono-causation? What if the world is really a field of interconnecting events, arranged in patterns of multiple meaning? (Roberts, 1976, p. 46).

We echo this and add to it a further two comments. What if not only the search for *mono*-causation, but even the search for *causation* itself, is based on an erroneous view of social reality? And also such a style of theorizing seems to us to be part and parcel of a 'masculinist world view'. Essentially sexist styles of thinking, of constructing the world, seem to us to be at the heart not only of these mono-causal theories but also of most feminist theorizing (and we do not exclude our own work from such strictures). What we are suggesting is that the 'masculinist world view' is so endemic, is so much advanced as the only 'scientific' way of interpreting social reality, that very few people are aware that it is a social construct and a part of sexism. However, this is to pre-empt an argument we shall discuss in more detail in later chapters and we introduce it here only as an appetizer!

What we find to be some of the most interesting and important strands within current feminist theorizing is very different from these. This work isn't concerned with the production of yet more causal explanations of women's oppression. Instead it is harder to categorize using conventional distinctions between kinds or types of theory. Some of it is concerned with working out in more detail these original causal explanations. The most obvious example of this is work carried out by various marxist and socialist feminists. Other work, however, isn't concerned with 'theory' in this way at all. Instead it is concerned either with 'theories of theory', in the form of typologies of feminism, or with simply describing particular theoretical positions. But another, and somewhat different, development is the current resurgence in radical feminist theoretical writing. We now look at these different aspects of contemporary feminist writing.

SOME CURRENT FEMINIST WRITING (OR 'HOW TO PROVE A POINT')

The proliferation of feminist writing from the mid–1970s onwards makes it impossible to treat 'feminist theory' now as a single body of work about which general statements can be made. This veritable 'explosion' has led to a body of work so diverse, and so vast, that we can neither make general statements about it nor hope to review it comprehensively. To do so would be neither desirable nor possible, we feel, and so our own interests seem as good a basis for choosing what to look at as any other. In any case, what we're trying to do is to show you, the reader, how we came to think the things that we do as we write this book. And so we use the following topics primarily as a means of demonstrating both what we think and how we came to think it.

Typologies of typologies of typologies of . . .

It is difficult to write about the enormous number of typologies of feminism which seem to have been produced over the last ten years without writing a list of these lists of types of theories. This would not only be boring to read, it would also be extremely boring to write. However, we're aware that we haven't altogether succeeded in escaping from list production. As we've said, the typologies we refer to are essentially theories of theories – they're concerned with categorizing and comparing varieties or 'types' of feminism. And so their particular concern is with emphasizing the differences between different 'types', rather than with what they all agree about because all are feminists.

It might be useful to point out, here at the beginning of this discussion of typologies, that we see them all as very similar indeed, whatever their apparent differences. For us, their similarity lies in the realization that each presents us with what is basically a spectrum: from the 'most left' to the 'most right', or from the 'most radical feminist' to the 'most politico feminist'.

The first spectrum is obviously based on conventional political distinctions. The second spectrum, we feel, is more covert in its approach but, we shall argue, it too conveniently points up for us who are the 'goodies' and who are the 'baddies', through the creation of a new, intra-feminist, set of political distinctions. We now outline, as a paradigm example of such a typology, one of the earliest of these – Shulamith Firestone's.

Shulamith Firestone's typology makes an essential distinction between 'politicos' and 'radical feminists', and the rest of her analysis is an elaboration of this (Firestone, 1971). 'Conservative feminists' are described as reformists concerned only with the more superficial aspects of sexism, such as the law and work. 'Politico feminists' are described as those women whose primary loyalty lies with the organized left rather than with the WLM. 'Radical feminists', in contrast, are categorized as women who refuse to accept left analysis. Radical feminism 'sees feminist issues not only as *women's* first priority, but as central to any larger revolutionary analysis' (Firestone, 1971, p. 684).

As we have said, within this early typology can be seen most of the features to be found within later ones. It describes each 'type' in clear-cut and definite terms. It suggests that each is separate from the others and that there is no overlapping between them. It implies that feminism 'on the ground', as it is experienced by individual feminists, is experienced in terms of these clear-cut types. And lastly, but not least, it clearly impresses on us what is to be seen as good, right-on, feminism and what is not.

Whatever the good intentions of the women who produce them, we feel that all typologies inevitably caricature. They do this because they comprehensively review feminism (what we've said we see as neither desirable nor possible) and so they over-simplify and introduce clear distinctions where these don't really exist. But Amanda Sebestyen argues that she isn't doing this (Sebestyen, 1979). She believes that it is necessary to produce such typologies in order to highlight the full range of theoretical possibilities within feminism. Doing this will show the complexities of feminism, Sebestyen feels, *not* simplify it.

Sebestyen is particularly concerned to use her typology to show the full complexities of theoretical understandings within radical feminism. She does this by using the basic 'politico' and 'radical feminist' distinction in order to outline a total of thirteen positions which can be subsumed under one or other of these distinctions.

But something which strikes us about this is that simply increasing the number of 'types' within a typology doesn't avoid the problems of simplification and caricaturing. It simply increases the number of simplified and caricatured types.

Having described the typology based on the politico/radical feminist distinction, we now turn to a brief examination of the other major form of typology. Alison Jaggar's typology is concerned with the 'philosophical' bases of various political positions within the women's movement (Jaggar, 1977). She uses 'political' here in the sense of left/right conventional political distinctions and with identifying 'types' of feminism in relation to these. A number of other typologies have been directly based on Jaggar's ideas, but all of these are so similar as to need no separate discussion. The basic point to note about them is that this kind of typology uses a 'political philosophy' framework for interpreting feminism, in an approach which lays out feminist philosophies from the 'most left' to the 'most right' along this one-dimensional spectrum.

In making some general comments about these typologies there is one obvious point that we must make. In essence, they are all concerned to lay out 'positions' from the most correct and to be identified with, to the least. But there are a number of other problems with them in addition. The definition of each of the 'types' is often arbitrary or eccentric. Women who would describe themselves as belonging to a 'type' frequently fail to recognize themselves in the descriptions provided. These descriptions fail to correspond to the actualities of life as experienced by feminists. Many women see themselves as adhering to beliefs and feelings derived from a number or none of the typologies described. Their production requires that complexities, ambiguities and contradictions are necessarily ignored. This is so whether a typology includes three 'types', thirteen or thirty. Increasing the number of types merely disguises the problem, it doesn't resolve it. Such necessarily bare and simplistic accounts present a static and fixed idea of differences and similarities within feminism. The lived experience is not only much more complex but also much more dynamic and fluid than this because, of course, people change.

We suggest that there are at least three ways of understanding these typologies. The first is to see them as they are by and large presented to us by their originators – as accurate descriptions of political realities and behaviours. The second is to see them as 'ideal types', as deliberately constructed abstractions which aren't meant to have any necessary connection with reality. This is an attractive interpretation for us, since it seems to provide a reasonable basis for their production. However, we're sure that the authors don't intend them to be 'ideal types' – indeed, rather the reverse. Each clearly implies that these *are* realistic and 'concrete', rather than abstract descriptions.

The third interpretation of such typologies, and our own feeling about them, is to understand them as deeply moral assessments based on largely conventional political concerns. We suggest that this is true, to differing degrees, of both kinds of typology. It is obviously true of the 'political philosophy' distinction, relying as it does upon conventional ideas about left and right political beliefs. But it is perhaps not so obviously true of the politico/radical feminist distinction.

This second distinction is presented to us as a reflection of real differences between feminists, because it hinges on the differences between women who align themselves with straight left groups in seeing women's oppression as one among many oppressions, and women who see women's oppression as primary. And yet, when such distinctions are examined more closely, what we see is a new left/right political spectrum, with the 'traditional left' portrayed as 'right' in its attitude to feminism. Sebestyen's chart of WLM 'tendencies' shows this clearly – traditional marxists and Althusserians nestle cheek-by-jowl with liberals, while the new 'left' within feminism has become the various 'tendencies' within 'radical feminism' as she sees it. We argue that both kinds of left/right distinction use one-dimensional forms of classification: both are concerned with pin-pointing differences; both portray political ideologies as clearly demarcated, fixed and unchanging. The most telling thing about them is that both portray what they see as right-wing as 'the other', and so as less revolutionary and less right-on. These, we feel, produce what are basically new dichotomous ways of construing reality – feminist reality here. And we have previously described this as an essentially masculinist way of interpreting it.

Theory from experience

We have said that these typologies of feminism oversimplify everyday experience. However, a number of attempts to derive 'feminist theory' from experience exist. Some of these try to construct feminist theory from descriptions of WLM policies and activities. Others do so by examining the personal beliefs and experiences of women who identify themselves as particular 'types' of feminist. We begin by examining two examples of the former approach.

For Rosalind Delmar 'feminism' is the political movement of women – women's response to their own oppression (1972). Historically feminism has been heterogeneous, and because of this different analyses and tactics co-exist. Basic to these analyses is that women's oppression includes psychological and biological aspects as well as the economic structures which contribute to it. Delmar also suggests that the operation of 'the family' is pivotal within such analyses. In addition she argues that the concept of 'sexism' is particularly important because it includes within it four distinct levels of women's oppression: the biological, the unconscious, the economic, and the ideological.

In so far as Delmar's description is purely that, a description, it covers the then existing (i.e. 1972) ways of working within the WLM and its style of analysis in a fairly unexceptional way. The women's movement *is* a political movement, composed of women, which sees itself as organizing around the basic fact of women's oppression; and this oppression *is* accepted as more than purely economic. But beyond this, whether the analysis of 'the family' is pivotal to the analysis of women's oppression for *all* feminists, and whether *all* feminists would agree that the concept of sexism necessarily includes these dimensions, are major points for discussion and argument.

A more recent description of beliefs and activities within the British WLM raises somewhat different ideas about what 'feminism' is (AWP *et al.*, 1976; AWP *et al.*, 1978). It suggests that the WLM is based on the belief that women are oppressed and discriminated against because of our sex; and this constitutes 'sexism'. It is this that the WLM is committed to change. However, it is not an organization to be 'joined'; it does not have a bureaucracy attached to it; and it is consciously non-authoritarian in its ways of working and its aims. Further, only women can be a part of the WLM and of the small groups which are its foundation. The 1976 AWP *et al.* document and its 1978 supplement describe the working aims and goals of the WLM in terms of the six (now seven) demands of the British movement, rather than in terms of any philosophy or ideology, or any analysis of 'why women are oppressed' beyond the simple description of this oppression as 'sexism'.

Personal belief and experience are also used as a basis for constructing 'feminist theory'. One example is the use of two women's descriptions of their beliefs, as a 'radical feminist' and a 'socialist feminist' respectively, in order to make general points about these positions within feminism (*Spare Rib*, 1978). It suggests that the differences between radical and socialist feminism are now less than they have been previously. Socialist feminists now accept the need for an autonomous WLM which excludes men from its ranks, while radical feminists now realize that change in people's personal life-style isn't enough and there is a need for 'larger political action'. It goes on to argue that the main remaining differences between these 'types' of feminism lie in *emphasis*, rather than anything more basic. Radical feminists, it feels, still tend to be rather more suspicious of all things 'male', while socialist feminists still tend to emphasize that women 'can't do it all alone'.

We feel that this attempt to get at the basics of these types of feminist theory has its own problems. These mainly concern whether personal statements can be used to generalize about ideological positions in this way. These statements undoubtedly describe the beliefs and feelings of the women concerned, and should be respected as such. But whether other women who identify themselves as socialist or radical feminists would accept what are described as essential to these positions may be doubted. For example, we doubt that all radical feminists accept that it is all men, as totally accountable individuals, who are the oppressors of women. And we doubt that all socialist feminists are so uncritical of 'the marxist method'. A better way to approach this problem, we believe, is simply to resist the urge to generalize in quite this way from some women's personal experience, so as to produce rigid and boxed-up categories of belief.

Brief selections from marxist-feminism

One interesting aspect of what we earlier referred to as the mid–1970s' 'explosion' in feminist writing is that ideas about 'theory' have changed. Increasingly the impression given is that only some feminists can be theorists, because 'theorizing' requires particular kinds of attributes and 'academic' training. Frequently 'feminist theorists', so-defined, are professional academics or 'professional theorists', and often they are also marxists of various kinds. Indeed, for many people marxism has come to be seen as the theory-producing part of feminism – for them 'feminist theory' and 'marxism-feminism' are synonymous (Page, 1978).

The development of this 'special relationship' of marxism-feminism to theorizing within feminism is one of the reasons why we wanted to write this book. Our ideas about 'theory' are very different from what we understand most marxist-feminists' to be. We also feel that this 'special relationship' prevents the participation of all feminists in the production of 'feminism'. And so we aren't at all concerned to describe the full range of theoretical work being carried out by marxist-feminists. Instead what we intend to do is outline particular aspects of it and suggest what we feel to be some of the main problems with these. In other words, what follows is our caricature of it.

Work carried out within marxism-feminism has included, as perhaps its main concern, an attempt to fit the idea that 'women are oppressed' into marxist theory (Barrett 1979; Barrett, 1980). In this sense, it is involved in 'fitting women in' to existing masculinist world views in the way we discussed in the last chapter. One key example of this often frantic 'fitting women in' has been the celebrated (or perhaps notorious) domestic labour debate. Whether domestic labour is productive or non-productive, in marxist terms, seems relevant only to marxists, and to rather few marxist-feminists at that. But in spite of this, inordinate amounts of time, effort, journal space and conference organization has been devoted to this issue.

Until quite recently we believed that we were simply being stupid in not being able to understand the 'feminism' within marxism-feminism. But lately we have come to feel that our 'stupidity' derives from our failure to grasp the simple fact that marxism-feminism's 'feminist theory' is *only* 'women are oppressed'; and the rest of it is traditional marxism (Thompson, 1978). One thing that has been extremely important in our failure to grasp this has been the opaque language and mystificatory approach of much marxist-feminist writing. To an extent this may be because much marxist-feminist work deals with abstractions which have no contact with reality as it is experienced; but to a much greater extent we feel that it is because marxist-feminists seem to believe that 'this is how theory is written.'

The prime example of this is the recent marxist-feminist concern with the extremely abstract and academic discussion of psychoanalytic ideas within the work of Lacan and other structuralists (Coward *et al.*, 1976). Most writing concerned with this is so jargon-ridden, mystificatory and elitist in its content and expression that it is difficult to believe that it is produced by feminists at all. A harsh appraisal perhaps, and yet one difficult to avoid making in the light of the kind of work being produced, and its elevation of male guru figures into prophet-like personalities whose every word is studied for the eternal nugget of truth and revelation it might contain.

Marxist-feminists have been primarily concerned with transforming conventional marxist grand theory through working out in detail marxism's causal explanation of women's oppression. Although a separation between theory and experience isn't sought by marxist-feminists, nevertheless we see such a separation as a consequence of their obsession with marxist grand theory. It is difficult to see how these abstract debates about psychoanalytic symbolism and the like connect with people's experiences in their everyday lives, but of course this kind of theory, by its very nature, isn't concerned with everyday experiences. What it *is* concerned with is the production of abstract ideas and concepts, and with relating these to yet more abstract ideas and concepts, not to experience.

It has been pointed out to us that a quite different strain exists within marxism, one which insists on the primacy of the relationship between theory and experience; and this now unfashionable 'dialectical marxism' is to be found in the work of men such as Sartre and Lukács. While we accept that this is so, we find it interesting and significant that few signs of this are to be seen in the work of academic marxist-feminists, except perhaps in the work of Sheila Rowbotham (1979). Most remain firmly immersed in the ramifications of grand theory.

Radical feminism revisited

The traditional and conventional grand theory definition of 'theory', as we have described, is that this is totally abstract and quite unrelated to the facts of experience. But a quite different interpretation is to be found in radical feminist ideas about the relationship between 'theory' and 'experience'. Commenting on the term 'radical feminist', Gail Chester suggests that accepting the traditional relationship between theory and practice leads us into a situation where we may also accept that there is such a thing as revolutionary theory which can be entirely separate from revolutionary practice. Consequently 'we can be led to believe that the development of theory alone is a sufficient revolutionary practice' (Chester, 1979, p. 13). She goes on to argue that the absence of radical feminist writings from feminist theory is no accident. Rather, she suggests, it is an inevitable consequence of the relationship between theory and practice within radical feminism because:

> Radical feminist theory is that theory follows from practice and is impossible to develop in the absence of practice, because our theory is that practicing our practice is our theory (Chester, 1979, p. 13).

By this she means that theory and practice, for radical feminists, are not separate things but are rather in a constant and dialectical relationship with each other. Experience leads to the refinement of theory, which itself feeds back into experience, and so on and so on.

In the previous paragraph we have used 'practice' and 'experience' interchangeably. This is because we see them as standing for 'all the things that we say, do, and feel, and have said to us or done to us, in our everyday lives.' Often 'experience' is seen as something which passively happens to us, and 'practice' as something we actively make happen. We make no such essentially sexist distinctions, and use these terms as synonymous.

Chester goes on to argue that 'theory' within radical feminism is quite different from the idea of theory we outlined earlier. For radical feminism, theory isn't abstract, unrelated to the facts of experience or the phenomenon examined. Instead the relationship between theory and practice is quite different from how it is understood in other revolutionary political beliefs. This is because radical feminists argue that 'the revolution' is occurring now, and can only occur by individual women taking positive action in changing their life-styles, experiences and relationships. It involves beginning a 'new reality' now:

It is a much more optimistic and humane vision of change than the male-defined notion of the building towards a revolution at some point in the distant future, once all the preparations have been made. . . . To bring revolutionary change within the realm of the possible is one of the most important attitudes I have learned from radical feminism – even though all the changes are unlikely to happen in my lifetime, the small advances I have contributed to will have made life better for some people, and most importantly, myself (Chester, 1979, p. 15).

The traditional notion of theory is concerned only with generalizations, and these inevitably lose the particularness of reality. Of course these aren't related to the real world, except tangentially. They *cannot* be related to it, because the real world cannot be conceptualized in its totality within *any* theoretical construction. And so such constructions always and inevitably deal with only approximations to reality.

Now, radical feminism suggests a quite different relationship between theory and practice, and a quite different notion of 'theory'. Simply by arguing that there *is* a relationship between them, and a necessary one at that, it is suggesting something rather different. It also argues that theory should be pragmatic, practical and everyday. It should be a set of understandings or conceptual frameworks which are directly related to, and derive from, particular facets of everyday relationships, experiences and behaviours.

Grand theory presupposes a particular kind of relationship between the individual and society, between the personal and the structural, which is in many ways alien to our understanding of feminism. It presupposes that the two are in some sense separate – that structures and 'the system' exist outside of individuals and collections of individuals. However, the radical feminist understanding of feminist theory is that 'the personal' truly is the political, and that there is both a direct and necessary relationship between theory and experience. 'The revolution' is within each and every one of us and it will come about – and is coming about – as a result of many 'small revolutions', many small changes in relationships, behaviours, attitudes and experiences.

This radical feminist understanding of the relationship between theory and experience is something we absolutely share. And this is why, of course, we have found much other recent feminist theorizing lacking. *You* may define what kind of feminists we are through reading this book; but we can do no more than say what we agree and disagree with, and what we find to be important and exciting. By this we mean that we adopt the label of 'radical feminists' only reluctantly, because we believe that so labelling beliefs and practices necessarily confines both present and future experiences and activities.

THEORY, EXPERIENCE AND RESEARCH

As well as the failure to discuss any possible relationship between theory and experience, much feminist and non-feminist work alike neglects to examine critically the relationship between theory and *research*. One view of 'theory' or 'research practice' (the 'deductivist' view of science) is that theory precedes research. Within this view 'theory' is concerned with the construction of abstract hypotheses which are later tested, usually using artificial or 'experimental' means of doing so. This is frequently seen as 'the traditional' view of science, but in fact its origins are comparatively recent. An older view (the 'inductivist' view of science) is that theory construction derives from 'experience', but in a quite different sense from how we use this word. Within the inductivist view of science pure, unbiased and objective knowledge is seen as something produced out of the scientific mind's experience of the world; and it is this which appears in 'theory'. Whether either of these two research styles are appropriately adopted by feminists ought to be a matter for discussion and argument. However, such discussions and arguments within feminism and feminist academic work have been strangely few.

Radical feminism argues that there must be a relationship between theory and practice which not only sees these as inextricably interwoven, but which sees experience and practice as the basis of theory, and theory as the means of changing practice. We argue that a similar relationship should exist between theory, experience and research. We feel that it is inevitable that the researcher's own experiences and consciousness will be involved in the research process as much as they are in life, and we shall argue that all research must be concerned with the experiences and consciousness of the researcher as an integral part of the research process.

For feminists 'the researcher' is a feminist researcher, presumably aware of problems concerning the power relationship involved in the research process. And this ought to include an awareness that 'the researcher', traditionally, has interpreted women's experiences through sexist eyes. The 'problem of sexism', however, can also be seen as 'the problem' that the researcher's self (including her values, likes and dislikes) is inevitably involved in the research process. Feminist researchers must not feel that 'being feminist' involves any easy escape from this, because feminists remain human beings with feelings. All human attributes are brought into the research situation by researchers, are *inevitably* brought into it, whether this is library research or research 'in the field'. In these terms 'feminism' can be seen as a direct parallel to 'sexism', because it similarly constitutes the presence of a distinct set of values within the research situation.

It is this which we argue must be made explicit within feminist research. We believe that the way to do it is to make 'the researcher' and her consciousness the central focus of the research experience. We refer to it as the 'research experience' because we see it as an experience like any other, not as something different, special or separated-off through the 'adoption' of special techniques such as 'objectivity'. As we have already argued in chapter 1, we see 'objectivity', as this term is presently constructed within the social sciences, as a sexist notion which feminists should leave behind. We echo Adrienne Rich in insisting that 'objectivity' is the term that men have given to their own subjectivity:

> Masculine ideologies are the creation of masculine subjectivity; they are neither objective, nor value-free nor inclusively 'human'. Feminism implies that we recognize fully the inadequacy for us, the distortion, of male-centred ideologies, and that we proceed to think and act, out of that recognition (Rich, 1979, p. 207).

But to argue that 'the researcher' should be the central focus of research might seem a completely ridiculous suggestion to make. However, we insist that the choice is of either including the researcher's self as the centre of research or of simply not talking or writing about it. It is impossible to 'do' research and at the same time 'not do it'; and 'not doing it' is the only way that the researcher's self can be excluded from the centre of the research process.

We have argued that it is impossible both to experience and not to experience, to do research and not to do research through the medium of one's own consciousness. We also suggest that this consciousness and experience should be made explicit within the research. It should not simply be taken-for-granted as its backcloth, because it isn't any 'backcloth' but instead the absolutely and totally central feature of any research process. And so it must be made a central part of the research report, not hidden from view and disguised through claims of 'objectivity' and 'science'.

Some people have suggested to us that such a style of research would be limited, but we don't agree with this. We're not suggesting that feminists should stop doing any of the kinds of research we are doing. Merely that our experiences of the research process should become explicitly present within research reports, as these are experientially central to the research process. It isn't necessary that feminists should stop doing research on mental illness, rape, depression, women at work, and so on. Instead, we suggest that the researcher's own experiences are an integral part of the research and should therefore be described as such. The kind of person that we are, and how we experience the research, all have a crucial impact on what we see, what we do, and how we interpret and construct what is going on. For feminists, these experiences must not be separated-off from our discussions of research outcomes. To the extent that we do this we merely repeat traditional male mystifications of 'research' and 'science', and by doing so we downgrade the personal and the everyday.

For us experience and feeling must be at the heart of feminist research or it is not 'feminism' as we understand it. We believe that 'feminism' if it is anything, is a re-evaluation of 'the personal'. This re-evaluation must not be something kept for nice safe feminist groups and gatherings, something only for friends and sisters. It must be included *within* our research, within 'feminist science'. As feminists, we should not be involved in traditional male academic routines for disguising our own feelings and involvements. Neither should we become involved in academic revelation of 'the personal' by publishing 'objective' research reports and then later publishing additional papers which purport to 'tell it like it was' (Bell and Newby, 1977). We feel encouraged that social scientists are, in some small measure, discussing more personal aspects of involvement within research. We're also very much afraid that feminist academics are beginning to do this in the same way. But that many feminist academics *do* separate-off experience, and treat it as different from and outside of 'the research proper', merely serves to point up the extremely conventional kind of research that is often carried out in the name of feminism.

FEMINISM, 'OUR WAY'

So far we have examined various ideas about what constitutes 'feminist theory'. We have also suggested something of our own ideas about the relationship between feminist theory and personal practice, and between theory, experience and research. For us 'feminist theory' and 'feminist research' ought to be concerned with the implications of *feminism* itself. This means examining the beliefs and values involved within feminism, and what these suggest for the conduct of research, rather than merely adding women in to existing theories and styles of research. We therefore now go back to what we see as the central themes of feminism, in order to describe them briefly. We use this later on to draw out what we see as some of the implications for research. The three themes that we see as central to feminist theory will come as little surprise to other feminists. What they might be surprised about is our interpretation of what these 'mean'. We feel that all feminists share the belief that these themes are important; what we dispute is the exact meaning and implication of these for theory, for research, and for how we live our everyday lives.

Women are oppressed

The most central and common belief shared by all feminists, whatever our 'type', is the presupposition that women are oppressed. It is from this common acceptance that there is indeed a problem, that there is something amiss in the treatment of women in society, that feminism arises.

This statement of women's oppression is a *factual* one for feminists and is not open to debate. All feminists accept that women are oppressed on the basis of their own experiences and those shared with other women. Also all feminists agree that women's oppression isn't inevitable, but that it can and must be changed. Even those feminists who may believe that women's oppression is connected to biological or other so-called 'natural' differences between the sexes, don't accept that either these differences and/ or their consequences are immutable.

Feminism also argues that the fact of women's oppression has consequences for *everyone* within society. It has consequences for children, as has been pointed out in a number of key writings (Firestone, 1970; Rush, 1974; Brownmiller, 1975). Many feminists and a handful of men believe that women's oppression has negative consequences for men too. The sexual political system oppresses women and men are in some sense women's oppressors, but they are themselves oppressed by their own status as oppressors. In addition, because women's oppression has consequences for the whole of society, it also has further consequences for the relationships between that human society and the natural world around us.

The personal is the political

A second key theme common to feminism takes up the previously argued point that feminists accept the fact of women's oppression on the basis of our own and other women's experiences. 'Oppression' involves an essentially shared set of experiences. And so this second theme is concerned with the nature of this experience as it is shared and understood in terms of 'the personal'.

These shared experiences include a growing awareness that there is something wrong, something amiss, within women's lives – what Betty Friedan memorably described as 'the problem without a name' (Friedan, 1963). It also includes the discovery and naming of this problem as 'sexism', 'oppression' or other similar terms, the essence of which is that they name the problem *as a problem*. The discovery and naming of this problem takes place in terms of the personal accounts that women provide, to be shared amongst us. This sharing involves experiences of the family, marriage, work, the education system, sex, death, and so on 'ad feminam', as Adrienne Rich says. Women's group's newsletters, conference reports, and collections of writings by various women involved in the WLM in the period of the late 1960s and early 1970s, all demonstrate the central concern with this process of describing, understanding and naming women's experiences for what they are now seen to be.

Within this process of naming and discovery there were two fundamentally accepted beliefs, although our next two chapters argue that these have been 'transformed' out of recognition. The first of these concerned the essential validity of personal experience. Feminism insisted that personal experiences couldn't be invalidated or rejected, because if something was felt then it was felt, and if it was felt then it was absolutely real for the woman feeling and experiencing it. The second was the feminist insistence that the traditional distinction between 'objective' and 'subjective' was false. The traditional male emphasis has been on objectifying experiences and so 'getting away from' the personal into some transcendental realm of 'knowledge' and 'truth'. For feminists the key consequence of this is that it denies validity to women's understandings of women's experiences, because these are 'merely' subjective, rooted in the particular. It also, of course, denies validity to the realms of emotion and physicality more generally, instead arguing that 'rationality' and 'mind' are superior to these.

The emphasis on the personal within feminism is summed up in the statement 'the personal is the political.' This argues that power and its use can be examined within personal life and, indeed, in some sense that the political *must* be examined in this way. It also emphasizes that 'the system' is experienced *in* everyday life, and isn't separate from it. And so feminism argues that systems and social structures, whether concerned with the economy, the family, or the oppression of women more generally, can best be examined and understood through an exploration of relationships and experiences within everyday life.

Although this awareness of the systematic, although everyday, basis of women's oppression can be gained by individual and isolated women, feminism believes that this can best be done through the process of women coming together. This 'coming together' focuses on meeting and talking in small groups in order to share personal experiences and feelings: women *hear* what each other are saying, they don't just listen and then ignore what is being said (Smith, 1978). From this group sharing comes the realization that what traditionally has been seen as 'personal problems' in fact have social and political bases and solutions.

From such 'consciousness-raising' activities has come an awareness that conventional ideas about 'politics' are lacking. Conventionally, 'politics' is seen in terms of traditional institutions and activities – political parties, elections, pressure groups and parliaments – rather than the experience of power within everyday situations. Focusing on power within the everyday points up that 'politics' doesn't lie beyond people's front door steps and outside of feelings, beliefs, relationships and behaviours.

Feminist consciousness

The third theme concerns the new understanding that women gain through consciousness-raising activities. This involves seeing the same reality differently. To express this another way, women's understandings of our lives are transformed so that we see, understand and feel them in a new and quite different way, at the same time as we see them in the 'old' way. This 'new way' of seeing the *same* reality, whilst also seeing a new reality, involves a situation in which women come to understand the (seemingly endless) contradictions present within life. Reality *is* much more complex and multi-dimensional than we ordinarily suppose it to be, and it *is* contradictory. And as Sandra Bartky has said, both ways of viewing the same reality, and the contradictions which result, are equally 'real' (Bartky, 1977). We shall later argue in chapter 5 that this 'double vision' of reality and our involvement in it is essential to the idea and the actuality of 'feminist consciousness'.

We have used 'feminism' and 'feminist theory' interchangeably because we believe that, by definition, feminism is not only a set of beliefs but also a set of theoretical constructions about the nature of women's oppression, and the part that this oppression plays within social reality more generally. We suggest that implicit or explicit in any set of beliefs are more general ideas about the nature of social reality, and these ideas are *theoretical* ideas. Feminism is no exception to this. Indeed, such theoretical constructions are more explicitly and more impressively present within feminism than within most other sets of beliefs. It will be obvious from this that we don't accept any grand theory interpretation of what 'theory' means, but prefer something much simpler which recognizes that we are all of us 'theoreticians' because we all of us use our values and beliefs to interpret and so construct the social world.

Beyond a basic acceptance of the three themes we have just outlined we believe that there is little which is commonly accepted and shared among feminists. How different feminists understand, conceptualize and theorize about women's oppression, and the actions necessary for women's liberation, differs a great deal. This basic acceptance may exist, but there is also an ongoing debate about what these themes *mean*, and what consequences they have for action. The statements 'women are oppressed', 'the personal is the political', and 'there is a feminist consciousness', do not have self-evident and inherent meaning for anybody. We interpret their meanings according to our own situations and understandings. As these differ, we suggest, so will our interpretations of them. 'The personal is the political' may be an idea commonly expressed by feminists, but how particular women interpret its meaning and relate it to producing theory, doing research, and living our lives, differs tremendously. We discuss in the next chapter these differing interpretations of the nature of the personal and its relationship to the political.

Chapter 3

Beyond the personal?

'The personal is the political' has been a key theme in contemporary feminism, we argued in the last chapter. This theme emphasizes the importance of the subjective, and rejects the traditional insistence that the objective and the structural are fundamentally different from this. Its adoption by feminists represented a marked break with conventional intellectual modes of thought. The western industrial scientific approach values the orderly, rational, quantifiable, predictable, abstract and theoretical: feminism spat in its eye. But more recently there have been attempts to justify a movement away from the personal by using it in order to produce a different kind of analysis.

We feel that many feminists now see 'the personal' as a stepping-off point, as merely the spring-board to theory (and practice) which is in some way 'more than' the personal. Feminism seems to be slipping back into what it previously rejected – 'expert' analytical and theoretical approaches which are seemingly divorced from personal experience.

But there is a price to be paid for this. Feminism appeals because it means something – it touches deeply felt needs, feelings and emotions. It makes a direct, emotional and *personal* appeal, or it means very little except as an intellectual exercise. But to what, we ask in something like despair, does 'expert' and abstract theorizing appeal? The answer, we are told, is that it appeals to the need to analyse in greater depth, and more sophistication, women's liberation. But we don't believe that such a form of analysis can do this because within it theory is provided 'for us' by an elite among feminists. This kind of work uses exceedingly conventional forms of analysis and constipated language, and by doing so it sets up a distinction between 'theorists', the elite, and the rest of us.

In this chapter we examine these developments, and also some of our worries about them. We examine a number of arguments about the need to 'get beyond' the personal, whether into 'real' political action and more 'effective' feminism, or new theoretical developments. And then we take one example of this kind of theoretical work – 'the family' and its crucial role in feminist theory – and look at how our own personal experience as feminists in the gay movement and within a lesbian group demonstrate problems with current feminist thinking on this.

THE PERSONAL IS THE POLITICAL – OR IS IT?

In the women's movement of the 1960s the statement 'the personal is the political' was an axiom with crucial consequences, both for the ideology of the movement and also for its organization and practice. Both WLM organization and the political practice of feminism were seen to lie within the small group structure. In America these small groups contained within them a variety of activities and functions, but they also maintained a consistent style. This included a conscious lack of formal structure, emphasis on participation by everyone, a deliberate sharing of tasks, and the exclusion of men (Freeman, 1975; Jenkins and Kramer, 1978). And a very similar description of the small group in the British women's movement, and of its use as a consciousness-raising device (Tufnell Park Group, 1972; Bruley, 1976), exists in pamphlets, articles and in a myriad of newsletters.

The basic values of the small group structure aren't confined to feminism alone. They are also those of other 'new left' movements, emphasizing as they do participatory democracy, equality, liberty and community. They also include the idea that hierarchy is wrong, the belief that everyone should share equally in activities and tasks, and the insistence that any kind of leadership is bad. And so when we use the word 'organization' in relation to the WLM, we do so taking its adoption of these values into account.

This lack of formal 'organization' has been criticized as the 'tyranny of structurelessness' which should be countered by adopting more openly structured forms of organization and procedure (Freeman, 1970). In contrast, many women have reaffirmed their adherence to the more traditional style of movement interaction (Levine, 1974), while others have argued that the basic structures advocated by Jo Freeman are in fact present within the 'structurelessness' she criticizes (Light, 1978). However, even at its most formal, the feminist style of political discussion and action is very different from that of other people. And where feminists are involved in formal and mixed organizations that is likely to lead to conflict, around precisely the basic values we have just outlined (Roberts and Millar, 1978). These values may be shared with other 'new left' groups, but how they are put into practice differs tremendously.

Later developments in the WLM include the continuance of consciousness-raising and also new forms of activity, particularly 'service' ones. These include the organization of newsletters, nursery groups and abortion campaign groups. Nevertheless, consciousness-raising retains its position as a central activity, one closely related to the existence of small group structures (AWP *et al.*, 1976). As we earlier outlined, discovering the relationship between the personal and the political involves women coming together in small groups to share our personal experiences, problems and feelings. Through this we discover that not only is the personal also the political, but *all* aspects of the political are necessarily and inevitably reflected within the personal. We say 'reflected' here, although later in chapter 4 we shall argue that this should be seen as 'constructed'.

At the same time that consciousness-raising has retained its central position within women's movement organization many feminist writers have expressed their dissatisfaction with all small group forms. Most of these dissatisfactions have hinged upon the felt-need to 'go beyond' what has been described as the 'constant repetition' of personal experience. And so we now examine some of the arguments for 'going beyond' the personal around these 'felt-needs'. We look at what is seen as the need for 'political action' and 'effectiveness', and the need for 'theory'.

Some arguments for going 'beyond' the personal . . .

1 The need for 'political action' and 'effectiveness'

Within the women's movement of the late 1960s and early 1970s political action was felt to lie almost solely within the process of consciousness-raising. It was believed that 'total revolution' could be brought about by many women making changes in their lives, effecting many 'small revolutions'. But later many feminists came to feel that this definition of 'political action' was too limited.

An example of this is to be found in the later work of Jo Freeman (1975). She argues that once the virtues of consciousness-raising have been exhausted then most feminists want to do something 'more concrete'. And she feels that anyway by the early 1970s consciousness-raising as a major activity had started to become obsolete. Freeman's arguments are based on a fairly conventional idea of political action and theorizing. She argues that personal change can provide a route for other and more concrete social changes, but if *only* personal change is aimed for then the impact of any social movement will be minimal:

> It is only when private disputes that result from personal changes are translated into public demands that a movement enters the political arena and can make use of political institutions to reach its goals of social change (Freeman, 1975, p.5).

In fairly similar terms Mitchell and Oakley reject the idea of 'sisterhood', an idea they see as involving three main facets (Mitchell and Oakley, 1976). These are the eschewing of leadership, the formation of small consciousness-raising groups, and the redefinition of the value and status of personal experience so that 'the personal' becomes 'the political'. They argue that statements of personal experience and the 'glories' of sisterhood 'by nature become repetitious'. They feel that these are useful as starting points, but after this they act as distractions from what they call 'going back to the drawing board'.

They also emphasize that this insistence on the correlation between personal experience and 'the political' has led to inflexibility in feminist practice. This is because it has involved a 'codification of personal insights as political rules' (Mitchell and Oakley, 1976, p. 13). In contrast to this they maintain that individual women's personal experiences of males, of marriage, and of the nuclear family, must not be elevated into political rules which are then applied to other women. Feminists, they say, should not be involved in a wholesale rejection of existing social practices. In particular they insist that the abandonment of marriage and the family, and other similar changes in life-style, are 'politically pretty useless' (Mitchell and Oakley, 1976, p. 12). And this, even though these may be identified as crucially involved in constructing and maintaining women's oppression.

A similar idea about the relationship, or lack of it, between the personal and the political is to be found in the work of Charlotte Brunsdon. She argues that, although 'the personal' is important in understanding women's subordination, nevertheless 'remaining within the politics of personal experience will not fundamentally transform this subordination' (1978, p. 23).

These writers present a very different analysis of the relationship between the personal and the political, and definition of what constitutes political action, than many feminists would have recognized in the 1960s. But such an emphasis on more traditional means of 'being political' appears to us to be an inevitable consequence of the idea that there is something 'beyond' the personal, something *more* than this. These writers seem to reject 'life-style' politics in favour of something they see as much more 'effective'. And 'effectiveness' is described, not in terms of widespread personal change, but rather in terms of mass action of a different sort, and consequent changes in public policy and 'social structures'.

A number of important points can briefly be made about this kind of work. First, we find Mitchell and Oakley's rejection of the idea that there is anything useful in changing life-styles very odd indeed. We believe that the essence of 'being feminist' is that it constitutes precisely such changes. Second, we reject the idea that 'the personal' can only be 'endless repetitions' of 'personal woe'; and in later chapters we discuss other ways of using the personal as a resource for feminists. And third, we see in such writings the reappearance of 'objectivity' and 'subjectivity' as dichotomous categories. Subjectivity is seen as limited, a stepping-off point only; and objectivity as the proper substance of theorizing. This latter point we now go on to discuss in greater detail; and we begin by looking at Mitchell and Oakley's ideas about 'going back to the drawing board'.

2 The need for 'theory'

'Going back to the drawing board' is what Mitchell and Oakley see as *the* alternative to continual statements about personal experience. This involves doing a number of activities, including rewriting history and reinterpreting the social world from a perspective that includes women. It therefore involves a reworking of all social science disciplines from a feminist perspective, as they see this. They recognize that their proposals are 'academic' ones – about producing feminist theory by working within and transforming the social sciences. They also argue that many feminists won't agree with this because, apart from marxism, we feel 'considerable scepticism' about all intellectual and academic work.

We have argued in the last chapter, and shall argue in the next, that this lack of criticism of marxism is lamentable. We feel it is based on a mistaken idea that marxism is somehow magically different from other male-defined and male-oriented theories. However, the main point we wish to make here is that what Mitchell and Oakley have done is to set up 'the theoretical' and 'the personal' as polar opposites, and they plump for theory as against 'woe', as they call it.

Although similarly arguing the need for 'theory', Sheila Rowbotham's recent work approaches this in what, we feel, is a rather different way, although her starting point is the same. She suggests that the slogan 'the personal is the political' contains inherent problems because 'it tends to imply that all individual problems can find a short term political solution' (1979, p. 14). She also argues that there is a need to theorize organizational experiences that have occurred within the WLM, because it becomes increasingly impossible to communicate the exact events involved in particular decisions – we 'can't keep telling it like a story', she suggests.

This is because she feels that the 'telling it like a story' means of communicating why things are as they are puts feminists in the position of continually refighting old battles – 'just going backwards and forwards, up and down the same hill', as she says (Rowbotham, 1979, p. 21). And she feels that theorizing also has additional benefits, mainly because it enables critics to be met with alternative and worked out theoretical positions. Now while we agree with much of this, we find the idea that 'theory' is a useful weapon, giving you an advantage with which to silence critics, not one that we subscribe to.

We should emphasize that when she says 'theory' Rowbotham doesn't mean a fixed and removed body of 'truth' which has universal validity. Instead, she suggests that it is useful to think of theory as 'maps': as a means of providing paths and footholds in the process of creating women's liberation. Although with Rowbotham we recognize that a problem exists, in terms of the need to theorize organizational rationale, we also feel that the kind of 'theory' current within feminism is definitely not of the kind she outlines. She argues that theory ought to be essentially practical, concerned with organizational activities; it should be fluid, amenable to frequent and continual change; and it should also be accessible to all women. A great deal of contemporary feminist theorizing appears to us to be the antithesis of these.

The kind of theory now being produced, as we've tried to show in chapter 2, is not concerned with movement organization but with 'higher' matters. And it appears absolutely not fluid or easily accessible. In arguing this we find ourselves agreeing with some remarks made by the Dalston Study Group, although what they said was about a particular conference (1976) and we wish to make the point more widely than this. Like them, we feel that much current feminist theory is expressed at a 'high' level of abstraction, in complex and technical language, in such a way that its often minimal content is carefully covered over, and it is presented with little tentativeness or exposure of method.

. . . And some brief responses

It seems to us that 'the personal' and alternatives to it are conceptualized in very limited and dichotomous ways. The alternatives aren't only consciousness-raising versus 'theory', or consciousness-raising versus 'real' political action; there are many others which remain undiscussed and unrecognized. However, before discussing these we'd like to emphasize what we see as the need for feminists to continue the so-called 'repetitious' and 'obsolete' practice of recounting personal experience in consciousness-raising.

The WLM doesn't have any well developed means of gaining entry into it. Women who wish to 'become' feminists, in the sense of joining the women's movement and participating in its small groups or other activities, are faced with considerable difficulties in finding out where and how they might do so. As a movement it appears curiously unaware of, or even uncaring about, these women and thus its future existence. In addition to this, 'new' feminists, women who are new to the WLM and/ or feminist ideas, still need to go through the same process of consciousness-raising as those who became involved in the 1960s and early 1970s. The need for consciousness-raising, whether in a 'formal' sense within small groups, or more informally, is something we *all* share. It would seem to us, therefore, that suggestions about the 'repetitiousness', 'obsolescence' and so on, of consciousness-raising, are really considering matters only from the viewpoint of women who have been involved in, and identified with, feminism for a comparatively long period of time. Such suggestions ignore the needs of women who are just becoming involved or who have been involved for only a short period of time, and are chauvinist in the extreme.

But there is a further point to be made about consciousness-raising. In the last chapter we suggested that feminist consciousness involves a 'double vision' and living out the resulting complexities, ambiguities and contradictions is difficult. It is difficult because this is a never ending process – a twenty-four hour a day, seven days a week job. 'Consciousness-raising', however, has been used in a very limited way, to imply that women 'go through' it, like a training course which brings them up to the standard of 'sorted-out feminists'. And sorted-out feminists, the further implication is, can live with this double vision without being continually hurt, continually afraid and continually in need of support. But if understanding oppression requires sharing, then surely 'doing feminism' must as well? For us, there's no such creature as a 'sorted-out feminist', because living as a feminist involves us in a continual and non-sorted-out struggle. All of our experiences need to be shared, discussed and analysed in order for us to make sense of our lives. And we believe that until the day that each of us dies we'll need the kind of support that consciousness-raising provides to keep ourselves sane in what is, in effect, an alien world.

It will be quite apparent from what we have just said that we don't see the feminist revolution as something which occurs in 'social structures', as these are usually defined. We believe that the daily 'doing' of feminism is what the revolution is, and that there is no other way for social change to occur other than through personal change multiplied many times. Although we discuss this again in chapter 4 we'd like to say here that we feel that many other feminist writers seem to equate social change with institutional change; and we feel that history is littered with examples of institutional change not leading to revolutionary social change, in the sense of profoundly affecting people's everyday lives.

We also argue the separate but related point, which we examine in more detail in later chapters, that there are means of using personal experience and subjective understanding other than those envisaged within the work of most feminist theorists. Subjective experience and understanding (as though there were any other) is seen as the basis for the development of a feminist consciousness. As such it is accepted as necessary for 'embryonic' theorizing about women's oppression, but as an inadequate basis for the in-depth theorizing that is thought to be necessary now. One example of this is Himmelweit's argument that placing importance on subjective and personal perceptions of oppression is done only 'at the expense of macro systemic, historical and class views' (Himmelweit et al., 1976, p. 3). This statement, like many others we have read, sees 'personal perceptions' and 'macro systemic, historical and class views' as mutually exclusive. One is concentrated on 'at the expense of' the other. Once again we find subjective and objective, process and structure, individual and society, presented as dichotomous, as distinct, separate and curiously unrelated.

We have already argued that the dichotomy between objectivity and subjectivity is false, because these are artificial constructs based upon essentially sexist thinking. But now a further distinction seems to be made by many feminists between the 'subjective' use of the personal and the 'objective' use of it in producing 'scientific' theoretical knowledge. We have already identified this as the traditional deductivist view of science and we reiterate this point here.

EXPERIENCE VERSUS 'THE FAMILY'

It has been argued that the earlier feminist emphasis on the personal is becoming or has become redundant, and that there is a need to 'get beyond' this into something more fitted to the times. We now go on to look at some more of the reasons why we feel that these arguments are not only mistaken, but are also part and parcel of an intellectual tradition that feminism once, rightly in our opinion, rejected. We shall do this by looking at some of our own personal experiences and how these have led us into not only rejecting one of the truisms of feminist theory but also the intellectual tradition in which it is located. That is, we have come to explain our lives in terms of our own experientially derived theories rather than in terms of other people's universalized theory.

Feminist theory and 'the family'

The experiences we want to examine are all concerned with our progressive movement away from feminism's universalized theory of 'the family'. For many feminists the operation of 'the family' is crucial in understanding the oppression of women. They have suggested that two fundamental sets of processes interlink to produce this oppression. The first concerns women in our roles as wives and mothers. These relationships, it is argued, fix women in a service and domestic mode of behaviour. Such relationships are highly routinized, privatized and influenced by a range of stereotyped 'ideals' exemplified in images presented through the media. The second concerns the family's role as the main means of 'socializing' children. This involves getting children to learn and enact what are seen as desirable attributes. In particular it involves socializing them into sexually stereotyped 'feminine' and 'masculine' attributes, so that they themselves will later engage in the same behaviours and so perpetuate sexism.

Rosalind Delmar, for example, has argued that such an analysis of the family is essential to what feminism is (1972); and most collections of feminist writings contain key sections on 'the family' (Wandor, 1972; Allen et al., 1974; Bristol Women's Studies Group, 1979). Such a view is continued in feminist and other writings about domestic labour within capitalism (Freeman, 1974; Gardiner, 1974; Magas et al., 1974). It is also contained in work on 'socialization' and the family (Chetwynd and Hartnett, 1978; Hartnett et al., 1979; Sharpe, 1976), and on links between the family, socialization and the economy within capitalism (Wilson, 1977).

Obviously, this view of the family as a repressive and oppressive institution isn't confined to feminism alone. One source of feminist thinking on this subject comes from pre-existing marxist frameworks. Another comes from 'radical psychology' and 'anti-psychiatry', which produced onslaughts on family life which pre-date current feminist thinking (Laing, 1960; Laing and Esterson, 1964). However, both these sources tend to see the 'oppressive/repressive family' as more or less synonymous with 'women-in-the-family'. These imply that it is women who socialize children, and so it is women who are responsible for all the ills of 'family life'. Feminist writings on the family borrow from both of these sources, as well as from more personal and grounded experiences, to analyse family life in a rather different way. These argue that the identification of 'women' and 'family' is the result of sexist thinking; and also that, contrary to straight male thinking on the family, *women* are the recipients of its most repressive, constraining and oppressive features. This is because they are most 'there', and are held by others to be most responsible for its 'proper functioning'. Such writings also argue that this responsibility is imposed on women from outside, as well as from inside by themselves and other family members (Comer, 1974; Wilson, 1977).

Feminist analysis of the family also goes further than this to include within it the oppression of children, and the similarities between this and the oppression of women, including children's frequent sexual exploitation inside and outside the family. It also includes an analysis of the repression of female sexuality within phallocentric definitions of sexual conduct, and the legal and other repressive aspects of marriage.

In short, in feminist writings 'the family' is seen to play a central role in the development and continuance of women's oppression. This notion of 'the family' includes the idea that the experience of family life is oppressive, and also the idea that the nature of this experience is *determined*. 'The family' is depicted as an institution and personal experiences within it as determined from *outside*. And this is seen to occur in a universal way. This is what it is like for us all, whether we accept it as an accurate description of our experiences or not.

This analysis has been rejected as a guide to personal change by many feminists, most publicly by Mitchell and Oakley, but of course by many others as well. Many women reject its universality, and they differentiate between *their* family and 'the family' as an institution. The experience of their *own* family is different from how theory tells them it should be. But instead of rejecting the theory altogether, they simply reject that part of it which suggests that family life must change. Behind this, we feel, lies a dichotomy between 'structure' and 'experience'. The structure, 'the family', must change; but this is interpreted as having no implications for changing experience, 'family life'.

Feminist accounts and analyses of sexual behaviour, marriages, families, has resulted in work on a number of important aspects of these. From this there are at least two possible directions in which theoretical work can proceed. The first is to *go beyond* the personal, into structural and more abstract work which develops these themes in more conventionally theoretical forms. That is, what we've just been talking about – the family as an institution. The second is to *go back into* the personal, back into the *experience* of it, in order to explore why, for example, women feel that *their* family is different from 'the family'. A myriad of questions need to be asked about everyday experience which get lost in the desire to generalize about things. Among these are: are these experiences oppressive for all women? in all their aspects or only some? at all times or intermittently? does the concrete experience of oppression vary? or is it the same for all women? if it is the same, in what ways? if it varies, why? and we could expand this list of questions many times without fully covering the complexities, ambiguities and contradictions that need to be described and accounted for.

We feel that feminists have been concerned with the first kind of theoretical work but have just about completely neglected the second. One consequence of generalizing, however, is that it often depicts 'the fact' of oppression as being the same for all women, at all times, and in all places. And this no matter whether the women are black or white, working class or middle class, heterosexual or lesbian, young or old. But we believe that we *each* of us have to find out the nature of our own oppressions in order to fight these; and we believe that the nature and dimensions of these differ according to our differing lives. Generalized thinking, we believe, leads to women's accounts of our lives being downgraded, and us being told we're wrong or falsely-conscious. In other words, if the facts of experience don't fit theoretical knowledge then these can't be 'facts' at all.

The second kind of theoretical work isn't 'theoretical' in the same way of course, because it is deeply rooted in variations in, and kinds of, *experience*. It is deeply related to the facts of experience, not to abstract and generalized concepts. Nor is it 'academic' as this is usually conceived of, nor is it of high status in the same way that abstract theoretical work is seen to be. But, we suggest, it can help us to understand, in a way that abstract theory can't, the complexities and contradictions of our own, and other women's, experience. We shall now try to elaborate this point by looking at some of our own particular experiences to show how we moved further and further away from abstract and slick phrases which gloss-over experience by saying 'the family this' and 'socialization that'.

Our experiences versus 'the family'

These experiences were ones which occurred largely as a consequence of our involvement, as women who were lesbian feminists, in the gay movement. Originally this involved a particular analysis of our oppression as women and gay women (and we use the word 'gay' deliberately here), an analysis drawn from the feminist theory of the family we outlined earlier. But as a result of various reactions to us this analysis changed radically. We came to realize that to be a lesbian is to be a particularly disturbing and threatening kind of woman, and to adopt a quite different kind of theoretical approach to our oppression. This different approach could be summarized by saying that we came to construe ourselves as lesbians, and *not* as gay women.

The feminist analysis of the family has been taken up, used and developed by the British gay movement. The London Gay Liberation Front (GLF) *Manifesto* consciously uses feminist ideas and analysis to argue that the 'patriarchal Family' is responsible for the oppression of homosexuals. It hammers home its point by insisting that:

> The oppression of gay people starts in the most basic unit of society, the family, consisting of the man in charge, a slave as his wife, and their children on whom they force themselves as the ideal models. The very form of the family works against homosexuality (GLF, 1971, p. 2).

It goes on to spell out the fundamental reason for society's treatment of homosexuality. This is the failure of gay women and men to conform to the most basic aspect of gender stereotypes – sexual orientation. The revolution sought by GLF is a feminist revolution – one in which 'femininity' and 'masculinity' come to have no meaning, where biological sex implies nothing more than biological sex, and where 'male chauvinism' no longer exists. And so the *Manifesto* argues that in order to achieve this:

> we, along with the women's movement, must fight for some-

thing more than reform. We must aim at the abolition of the family, so that the sexist, male supremacist system can no longer be nurtured there (GLF, 1971, p. 10).

GLF has been characterized as the radical wing of the British gay movement, but it is interesting to note that the self-same analysis was also adopted in what has been characterized as its conservative wing – the Campaign for Homosexual Equality (CHE). CHE's *Introducing CHE* similarly identifies marriage and the family as the key embodiment of sexism, and also as the source of the oppression of gay people.

> Society's treatment of homosexuality is rooted in its attitude towards sexuality, social acceptance of which is based upon heterosexual marriage. Within marriage, distinct tasks are assigned to husband and wife, and similarly within society for male and female. . . . These distinct expectations, known as 'gender roles', together with the economic, political and social privilege accorded to the masculine role, make up what has been termed 'sexism' (CHE, 1972, p. 2).

Both of us wholeheartedly accepted such an analysis of anti-homosexual feelings and beliefs – indeed, one of us was involved in producing the CHE leaflet. And a later discussion of matters of interest to women in the women's movement and women in the gay movement (WCC, 1974), in which both of us were involved, argues that it is the family which socializes children into gender roles. And again, the central part of gender role is seen as sexual orientation; as it says, 'masculine = fucks women, feminine = fucked by men' (WCC, 1974, p. 3).

Now one of the things that strikes us about these statements, and the documents from which they derive (apart from embarrassment), is how they see 'oppression' as something an institution – 'the family' – *does* to people. This is presented to us as, at the same time, an obvious truth and a revelation. And such thinking is blindingly simplistic in its adherence to a causal, deterministic, social reality. This kind of analysis sees structures as causal, as determinants of human personality and behaviour, but also as somehow existing outside of human agency. It suggests that 'the family' oppresses all gay people, because sexually stereotyped heterosexuals internalize anti-homosexual prejudice as well as other nasty things. And gay people too, brought up as heterosexual, internalize at least one part of the gender stereotypes thrust upon us – thus gay self-oppression.

Within this analysis it isn't *people*, gay or heterosexual, who make decisions and carry these out, who are agents within our own lives. This is because it depicts a world in which what people think and do is *determined* by our upbringing, our 'socialization'; and so we then enact 'the family' among ourselves and on others. All children, this argument suggests, are rigidly socialized within 'the family' – if we are heterosexual. But if we are homosexual or bisexual then this (magically?) enables us to escape from the central aspect of gender stereotyping and so in adulthood we are more liberated, more free. However, we argue that *many* people, irrespective of sexual orientation, don't embody or adopt gender stereotypes. Otherwise there would be no women's movement, no men against sexism, as well as no gay movement. And this is the minimum statement of such exceptions – many people other than these don't behave or feel in gender stereotyped ways. And also being gay doesn't involve any easy or necessary escape from sexism, in the way that it was thought to then. Indeed, it is quite possible to make out a good case for saying that gay men are frequently more sexist than many heterosexual men (Stanley, 1982), and certainly many feminists have complained about the sexism of lesbians involved within the WLM.

Implicit within this analysis is also the comforting message that 'the family' is not us, people in the gay movement. 'The family' is composed of heterosexuals who have internalized sexism, anti-gay prejudice, and so on. *We* have escaped this, unless we are self-oppressed, of course. This kind of analysis is very appealing – it was certainly very appealing to us. It seemed convincing because we wanted to find an explanation of gay oppression in feminist theory. It links the oppression of homosexuals to the oppression of women because it utilizes feminist analysis of the crucial role of the family in this oppression. But the reasons why it seemed so convincing to us are worth looking at more closely.

Here we have a very simple solution to the 'problem' of finding a feminist analysis of gay oppression and self-oppression. It 'adds in' homosexuality to the oppression of women in a very neat sort of way. It does this in such a way that the centre of this action is a structure, a social institution. This is what makes 'them' oppress 'us'. It externalizes everything and places blame and responsibility on 'the system'. And last, but by no means least, it manages to produce an analysis with a very comforting message to those people who adopt it. Just like much feminist theory, it contains the implication that those who adhere to the theory are outside of the analysis produced.

By this we mean that present feminist theories about the oppression of women can't explain why *feminists* haven't internalized this oppression in the way that other women are described as doing so. And, similarly so, gay theory of the oppression of homosexuals can't explain why homosexuals, brought up in 'the family' just like everyone else, aren't ourselves anti-gay heterosexuals. In other words, these theories aren't 'reflexive' – they do not and cannot explain their own production. But a more obnoxious thing about them is that they're very arrogant – 'the family' does this to people; but *we're* different, it doesn't do it to *us* because we're special.

Two objections might be made to our arguments here. The first is that such theories make probability statements only, and that they aren't claiming 'the family' determines. The second is that 'the family' is one factor only in the determination of 'society', and that it is all these factors combined which produce feminists, gay people and so forth. About the first objection, we detect no such tentativeness in the body of work we're concerned with. It is written as a deterministic argument. It may be that all exceptions are simply seen as unimportant or irrelevant in such work, but this in no way undermines the point we're making. And about the second objection, we detect no signs of any such sophistication. It makes simplistic points and presents an entirely simplistic argument.

Our combined experiences of consciousness-raising in lesbian groups, of more conventional political activities, of attempting to work with men in the gay movement, and of reading and attempting to 'live' feminism (as well as numerous other experiences for which we have no name or convenient label), finally led us to reject the analysis of oppression we were previously involved in making and promoting. We now describe some of the events and processes involved in our changing understanding of the oppression of lesbians/women. A number of important themes exist within this: compulsive monogamy, men in the gay movement, obscene phone calls and consciousness-raising.

1 How to lose friends and influence people

Coming into the gay movement at the time of the greatest influence of GLF, first one of us then the other came to reject what the *Manifesto* calls 'compulsive monogamy'. That is, it was believed that monogamy in gay relationships was a product of aping the heterosexual family model. This behaviour was seen as sexist and was thought to prevent gay people from being truly liberated. Both this 'theory', and people who we loved and respected, assured us that some forms of relationships were inherently confining and oppressive (monogamous ones) and others inherently liberating (non-monogamous ones). And so we both tried very hard to have non-monogamous relationships. But it didn't work for either of us – it made us feel miserable failures. Although we knew 'non-monogamy' wasn't working, we thought this was because *we* weren't liberated and right-on enough. We still didn't see that there was anything wrong with the theory – we thought that whatever was going wrong was *our* fault.

Later we came to have a monogamous relationship with each other, not because we chose to do so but because we'd failed at being 'sexually liberated'. We decided that this was the only way we could carry on living together. And this to the amazement and sometimes disgust of more revolutionary friends and acquaintances. We were made to feel that we were letting the side down!

But, somewhat to our amazement, we found living together in our romantic haven wonderful. We didn't feel failures, and we both realized how very liberating a totally committed and mutually dependent relationship could be. This was because we came to define 'liberation' in terms of how a relationship felt, and not how it was structured. Both of us came to feel, to state, and to write, that 'structures' aren't inherently anything; and that what relationships are like depends on the people involved in them. What may be totally liberating for one person may be totally the opposite for someone else. And what may liberate at one point in a person's life may come to be seen differently at another.

Later still, as our relationship changed again to become non-monogamous, we came to realize that another set of people had interpreted our statements about the lack of inherent meaning in structures as, instead, a defence of monogamy as an 'institution'.

And they reacted towards us with amazement and disgust! The most galling reaction of all, however, was when liberated friends took this as a sign that we'd finally made it, finally made sexual liberation. They treated us as though we were the same people having the same relationship; and, of course, six years on, we weren't.

2 Close encounters of the fourth kind, or how to cope with gay men

In the early 1970s both of us emphasized the need for gay women and men to work together against the common enemy of 'hetero-sexism'. The oppression of gay women and men is, we insisted, in all important respects the same. 'The family' sexually stereo-types people. It is here that people internalize a whole variety of values, including anti-gay ones. The substance of our argument was that there was a *common* oppression and that gay men could – and would – reject sexist treatment of women and of other men.

Experiences, a very bitter set of experiences, in the gay move-ment nationally and in our home town, changed this (Stanley, 1982). Our changed feelings coalesced around the reactions of our male friends and 'comrades' to 'gay' clubs that either totally barred women or which allowed only small numbers to enter as the guests of male members.

The earlier gay movement had rejected the 'gay scene' of pubs, clubs, discos and saunas as sexist and capitalist, and concerned only with profit, the perpetuation of the 'youth cult' and sexual exploitation. But this later gave way to something very different. To our horror, our gay male revolutionary friends left political meetings with us, only for them to go to such clubs – although it must be said that they offered to sign us into them! We have our 'male needs', these revolutionary shock troops proclaimed as they surveyed their polished shoes, carefully blow-dried hair and crutch-hugging trousers. Their proclamation of 'male needs' – gay male retention of gay male privilege and sexist attitudes and behaviours towards other men – brought about a change in our feelings about the 'common' root of oppression.

These men were supposed to be our friends and comrades in the gay movement. But gradually we found out that they had, in effect, 'secret lives' – they said one thing to us while living quite differently. And we also heard their excuses, explanations and legitimations for their simple refusal to live out their professed beliefs – the 'talking head' phenomenon. What we found particularly nauseating about it all *wasn't* this refusal, but its heavy disguise in a variety of political and theoretical statements. It was in relation to such formulations that 'male needs' made its appearance and, stripped of rhetoric, it means 'the needs of men who are ruled by their penises.' Expressed a bit differently, if gay men are asked or expected to do something which cuts down the time and opportunity they get for fucking each other then they won't do it.

These experiences with gay men have been painful because they've involved some men we've been very fond of, and who have been very fond of us. But even with these men we've also experienced another phenomenon which fascinates us; this we call 'the Andrew phenomenon'. Gay men may be close to, love and respect, women, but as soon as another man walks in the room it seems to go straight to their crutch. Immediately their attention is diverted from women to whatever man it is. Perhaps gay men too have a double vision of reality, but this is for them to explore and not us.

We began to connect these experiences with others. The 'talking head' phenomenon is not peculiar to gay men. Increasingly we felt that something very similar lies at the back of structural analyses of all kinds. By their very nature these externalize and objectify in exactly the same way the notion of 'male needs' does. Such analyses encourage us to believe that any change has to come from outside the personal and the everyday – that change too must be 'structural'. Personal change, small piecemeal change in everyday life, such analyses tell us, are irrelevant and useless. These are not the revolution. And they are worse than useless, because involvement in them distracts us from real revolutionary activities.

3 On the receiving end

Our experiences of sexism, in the form of the obscene phone calls we received while our telephone was the contact number for the lesbian group to which we belonged, is something we've written about before (Stanley and Wise, 1979; Stanley and Wise, 1980). These calls dominated our lives in the sense that they could, and did, occur at all times of the day and night over a long period of time. The content of these calls immediately and vividly demonstrated the threat of lesbianism for many heterosexual men. These calls were horribly and terrifyingly violent, while this violence was dressed up in sexual terms. As Sheila Rowbotham argues, the 'fantasy of free women' is to be seen through the projection of male fears (1973, p. 34). Lesbians are 'free' in the sense of not being dependent (in sexual, economic, emotional ways) on men; and so lesbianism forms one important projection of male fears.

The reactions of gay men, together with the reactions of male academics and colleagues, as we discussed and wrote about the obscene calls, brought home to us that many of *them* experienced the calls as sexually arousing, in the same way that the callers did. What these men found arousing wasn't anything about women in them, but their phallic imagery, and their expression of sexuality and violence as synonymous. What they found so arousing were verbal expressions of physical violence, pain, and with the enactment of these on people who were unwilling. We came to believe that gay men shared more with heterosexual men, more about violence and power, than we'd previously believed. We came to believe what they shared was their common experience of the penis in a particularly phallocentric and sexist fashion – as a weapon. In other words, we came to feel that gay men were in no sense different from heterosexual men in their ideas about power and the penis.

4 To pass or not to pass, is that the question?

At the same time that each of the above experiences occurred, they intermingled with our long involvement in lesbian consciousness-raising groups. We were both, separately, involved in a long succession of these groups over a period of about three years. During this time we came to feel that 'the oppression of lesbians' was very different from how we had earlier understood it. The central problem, we came to realize, wasn't 'the family', 'capitalism' or even the 'self-oppression' described by the GLF *Manifesto*. Instead we came to eschew structural explanations altogether.

People who smoke can't imagine what reality would be like without smoking. Often they can't believe that such a reality could exist for them. And similarly lesbians who pass, who behave and allow ourselves to be treated as heterosexual, can't imagine what it is like to live openly as a lesbian. Part of the problem lies in 'self-oppression' perhaps, in not really believing that 'gay is good', and in really believing that lesbian means inferior. But much more than this, for the vast majority of women we have known, it is not being able to envisage people's reactions to lesbianism – or being able to envisage these *only too well*. These women fear rejection, abuse, biblical scenes of denunciation, or even physical attack. These things happen, of course. But not very often. In our and many other people's experience, calm acceptance, lack of interest or mild curiosity are more frequent. Underlying these may be darker, less pleasant, feelings and thoughts, but these are infrequently expressed to lesbians convinced that lesbianism is perfectly acceptable.

It was around discussions of how to achieve a social reality in which it is possible to be openly gay, and in which people don't react negatively to lesbianism, that our 'small groups' were based. Sometimes these discussions occurred directly, sometimes obliquely; sometimes they occurred easily, and sometimes in a painful and upsetting way; but these were always the issues that, sooner or later, were arrived at.

It would be untrue to suggest that 'consciousness-raising', in the sense in which the WLM tends to use this term, always occurred in these small groups. The term is based on the idea that there are *levels* of consciousness, that there is a hierarchy of consciousness with some levels better and 'higher' than others, and with 'feminist consciousness' better than its absence. We do not accept such an elitist conception of consciousness, such a patronizing assessment of other women's understandings. We feel like this because we believe that any 'state of consciousness' is deeply rooted in particular sets of experiences. It isn't produced through effort of will, nor is it resisted out of sheer bloody-mindedness, stupidity or malevolence. If people do not share the same experiences, they will not share the same consciousness.

This was true for the women in our small groups. All lesbians we might have been, but we didn't all share the same experiences and, even where we did, different women interpreted and related to the same experiences in often quite different ways. We cannot say that this was wrong, that some women 'failed' to have their consciousness raised, or to raise them themselves. What we can say is that these small group experiences changed us all; where and what we changed to differed considerably.

Here we are a long way from 'the family oppresses women and homosexuals.' We have outlined these four sets of experiences in some detail to show how they were important for us in informing and changing our understanding of 'the oppression of lesbians' and also 'the oppression of women'. It wasn't any theory about 'the family' that helped us make sense of the things we were involved in, although we started out believing it. And so we'd now like to outline what we feel are the most important things we learned from these experiences.

These experiences led us to understand that ideas about how 'structures' impose themselves through 'socializing' various 'internalized' behaviours and attitudes are, quite simply, irrelevant. What is relevant, and should form the basis of our theorizing about oppression, is our *experience of oppression itself.* How we experience oppression tells us a great deal about what this oppression is and how it operates.

Oppression we see as quite different for lesbians than for gay men. Gay men we see as 'men', frequently more sexist and certainly more phallocentric than many heterosexual men. We also now understand how gay men have attempted to take over and use feminist theory of the family in order to absolve themselves from any responsibility for the oppression of women. By portraying themselves as oppressed by 'the system' in the same way that women are oppressed by it, they seem to be freed from blame.

This is achieved through the manipulation of dichotomous terms and frameworks of the kind we've already discussed, and in particular the dichotomy 'oppressor/oppressed'. The oppressed are oppressed – they can't at the same time be the oppressors. It isn't of course just gay men who've used this analysis. We used it too; and we feel cheated because we used it in good faith, and we believe that they used it dishonestly.

We used to believe that lesbians were oppressed because we are homosexual. All homosexuals, whether women or men, are oppressed in similar ways because of the way people feel about homosexuality. We also believed that lesbians are oppressed because we are women. All women, whether heterosexual or lesbian, are oppressed in similar ways because of the way that men feel about women. But the experiences we have outlined led us away from this analysis to something rather different. We now believe that lesbians are oppressed because we are particularly threatening women – women who aren't dependent on men and, in this sense, 'free women'. We feel that many men react to what they experience as threatening by 'sexualizing' it. If nothing else, that the penis can batter lesbians into submission is what our obscene callers told us in no uncertain terms.

In addition to all of this, we also suggest that 'the oppression of lesbians' will differ for different women in different situations and at different times in our lives. It will also differ for women who live openly as lesbians and those who pass as heterosexual. What differs is not 'just' our understanding of oppression, but the concrete material form of oppression itself. This is because it is understanding, consciousness, which shapes the material world. The shape, the *form*, of oppression will be similar for all lesbians, but its concrete expression, its *content*, may differ.

Where, one might ask, does all of this leave 'the family' in our analysis? The answer is 'nowhere very much'. Indeed, how we see 'the family' more generally within feminist theory is very similar to this. We see it simply as an institution within society, as a 'social structure' if you like, but without any of the semi-mystic connotations that this term often has. It has a role in legislation, in the welfare system particularly; and some aspects of its functioning are forced upon women (and children and men). And people who live within families may be oppressed. But we don't agree that it is this, 'the family', which is responsible for the oppression of lesbians and other women.

We see such a line of argument as simplistic, borrowed from structural analyses with little consideration of whether it is adequate for feminist analysis. It ignores the *fact* that different women *experience* oppression differently. We stress 'fact' and 'experience' here because we see them as synonymous, and reject the idea that there are 'real' conditions of oppression outside of experience and understanding.

THEORY AND EXPERIENCE

To return to our starting point, we emphasize that, *experientially*, the analysis of the key oppressive role of 'the family' in the oppression of lesbians is, to say the least, lacking. But the rejection of theory on the basis of experience is what many people won't accept as a proper basis for the evaluation of theoretical adequacy. Experience? Subjectivity?

Because we believe that 'experience' is the basis of all analysis, and for all evaluation of analyses, in an odd sort of way we find ourselves saying something similar to Mitchell and Oakley – that *my* family, husband, gay oppression, may indeed be different. And so we too feel that other people's experientially based theory shouldn't form the basis of one's own actions. However, where we part company from them is in our argument that it is one's *own* experience which should form the basis of both theory and practice. Experience, theory and practice should exist in a mutual and immediate relationship with each other.

What we have tried to do in the last part of this chapter is to take a key theoretical idea, one derived from feminist thinking and adopted within the gay movement, and one which we were both involved in producing and promoting. We then examined a set of experiences which led us to reject our previously accepted theoretical analysis. We've done this because we want to demonstrate two closely linked things. The first is that 'the personal' is centrally involved in the evaluation of theoretical analysis and in the production of new theoretical analysis. Ideas don't come from nowhere into people's heads, nor does criticism. And the second is that as much as the personal is involved in theoretical analysis, so it is in oppression itself. Institutions, structures, do not oppress. *People* oppress people – they make decisions to do so, and the oppressed sometimes comply in acts of oppression.

We are not, we must emphasize here, trying to deny that lesbians and homosexual men are murdered, assaulted, raped, beaten-up, mutilated, attacked, persecuted, discriminated against, poked fun at. All of these things we know happen to people just because we happen to be, or are seen to be, lesbians or gay men. But what we are trying to do is to point out that it is the idea that these things will *inevitably* occur that chains most gay people to our own secrecy, our own pretence at heterosexuality, our own shameful silences – and our own oppressions.

Closely related to all of this is our insistence that there is no 'going beyond' the personal, that chimera of contemporary feminist theory. To talk about 'going beyond' is to posit a false distinction between experience and theory and between structure and process. But in another sense our arguments might be objected to as unfair, as an undue misrepresentation of a very real need to theorize women's experience. The insistence of 'getting beyond' might instead be seen as a more general equivalent to Sheila Rowbotham's 'maps'. However, while accepting the 'maps' view of theory, we stick by our interpretation of the 'beyond the personal' argument for reasons we now elaborate.

For a start, the kind of theory generally proposed is something very different from the experientially grounded kind we prefer. It is abstract, generalized, 'objectified' theory which bears little relationship to anything very real. It is concerned with abstract ideas abstractly related and 'standing on behalf of' lived experiences. And underlying it is an assessment of the personal we profoundly disagree with – that the personal is limited because of its particularness and is merely the product of the person whose 'personal' it is. And closely connected to this is the idea that if experience clashes with theory then it should be discarded as 'false', limited and too partial. However, we feel that the generalizations involved in 'theory' as many feminists would have it don't escape from subjective experiences. Instead these are multiplied. This kind of theory is produced by multiplying subjective experiences and generalizing from them in order to produce an 'objective' account.

Feminism must look for an alternative. And this alternative ought to include an understanding of 'theory' which doesn't present 'the expert's theory' as an alternative to, and test of, the adequacy of 'the person's theory'. We feel that much feminist theory and research tends to do this, to treat women whose experiences don't correspond with theory as falsely conscious or otherwise inadequate. When looked at from the viewpoint of these women this is offensive and patronizing – not a good basis for sisterly solidarity. Feminism's alternative to conventional theorizing must reject collecting experiences merely in order to generalize them out of all recognition. Instead it should be concerned with going back into 'the subjective' in order to explicate, in order to examine in detail exactly what this experience is.

And as for why theorizing should be like this, we see it as a more humane, less 'scientific' and patronizing approach than one which uses people's lives as merely research fodder. The traditional approach *uses* people, but sees us as more inadequate in understanding our lives than the researcher, with her fleeting and partial acquaintance with these. We also feel that women's liberation requires something it doesn't yet have – an adequate analytic understanding of women's oppression. The way to gain such an understanding is to listen much more carefully, take much more seriously, what women and men have to tell us about their lives. There's little point in *us* telling *them* that they've got it wrong, that they haven't understood it properly. Apart from all other considerations, this would simply confirm feminism in a quite unacceptable elitism – *is* confirming it in this. It is confirming it in a belief that feminists, having read a few books, done a bit of consciousness-raising and talked a lot about 'the working classes', have got the answers and have nothing to learn from other people's experiences beyond 'transcending' them through adding them into many others, and so producing 'theory'.

Chapter 4

Socialization and gender role
A sort of critique

In the previous chapter we suggested that one of the most important aspects of feminist theory – that concerning the critical role
of the family – is inadequate. We argued its inadequacy on a
number of grounds, principally that personal experience should
be the prime test of theory.

In this chapter we go on to apply our arguments to some other
aspects of feminist theory. Feminist theory of the family includes
within it two key theoretical concepts. The first of these is the
concept of 'socialization', the second the concept of 'role'. We
find the feminist adoption of these concepts a good example of
the problem with 'adding women in' to existing theory. One of
these problems concerns what happens when we 'go beyond' the
personal to make generalized statements which are applied to all
people. These statements necessarily move away from people and
experience because of their abstract and generalized nature. They
'go beyond' people and into structures, and by doing so we
cannot personally evaluate them.

But structural accounts aren't merely removed from experience
and the everyday. They deny the validity of these in sometimes
subtle and sometimes gross ways. We feel that important within
this is their positivist character. They externalize explanations of
personal experience away from this experience and into something
which attempts to transcend it. And they also rely on the series
of dichotomies we discussed in chapter 1. The subject/object
dichotomy is basic to positivism; and we shall discuss feminist
objections to this particular dichotomy and to those theoretical
explanations which grow out of it. But where we begin is by
outlining some of the links which exist between feminist ideas

about 'the family' and feminist thinking about 'socialization' and 'gender role'.

'THE FAMILY', SOCIALIZATION AND GENDER ROLE

In the last chapter we briefly outlined a feminist theory of how the oppression of women occurs and argued that feminist ideas about 'the family' were central in this. These ideas hinge on feminist accounts of the relationship between the individual and society. It is within 'the family' that the values, norms, expectations and ideologies of society as a whole are internalized by individuals – 'the family' turns individual egos into social beings.

Whether feminist explanations are labelled 'marxist', 'liberal' or anything else, it is interesting to note that the emphasis on 'the family' remains the same, even though 'in life' there seems such vast and unresolvable differences between different 'types' of feminists. But we feel able to present a composite picture of how processes are seen to operate within 'the family' because of this common emphasis within feminism generally. This composite picture is drawn from a number of feminist writings, but particularly from the work of Lee Comer, Elizabeth Wilson, Ann Oakley and Sue Sharpe (Comer, 1974; Wilson, 1977; Oakley, 1972; Sharpe, 1976).

'The family' expanded

Within feminist theory of 'the family', women's roles within family life are seen as absolutely crucial to the perpetuation of 'the system'. And this is so whether that system is seen to be capitalism or patriarchy. Women are seen as central in this way because of our two roles: our biological role as childbearers and our social role as the family member most responsible for 'socialization'.

'Socialization', briefly, is that process by which children are transformed into social beings who have taken on particular norms and values, and know what kinds of behaviours are expected of them. Most feminist writers seem to see socialization as a kind of 'self-fulfilling prophecy': a self-perpetuating system which goes on from generation to generation. But the main focus of feminist concern is not this entire process, but rather that part of it which is seen to be particularly important in women's oppression – sex role socialization. Sex role, or often gender role, socialization is that bit of the process by which children come to be not only social beings, but either 'feminine' or 'masculine' ones. And here, of course, 'femininity' and 'masculinity' – gender – involve clusters of attributes and behaviours seen, within particular societies, to be appropriate for females and males respectively.

What is seen as the 'content' of this process – norms, values, behaviours and so forth – is also seen as a content which derives from the needs of 'the system' we earlier referred to. It is the perpetuation of *capitalism* or *patriarchy* which requires that people should behave, think and *be* in these particular ways, the argument goes. Closely connected is the idea that the demands and requirements of the system translated through an ideology of family life constitute reality. Whether family life is experienced as the embodiment of love and support, or as a destructive hell, is neither here nor there: its *reality* is its particular function within 'the system'. Embedded within ideas about the family are a further two concepts: 'socialization' and 'gender role'. We shall now go on to examine, in the form of composite descriptions, some important although general aspects of feminist thinking about these concepts.

Most feminists argue that at birth all children are assigned a gender which is based on the appearance of their genitals. Gender is then inculcated, at first by their mothers differentiating between children of different sexes through their behaviours towards them. Most feminists also argue that mothers respond differently towards their children on the basis of preconceptions about what biological sex differences are supposed to exist; and these differences include touching, soothing and differential ideas about the autonomy (or lack of it) of boy and girl children.

Some feminists believe that the direction of personality, more specifically its femininity or masculinity, is set in the very earliest interactions between an infant and its parents, more particularly its mother.

Women who believe this suggest that the universal mothering role of women differentially affects boys and girls. For girls there is a universal internalization of certain features of the relationship between them and their mothers; and 'Through this process the individual characteristics of society are reproduced' (Sharpe, 1976,

p. 74). The mother/daughter relationship is based on a mutual interaction in which each identifies with the other. However, the mother/son relationship is seen as quite different, because a mother is described as stressing the opposition between herself and her son.

These early processes may be described as unconscious or conscious in nature; whichever, they are seen as the prime determinants of later interactions within the family and as the basis of adult personality. Both interpretations recognize the existence of conscious socialization behaviours, and usually draw on the work of Ruth Hartley in order to describe these (Hartley, 1966). One consequence is that 'learning gender' here isn't seen as verbal or disciplinary in nature, but rather as 'kinaesthetic'. Kinaesthetic processes involve, in essence, a number of ways in which children are directly manipulated into 'being socialized'.

The effects of these processes, this argument suggests, is that by the age of four children know their sex identity and are also aware of the fine distinctions of gender. And the extent to which they are sexually stereotyped is seen as directly affected by parental behaviours. In other words, the more parents treat their children in sexually differentiated ways, for example in exposing them to particular kinds of toys, the more it is believed that a child will reflect such stereotypes.

We have already hinted that parents are seen as able to influence directly the extent to which their children are sexually stereotyped by many feminists. From this it will be apparent that much feminist theorizing sees events within the family, and parent (or mother)–child interactions, as the means by which these kinaesthetic processes occur and are effected (and effective). This is because most feminist writers argue that children identify with their parents through either 'imitation' or 'identification'. Which of their parents they imitate, and, more importantly, identify with, is strongly influenced by the relative power of the two parents. Many feminists believe that, generally, both girls and boys identify with the one they always describe as the more powerful of the two – their fathers. However, the later identification of girls with their mothers is described as occurring by puberty at the latest, because it is at this point in their development that girls experience much stronger peer and other pressures on them to conform to sexual stereotypes.

The most important later sources of gender stereotypes are seen as other children and, especially, the mass media. Children tend to internalize stereotyped images, identify with them, and then enact them (how on earth anyone managed to become gender stereotyped in the days before the mass media is an interesting point to ponder). The result of such processes is that gender roles become a central feature of adult personality.

Basic concepts in feminist descriptions of the processes involved in 'learning gender' include 'imitation', 'identification' and 'internalization'. Children *imitate* the behaviours of those people they identify with. They tend to *identify* with one or other of their parents and usually their fathers, although for girls a sexually differentiated form of identification is later brought about through the internalization of outside pressures. This particular interpretation of *internalization* suggests a direct and in many cases one-to-one relationship between what children are presented with and what they later enact.

One exceedingly interesting point about feminist ideas about 'socialization' and 'role' which we hope will have been detected by readers is the very great emphasis placed on the part that *mothers* play in socialization and thus in women's oppression. We're told that it is *mothers* who are involved in the earlier unconscious stages of socialization; and that it is *mothers* who are primarily involved in effecting the kinaesthetic processes. *Mothers* treat little boys and little girls differently, and so it is they who produce sexually stereotyped children and adults. Blaming the victim?

We have said that an amazing agreement about these aspects of 'the family' exists among feminists. We believe that two things account for this, the second much more important than the first. The first is the common use of sources. By and large most feminist writings on this subject seem to rely on the same research, carried out mainly by non-feminists, and now rather dated research at that. The second is that this great unity in thinking derives from the adoption of what is basically the same model of socialization.

This model is one in which the processes of socialization are seen as those by which 'social structures' are internalized by children. Parents are seen as a kind of funnel through which stereotyped behaviours of all kinds are presented to children who then obligingly internalize them. There is a great reliance on the concept of 'internalization': 'gender' as systemized behaviours and attributes derives from this. Some accounts, we should point out, do state that an enormous variety of behaviours and attitudes exist in the real world, even in relation to gender-associated phenomena. But, in spite of this, all such complexities are left behind as of no great importance. This model stresses the paramount importance of generalities, stereotypes, and the common processes of socialization; and portrays variations and differences as theoretically unimportant.

We shall go on to argue that this model is one which feminists have taken over and used, practically unchanged, from monocausal structural approaches within the social sciences. But before doing this we'd like to make one further comment about what we've written so far. At the beginning of this section we said that our 'composite picture' was derived from the work of many feminists, but four in particular – Lee Cromer, Elizabeth Wilson, Ann Oakley and Sue Sharpe. These women could, quite legitimately we feel, point the finger at our descriptions and say that these bear little or no resemblance to their work, which has been caricatured out of all recognition. We feel that this is a legitimate point to make because what we've presented *is* a caricature. And this is because what we've done is to make generalizations, to produce universalized statements out of individual accounts. In the last chapter we argued against the production of universalized theory, and we let what appears in this section stand as part of our evidence for arguing so.

'Socialization' as a feminist form of functionalism?

We now move away from describing feminist writings on socialization and role through composite pictures, generalizations. Instead we focus on the work of two people who have written about socialization, sex role or gender role socialization in particular. One of these people is a feminist and the other most decidedly not. However, we look at the work of both to suggest that both feminist and non-feminist accounts utilize the same basic model of the processes involved in socialization.

The feminist work on socialization we examine is that of Helen Weinreich; and we do so in order to look at some of its strengths and also some of what we feel to be its limitations (Weinreich, 1978). We haven't chosen it because we particularly wish to criticize it. Indeed, rather the reverse. We see Helen Weinreich's examination of socialization as much more complex and highly developed than those of other feminists because it includes within it, in a complex and complementary way, a number of different ideas and concepts which are usually used as opposites, as mutually exclusive, in other accounts of socialization. The reason we've chosen to discuss it is precisely because it includes the strengths of other accounts and excludes many of their weaknesses. It will become clear later that the substance of our feelings about its limitations stems from the *kind* of approach adopted, its basic model of socialization, and indeed the notion of socialization itself; and not more specific features of it.

Socialization, Weinreich suggests, is concerned with the 'transmission' of behaviours, roles, attributes and beliefs to the next generation and has three key facets. The first focuses on internalization through direct proscription, example and expectation. The second emphasizes the part played by 'socializing agents' (primarily but not exclusively the family), who hold stereotypical beliefs about sex-appropriate characteristics which are reflected in their socialization practices. The third points out that many aspects of socialization are particularly concerned with sex roles and these are mainly cultural in origin although 'undoubtedly', Weinreich feels, some are biologically based.

Weinreich uses material drawn from Maccoby and Jacklin's review of the literature on psychological sex differences in order to examine actual measured sex differences and stereotypes (Maccoby and Jacklin, 1975). She too concludes that there are very few established behavioural differences between males and females, and those that do exist generally become established after early childhood.

The main four aspects of socialization for Weinreich are the process of *learning*, the use of *models, identification* with the same-sex parent and *self-socialization*. In relation to this fourth process, Weinreich uses the work of Kohlberg to suggest that gender is an important category for making of the world (Kohlberg, 1966) because it facilitates the easy categorizing of events, people and behaviours; and this is seen as the basis for children's very swift adoption of sex roles and sex-stereotyped behaviours.

Finally, Weinreich outlines a number of the problems which arise from sex-role socialization. She suggests that such problems are experienced by both females and males, although they may occur at different stages and in different ways. She also discusses the conflict that exists between the covert and overt demands which are made of children, using as an important example of this the conflicting demands made on girls within the educational system.

The decidedly non-feminist work on socialization that we now look at is that of Talcott Parsons, one of the key figures involved in the development of functionalist theory. We're particularly interested in his work on socialization because we think that a comparison of feminist work with that of a key figure within functionalism, one of the main targets of feminist criticisms, is particularly illuminating.

Parsons' account of the relationship between socialization and family structure borrows heavily from Freudian terminology, although he uses this in an idiosyncratic way (Parsons, 1956a; Parsons, 1956b; Parsons, 1956c; Parsons, 1956d; Parsons and Bales, 1956). Taking the Freudian concepts of the id, the ego and the super-ego, Parsons relates them to his own belief that there are four key phases of socialization which occur within the family. And so, in order to relate Freudian ideas to his own, he develops and adds on to them the concept of 'identity'. As with most other accounts of socialization, Parsons too emphasizes the crucial importance of 'primary socialization', that aspect of it which occurs in early childhood. And it is because of this that he is so concerned with the processes involved in sex role identification.

A key concept in the Parsonian scheme is that of 'role differentiation'. Parsons maintains that different roles must exist in the relationship between spouses, and that the development of sex-role identification in childhood mirrors the different roles which exist between a child's parents. The 'instrumental' role involves 'universalistic norms' of various kinds and is concerned with the relationship between the family unit and the outside world. The 'expressive' role involves 'particularistic norms' and is concerned with the nexus of relationships within the family. There are no prizes for guessing that Parsons identifies the instrumental role with males and the expressive role with females.

In summary, then, Parsons sees the processes of socialization as intimately concerned with the internalization of sets of *reciprocal* expectations which exist between the child and others. In many ways this is a 'learning theory', in which the child takes over specific behaviours of various kinds. But Parsons also uses the idea of identification, and the existence of 'identificands' within the family. And as well as this he retains some allegiance to an 'action' perspective in which the individual is seen to be active in construing and 'making' their own social reality. A result is that Parsons sees the child as itself active in the entire process. It is the child who makes choices and then enacts these, rather than being merely passive in a process of simple internalization.

We feel that there are a number of important ways in which Parsons' and Weinreich's accounts are similar. These include their common complementary use of facets of each of the existing socialization theories, their common adoption of a bi-polar notion of gender role, and their common belief that the sex role socialization they describe is essential to 'the system' that each depicts.

Parsons takes over and combines various aspects, concepts and ideas from the three main kinds of socialization theory that exist (Mussen, 1971), as well as from Freudian theory. Weinreich borrows from each of these three main kinds of socialization theory in her complementary use of them. She doesn't use Freudian terminology. However, she does utilize a psychoanalytic explanation of the basic processes seen as underlying the more overt learning processes. And this, of course, ultimately derives from Freudian psychoanalytic thinking.

Within Parsons' work the reciprocal 'instrumental' and 'expressive' roles are approvingly described as belonging to and describing two quite separate 'worlds'. The first is the world of work and the economy; the second that of home and love and child-rearing. Weinreich too sees gender as involving polarized clusters of attributes, masculinity and femininity. However, she argues that this polarization involves, particularly for females, problems and conflicts, while Parsons' work emphasizes the functional necessity of the processes he describes. Sex-role socialization is seen as essential to the continuance of the reciprocal role relationships involved in instrumentality and expressivity. And these role relationships are seen as essential to the maintenance of the social system. Now, although Weinreich's account is no overtly functionalist one, we believe that some of its arguments are very similar indeed to those we have just outlined. For her, sex-role socialization is essential to the continued existence of highly differentiated gender roles. And highly differentiated gender roles are similarly seen as essential to the perpetuation of 'the system' she is concerned with. This is, of course, sexist society in which women are treated differently because of their supposed inferiority.

We believe that the main difference between Parsons' and Weinreich's work is the moral assessment that each makes of what they describe. Parsons believes that what he describes exists in the real world, that the continued existence of this is necessary for the perpetuation of the status quo, and that this is essential and desirable. Weinreich believes that what she describes exists in the real world but, in marked contrast to Parsons, she objects to what exists on moral grounds. She doesn't agree that it is good or necessary that males and females should be differentially treated, and she believes that this ought to be changed. But there is an important difference here which we have glossed over. Parsons explains socialization as the product of society – of society's needs and requirements; and Weinreich explains society as the product of socialization. So it might be more accurate to emphasize not only the moral difference between them, but also that they use rather different types of explanation, in terms of what explains what. But in spite of this we feel that in most important respects their ideas are very similar indeed.

'Socialization theory' exists in feminist and non-feminist varieties; but in important ways these are varieties of the *same* theory – the 'socialization model'. We believe that the socialization model is 'psychologistic'. It suggests that there exists *within* the child various innate processes. It postulates a pre-formed and almost autonomously unfolding ego which develops independently of the social. We say 'almost' because it also identifies the existence of parental, and especially mothering, socialization practices which act as 'stimulus', so encouraging this 'response'. Apart from this, it sees what happens in social reality 'outside' of the child as independent of these processes and irrelevant to them. Of course self-socialization theory, as a variant within this model, isn't psychologistic in this way; and it does see action and interaction within the child's life as very important. However, self-socialization theory retains a psychologistic 'underbase', because it argues these social processes are based on innate sex differences which become established by the age of two or so (Stanley, 1976).

To us, the socialization model also seems overly deterministic. It presents us with what has been referred to as an over-socialized conception of people within a too deterministic view of social reality (Wrong, 1961). People are presented as totally passive and totally malleable and entirely determined by 'society'. There are, of course, some variants within this model which recognize that

'exceptions' exist and that all individuals aren't entirely programmed in this way. However, more often than not these are
accounted for by simply saying that 'proper socialization' has
failed to take place.

In explaining 'exceptions' these variants aren't adopting probabilistic statements rather than claiming universality. If they did
so they would be less objectionable. Instead we see them as
both claiming universality and at the same time recognizing that
universality doesn't exist. They have their cake and eat it too
because they quite simply reject any notion that the existence of
'exceptions' might be important, something for theory to explain.

Instead of looking for explanations, 'exceptions' are simply
labelled as 'deviance', the result of 'mal-socialization' and so forth.
They do this because, of course, they look at the world through
the framework provided by the socialization model. And at
the heart of this we find the dichotomy 'properly gender-
stereotyped'/'not properly gender-stereotyped'. What feminists
who adopt the socialization model seem unwilling to confront is
that this model embodies the values and power divisions of sexist
society. Conform and you're acceptable; dare to be different and
you must be a freak of some kind, are the ideas this model
enshrines and perpetuates.

That we've described the socialization model as both psychologistic and presenting an over-socialized view might seem
contradictory. After all, 'psychologistic' suggests the natural
unfolding of innate processes already 'in' the child; and 'over-
socialized' quite the opposite – that the child is totally malleable.
We agree: these *are* contradictory things to say. However, we
believe that this is a contradiction which exists within the socialization model and not just in our description of it. Although we
recognize this contradiction exists, we don't feel that most of the
people who adopt the socialization model do. They seem quite
happy saying both that gender is psychologically innate *and* that
gender stereotyping is dependent on 'agents of socialization'.

The socialization model is also reificatory. By this we mean it
suggests that 'the social system' somehow 'demands' that certain
things should occur. Within this 'the family' is the means of
ensuring that these demands are fulfilled. Such an approach sees
social systems existing over, above, and beyond the collection of
individuals and artifacts which compose them. It sees the whole
as more than the sum of its parts. Later we shall suggest some

implications for feminists in adopting an approach which reifies in this way. But before doing this we'd like to look at what we think is the most important criticism to be made of the socialization model.

We believe that the most important criticism to be made of the socialization model is that it is 'non-reflexive'. By this we mean that it explains obviously 'mal-socialized' or 'un-socialized' people as mistakes within the system; and feminist adoptions of this model let such labels and categorizations stand. The basic dichotomy we've identified within this model is one which sees *feminism*, along with lesbians, 'effeminate' men, career women, and a myriad of other people, as 'mistakes' whose existence can't be explained except by reference to 'mal-socialization'. That the feminists who use this model don't confront or seem to notice this issue comes, we believe, from their take-over of it in a practically unchanged form. They merely add women into it rather than critically focusing on the premises of the model itself. However, rather than continuing this discussion about non-reflexivity around the socialization model, in the next section we consider reflexivity and non-reflexivity more widely.

REFLEXIVITY AND 'ROLE'

In the last chapter we briefly outlined feminist thinking about 'the family' and we responded to this by saying that our own lived experiences form the basis for our own theory of oppression. We said that it was *our* experientially-based theory, and *not* feminism's universalized theory, which was important to us. In a way responding like this side-stepped the issue of how we felt about specific aspects of feminist theory. What we've tried to do in the previous section is to describe in more detail how feminist theory describes the *processes* of socialization (and thus oppression). We responded there to this universalized, generalized, approach largely in its own terms. That is, our response consisted of logical points and arguments about similarities between ostensibly different models. In this section we try to move away from responding to this approach in a more technical way. We try to break out of the framework it imposes on our thinking, and respond to it in our terms through looking at it in relation to what we believe feminist theory ought to be like.

The most important criticism of feminist adoption of the socialization model is that in a particularly curious sense it is non-reflexive. Because it turns on the socialized/not socialized dichotomy, it explains all 'not stereotypically socialized' people as failed products of socialization – all people who aren't stereotypically feminine or masculine are 'deviant' in some sense. Perhaps feminist uses of this theory don't accept this kind of labelling of 'exceptions'. But what they *do* do is to imply that 'exceptions' are unimportant irrelevancies by simply ignoring the existence of these.

One consequence is that feminist explanations of women's oppression ignore the existence of feminists, lesbians, men who oppose sexism, and other people who aren't like the stereotype for their sex. Now a feminist theory which ignores feminism because it isn't important enough to include is a very peculiar feminist theory. But even more objectionable to us is that, by failing to take a stand against the portrayal of all exceptions as 'deviancies', feminist theory leaves undiscussed and uncriticized the *political* phenomenon in which lesbians, among other 'deviants', are oppressed. And as lesbian feminists we register our protest at our sisters' failure to confront heterosexism within the theories they utilize.

Another consequence arises out of the construction of 'socialization processes'. These are described by feminists and non-feminists alike as those processes which normally, typically, happen in normal, typical, families. But such vast generalizations gloss over, don't see as existing, the possibility that these abstractions, generalized statements, are *only* generalized abstractions and aren't even an approximation to lived experience. Such statements are often based on inadequate research, in that it is work on white, largely middle-class, nuclear families, and largely ignores fathers as unimportant in socialization (Maccoby and Jacklin, 1975). And, in addition to this, the abstractions derived from this work – 'canalization', 'identification' and the like – are those which researchers, *adults*, place on their constructions of *children's* responses to the adult world. To respond in experiential terms here is very difficult; we can only 'remember' our childhood pasts through constructions provided by our adult present-day selves. And as for us so for all other researchers. So then, we see this approach, and the mystic 'processes' it throws up, as a good example of adult chauvinism and fantasy. That most of us reach adulthood is indisputable; what can and must be disputed are the definitions of 'child', 'adult', and of the processes which link these two stages in our being.

We have said that feminist uses of socialization theory are non-reflexive in a particularly curious way, and pointed to our objections to this as lesbian feminists. We feel that a feminist theory which is set up as a means of explaining 'other people' isn't 'feminist' as we understand feminism, for a number of reasons. First of all, it separates-off 'feminists' from 'people', and it goes on to depict families as making theories about 'people', always *other* people. Second, it implies that feminists are different from the 'other people' they make theories about. And, third, the end result is 'theory' as a massive generalization that applies to no one in particular.

Our first objection could equally well apply to social theory produced by other 'experts' as well as feminists. 'Experts' make theories about 'people'. We fear that the result of adopting this kind of approach by feminists will be a situation in which feminists become part of a new power structure, in which we, feminists, become the new experts. We become experts on women, on sexual divisions, on sexual oppression. And 'women' – the *objects* of our expertise – become seen as merely 'falsely conscious'.

Our second objection is closely related to this. If feminists become the experts, the theoreticians about other people's reality, then we distance ourselves from them. We mark ourselves off as different, as those people who see the real reality of sexual oppression, who are not stereotyped and falsely conscious like 'them'.

Our third objection follows Margrit Eichler's critical discussion of role (1980), in which she suggests that the global nature of the concept, and of the research conducted around it, means that it is absolutely not applicable to *individuals* at all. We feel that feminists who produce theories which do not apply to people, and to feminists as well as to other people, are strange. Surely feminism should be concerned with making *experience* the basis of theory, and not with making a fetish out of 'grand theory' which, by its very nature, can't be applied to specific situations?

We believe that if theory can't be applied to people – some people somewhere – then it is of little use to feminism. Indeed, we feel that it runs counter to some of feminism's most fundamental beliefs and practices. We don't mean that theory should be capable of encompassing every aspect of someone's unique personality and experience. But we most certainly do mean that feminism should attempt to dissolve the power differentials between 'experts' (who usually just happen to be male) and 'people', including the power differentials between those who produce 'grand' and abstract theory and the rest of us. And we believe that feminism should pinpoint the fallacy (or perhaps phallacy) of grand theory – that it ignores or does not see that 'reality' is experienced differently from how this kind of theory portrays it. 'Theory' based on abstract misconceptions unconnected to experience is, surely, something which feminism ought to reject as an example for its own theoretical work. Feminist theory, we feel, ought to be much more concrete, connected and everyday.

We feel that the kind of socialization theory produced by feminists is 'feminist' only in the sense that it is concerned with adding women into existing models, theories and understandings within the social sciences. It is, we feel, a feminism concerned with taking over an existing view of reality, and building into this a portrayal of the situation of women. The appeal of such an approach, particularly in relation to socialization theory, is that such theories are neat, simple, and appear to have great explanatory power. Their problems, as we have already outlined in chapter 2, is that they simply add women into existing masculinist world views, and by doing so they distort and control women's experience.

'Role' or stereotype?

The concept of role, like the concept of socialization on which is it logically dependent, derives from existing social science theory. Some social scientists distinguish two basic ideas of role; and these are frequently referred to as 'role-making' and 'role-taking'. We begin our discussion of role by looking at these and comparing them with feminism's use of the 'role' concept.

'Role-making' emphasizes the importance of situation, personality and context in influencing events and behaviours. This approach doesn't see 'role' as anything which is 'internalized'; nor does it accept that any consensus about 'role content' exists, apart from in a few specific exceptions. Instead it sees 'role' as something which can be constructed and analysed only *after* the event. Only after something has happened can we know what has happened, and even then 'what has happened' may seem very different to the various participants within it.

However, 'role-taking' sees social reality in a rather different way. Here role is seen in functionalist terms, and this approach is frequently referred to as 'role theory'. Role theory, like functionalism, describes a determinate reality in which absolute order exists and prediction is possible. It believes that role content is generally agreed upon and that this content is internalized and then enacted. And role theory goes further than this, for it has been argued that people *are* the roles they inhabit (Frankenberg, 1966). Such arguments suggest that no distinction exists between 'self' and 'roles', because these roles combine to 'make up' the person.

Feminist ideas about 'gender roles' appear to us to adopt this 'role-taking' approach. For many feminists socialization is the means by which little girls and little boys become stereotypically feminine and masculine entities. The result is the sexual division of labour within the family reproduced in the next generation and so within society generally. For us this approach to role is one which is epitomized by the cover of Leanore Weitzman's introductory text on sex role socialization (1979). This shows a rubber stamp embossed with the word 'girl', and the cover of the book stamped with this word. Doubtless Weitzman had little control over what appeared on the cover, but what does appear implies that we are stamped in some way (perhaps by the great rubber stamp in the sky), and this then determines the form that we take on the printed page of our everyday lives. What could be more deterministic than this?

Many social scientists, working from a variety of perspectives, have noted the simplistic and over-deterministic aspects of role theory. Popitz, a role theorist himself, argues that role theory should be principally applied to institutionalized occupational roles and not to every aspect of behaviour which can be expressed in the form of a noun (Popitz, 1972). And from a quite different perspective Coulson, a marxist-feminist, insists that limiting role theory to an analysis of institutionalized roles is an irrelevancy. Discussing this suggestion, Coulson asks:

> does not the reduction of the concept to this level place it totally in question as a useful category? If the essential point is to explore the various expectations which different groups have

about the incumbents of particular social positions, then we may be able to approach this more directly if we do *not* introduce the concept of role at all (Coulson, 1972, p. 109).

These of course are criticisms of role theory generally, not of 'gender role'. However, many people have noted problems with the notion of 'gender role' itself.

Myra Komarovsky has carried out research on the masculine stereotype and also attempted to rebut Coulson's criticisms of the role concept around this research (Komarovsky, 1973). Her research was concerned with the nature and extent of the strains that men experienced 'in a given social milieu, at a certain stage of their life cycle, precisely because they are men and not women' (1973, p. 655). This 'strain', difficulty in fulfilling 'role obligations' and/or a sense of 'insufficient rewards for role conformity', was experienced by about half her sample members. And Komarovsky goes on to suggest that it would be a mistake to assume 'that the half of the sample who did not express anxiety on this score was composed solely of men who in fact exemplified these virtues' (1973, p. 655).

In spite of this, Komarovsky fails to question social science use of the concept of role. Indeed she argues for its continued usefulness which she feels lies in its ability to enable the identification of the 'intrusion of self into the role'. We're not at all sure we understand what she means by this. But what we do feel is that it would be sensible to use her research to conclude that the 'masculine role' (like the 'feminine role') exists as a *stereotype* to which the self may feel lesser or greater similarity and adherence, depending on a multitude of circumstances. But we feel that Komarovsky explains away the 'distance' between the role and these men's experiences, rather than confronting the issues which, for us, her research so plainly raises. She does this by arguing that this 'distance' is 'successfully resolved' through two processes. The first is by them avoiding all women who challenge their 'ideal' of masculinity. The second is by them concluding that for practical reasons women must retain their traditional 'feminine' responsibilities and tasks.

But we see this as not so much a 'resolution' as an avoidance of those practical circumstances which lead these men to feel 'distance'. We don't feel that Komarovsky's argument about 'distance' is very convincing. A much more straightforward approach is to start from the notion of 'distance' and not from role. We believe that 'roles' aren't internalized, do not 'become' the self. Instead we argue that the clusters of norms, attributes and so on that are referred to as 'gender' exist and are related to as *stereotypes* – as simplistic and stereotypic representations which people relate to in a myriad of ways. These are not in themselves 'reality' as people experience it; they are but one facet of what people construe this as.

Research carried out by one of us some years ago now (Stanley, 1976) certainly suggests that the 'distance' so well-documented by Komarovsky isn't confined to males or to America. This research was concerned with examining the two different views of 'role' that we earlier outlined – role-taking and role-making. More particularly, it looked at 'gender role' in relation to these. The results of this research suggest a number of interesting things. The first of these is that people do not willingly use sex-role stereotyped items when describing themselves. The second is that, in spite of this, when people are provided with stereotypic descriptions, they can easily and stereotypically describe 'masculinity' and 'femininity'. The third is that even when people are constrained into using stereotype items to describe themselves, they do this in a very different way from the way they describe a stereotyped person of their own sex.

These results corroborate Komarovsky's suggestion that many people experience a difference between 'themselves' and their 'femininity' or 'masculinity'. But of course we have drawn different conclusions from this than Komarovsky does and we believe that other criticisms of the 'role theory' approach to conceptualizing gender can be added to these.

Feminist ideas about gender see sexual stereotyping as something which happens in 'family life'. But feminists aren't sexually stereotyped as the stereotypes have been analysed and described. So why on earth doesn't feminist thinking about socialization and gender role ask questions about how feminists come to be feminist? And indeed why doesn't it go on from there to question whether other people might not be so stereotyped, and ask why and how? The answer – and a gloomy sort of answer it is – is that feminist ideas about gender role can't be applied to feminists except through various contortions, all of which involve identifying feminists as 'special'. And we've already outlined our feelings about 'specialness' in discussing the gay movement's use of feminist theory of 'the family' in the last chapter.

We believe that just as feminist ideas about gender role don't fit feminists, so they don't fit anyone in the way they're supposed to. Our approach is to emphasize the *making* and retrospective approach to 'role', and to argue that particular combinations of people and circumstance will see different 'displays' of behaviour of all kinds. Some will include gender displays, others not. And such gender displays will themselves vary. We echo what Erving Goffman has said about the belief that gender as a role is 'there', somewhere within us, and always expressed:

> we are led to accept as a portrait of the whole something that occurs at scheduled moments only, something that provides . . . a reflection not of the differential nature of persons in the two sex classes but of their common readiness to subscribe to the conventions of display (1976, p. 8).

The main point we want to emphasize here is that what we often construe as fixed and immutable, gender socialized *in* someone, should rather be seen as situationally variable. But feminism's adoption of the notion of role within its ideas about 'the family' leads it into producing massive generalizations which can be applied to only very few actual people. The search for universalized theory means there is no time or inclination to include – and little respect for – individual experience and individual variation. Too often this is treated as but so much grist to the ever turning mill of 'theory'. In contrast to this, we believe that a feminist approach should recognize, indeed begin from, the existence of variations and complexity. This doesn't mean that we believe that *all* 'structural' or general analysis must be eschewed, as we'll try to show in chapters 5 and 6, just that particularly simplistic version of it presently dominant within much feminist analysis.

FEMINIST THEORY OF 'THE FAMILY' AS A STRUCTURAL THEORY

Feminism's use of 'socialization' and 'role' as two key concepts in explaining women's oppression is a *structural* use of them. We are aware that there are many different kinds of structural approaches, of varying degrees of complexity and sophistication. However, we believe that the feminist use of the structural approach is a simple and unsophisticated one. This may be because feminism is just beginning to adopt this approach in its theorizing, and it might later produce more sophisticated versions. We would find this altogether regrettable, because the message we want to put across is that feminism should have no truck with conventional structural approaches, whether naive or sophisticated.

We believe that feminist use of structural approaches can be characterized as one in which social structure, institutions and social processes influence people in deterministic ways. The feminist kind of structural approach (and we include within this its marxist and other variants) sees human action as 'shaped' or determined by 'social forces'. These 'forces' are the product of structures and they exist outside of the people they 'shape'. What the individual says/does/thinks can be explained or even predicted by reference to whatever particular 'social structure' moulds them. Within this, 'socialization' describes the processes by which we, people, internalize sets of norms, values, characteristics and behaviours which 'society' wants us to.

The feminist kind of structural approach also suggests that, underlying the 'ideology' or 'sets of roles' that we internalize and enact, is a quite different, *real*, reality from the one we think we inhabit. People may tell us what their class position is; but *really* their objective position in the class structure may be different. Some women may reject the idea that they are oppressed; but *really* we know that they are.

We have included marxism-feminism along with other feminist uses of the structural approach quite deliberately in previous paragraphs. Along with Mitchell and Oakley we believe that many feminists, although rejecting other conventional wisdoms, have a very uncritical attitude towards all of the different varieties of marxism. We believe that much of this lack of criticism derives from fear, or something very like it. Many women appear to be very wary of standing up to marxist-feminist 'heavies' who in all circumstances appear to remain absolutely convinced of the total rightness of what they say. They are also worried about their tentative remarks being met by a barrage of superficially convincing theoretical rebuttal. But much of this lack of criticism derives from a feeling that marxism's radicalism about class can be extended so as to conceptualize women's oppression adequately. We ourselves reject such a starry-eyed attitude to it.

If feminism is critical of other systems of thought then it should also be critical of marxism. Quite simply, there is no reason for it not being so. Marxism hasn't been any great ally of women, either in theory or in practice. Its current enthusiasm for 'women's issues' is a response, often partial and grudging, and for which not always pure motives exist. But we suggest that there are other and more important reasons for developing a more critical attitude to it.

The dominant version of marxism, as we have pointed out, is a structural theory of the world (Worsley, 1980). Such theories see structures as 'more than' people and as self-perpetuating once in existence. Also they frequently describe systems as 'demanding', 'requiring', as though they had life of their own. In addition to this, they accept that one real objective social reality exists. The clear implication is that proponents of such theories know what this objective reality is, and so people who reject their explanations are falsely conscious. Such a patronizing insistence on the expertise of those accepting these explanations at the expense of those who don't ought to be totally offensive to all feminists. It appears not to be.

We have another objection to structural explanations. These enable people to hide in collectivisms, in the sense that they can avoid taking responsibility for their own lives and actions. 'The revolution' they envisage is a revolution of structures – economies, polities. These are seen as lying outside of everyday life, in the sense that they are conceptualized as self-perpetuating and so outside of ordinary human agency. But such an idea about social change is absolutely antithetical to the feminist insistence on the political importance of the personal, and the necessity of effecting political change through personal change. We find it useful to think of this kind of structural approach in terms of the 'talking head' phenomenon we referred to earlier, in which people's mouths speak liberated sentiments but their lives show no signs of these being put into practice. But, more than this, it simply isn't thought necessary for political sentiment and everyday life to be synonymous.

Within structural approaches 'the researcher' of the social scene plays an important part. These see research, if conducted 'properly', as a process of objective truth-gathering and truth-uncovering. And if the researcher's and the participants' accounts differ, then the researcher's is to be preferred. This is because participants are involved, their emotions cloud their judgements, they adopt partial viewpoints. But in contrast to this the researcher is trained, is an expert, and is an outsider who isn't involved and so can be objective about what's going on.

The underlying description of social reality contained in such structural approaches is positivist. Positivism sees social reality, social 'objects' and events as 'like' physical reality, objects and events. Positivism also accepts the existence of an 'objective' social reality. It argues that just as there is a real, kickable, irrefutable, physical reality, so there is one, equally real and irrefutable, social reality. When examining social events of various kinds, if we use the right methods, the most appropriate techniques, develop the best possible set of hypotheses/explanations, carry out this research without fear or favour and remain objective in doing so, then we shall eventually arrive at 'the truth' about it. And almost invariably we find that, within positivism, 'the truth' that is discovered is exactly what the researcher thought it might be right at the beginning.

That there isn't *one* true social reality 'out there' to be discovered, but competing truths and realities competently managed and negotiated by members of society, is rejected by positivism. This is because positivism knows that 'the truth' exists and that those people who don't believe this are, quite simply, wrong or misguided. They may be inadequately socialized, falsely conscious perhaps, or even deluded, but ultimately they are wrong.

We reject positivist views of social reality. First of all we reject the idea of 'the researcher' as a god-like creature who is able to leave behind subjective involvements while conducting research. We also believe that there are many (often competing) versions of truth. Which, if any, is 'the' truth is irrelevant. And even if such a thing as 'truth' exists, this is undemonstrable. This is because 'truth' is a *belief* which people construct out of what they recognize as facts. When other people reject our facts, insist that their own are the 'real' facts, this doesn't usually mean that we agree with them. Instead we use the same arguments that they do: *their* facts are wrong, *they* must be mistaken, we reject *their* interpretation.

Accepting the validity of other people's experiences, and rejecting the belief that there is *one* truth in social terms, ought to lead us to a position in which we do three things. First, we should reject positivism's interpretation of the 'researcher/subject' dichotomy. Second, we should take other people's truths seriously, even when we disagree with them. And, third, we should recognize the importance of examining and learning how people 'do' the truth – how people enact the 'objective reality' that we all inhabit.

The researcher/subject dichotomy

Social science researchers are defined as scientists, as people who set goals, devise rational means of achieving these, investigate social reality by using scientific techniques and modes of thought, in order to uncover the truth. In contrast to this, 'subjects' are defined as irrational, incapable of scientific thought or the use of scientific techniques, and instead have 'commonsense understanding' (read 'misunderstanding'). But, more than this, the 'science/life' dichotomy at the centre of the positivist approach suggests that people are more like *objects* than subjects. It portrays people as 'out there', and the researcher goes out and does research 'on' them.

However, that these 'objects' think, decide, react and interact within the world in general, and within the research processes in particular, is dismissed or its implications minimized by 'controlling for bias'. Discussing this point, Don Bannister writes of natural science scientists and their research objects, and contrasts this with the position of the psychologist. Of the natural scientist, Bannister suggests:

> He sits alone in his laboratory, test tube in hand, brooding about what to do with the bubbling green slime. Then it slowly dawns on him that the bubbling green slime is sitting alone in the test tube wondering about what to do with him. This special nightmare of the chemist is the permanent work-a-day world of the psychologist – the bubbling green slime is always wondering what to do about you (1966, quoted in Bannister and Fransella, 1971, pp. 188–9).

But for many social scientists, including most psychologists, this is *not* the 'work-a-day' world. Within the work-a-day world of research the person *is* treated as an object, including within much of that research conducted by feminists. And, in addition to this, the *presence*, complete with likes, dislikes and other subjective feelings, of the researcher within all research is a rarely discussed phenomenon. This is the mythology of 'hygienic research' in which the researcher can be 'there' without having any greater involvement than simple presence. Part of this mythology, which we shall discuss more fully in chapter 6, is that research can be carried out in such a way that 'the researcher' is unaffected and unchanged by the people she does research 'on'. That the researcher might affect the researched is a constant source of worry – this after all is what constitutes 'bias' – but that *they* might affect *her* is unthinkable.

It could be argued here that we have rejected the positivist view of research reality as invalid, as in some sense 'not true', and that this contradicts our earlier contention that views of reality can't be invalidated. We make two responses to this. The first is that what we're objecting to most strongly is the privileged status of the positivist view of reality – that this is seen as the only possible valid way of viewing it. The second is that we see positivist reality as invalid – but only for us. What we mean by this is that positivist reality isn't just 'reality for positivists' – 'positivist reality' is *their* generalized, universalized, view of *our realities*. We object to our lived experiences being turned into generalized mush.

Other people's truths

When people react to feminists and feminist arguments they typically do so on factual grounds. They either suggest we've got our 'facts' wrong, or that we're not interpreting the facts 'correctly' or 'objectively'. Both responses deny validity to women's experience, because they say that 'you may think you feel this, that you know this, but really you don't.' Doing this downgrades experience from 'valid and true' for the woman experiencing it, to 'irrational', sometimes 'neurotic' or even 'paranoid'. Frequently the product of research does exactly this, because it purports to unfold the truth for us. It says that 'what is really going on here (though the participants but dimly appreciate it) is this. . . .' This occurs, we feel, because 'the researcher's account' and 'the participant's account' are seen as *competing* attempts to get at *the* truth of a situation. Data are elicited by the researcher, who then evaluate them in relation to her assessment of the participant's competence in 'properly' understanding what is going on. This, of course, constitutes one of the major ways in which power is exercised in research situations, and we discuss it in more detail in chapter 6.

How people 'do' 'objective reality'

We have emphasized that different and competing explanations, understandings and interpretations of social reality exist. None of these, we believe, is 'the truth', because 'the truth' is undemonstrable even if it exists. This doesn't mean, however, that we deny the existence of 'objective reality'. We, as well as other people, base our lives on our belief that 'social facts' exist. Social events and behaviours have an objective and constraining reality for us as much as tables, chairs and corporation buses have for us. *But* we argue two things about this 'objective and constraining reality'.

The first is that this doesn't exist in and of itself, 'outside of' or 'beneath' everyday events as a 'social structure' or 'social force', as depicted in traditional structural accounts. Instead we argue that it is *daily constructed* by us in routine and mundane ways, as we go about the ordinary and everyday business of living. The second is that frequently there are conflicts between different realities, which people experience as such in their encounters with others. Such a conflict occurs in interactions between feminists and arch-sexists, and this constitutes one such break in our shared construction of 'reality, for all practical purposes'. We feel that seeing 'feminism' as the construction of an alternative reality, and as an alternative construction of sexist reality, is interesting and useful in understanding the nature of 'feminist consciousness', and so we look at it again in more detail in the next chapter.

One problem for researchers is what to *do* with these conflicts, these disagreements about 'reality'. We believe that to evaluate them on a single bi-polar scale of 'right/wrong', or 'rational/irrational', is pretty useless. Of much more interest and, in the long run, of much more use to us as feminists, is to attempt to understand how people 'do' their particular reality, whatever their and our evaluation of it. To take one example. If a housebound, depressed, battered mother of six with an errant spouse says she's *not* oppressed, there's little point in us telling her she's got it wrong because of the objective reality of her situation. Her construction of the facts in her life are different from our construction of them. And what she sees as the facts of her life is *truth* for her as much as any alternative account is truth for the onlooker. To swap arguments about 'I'm right and you're wrong' is silly and patronizing. What we feel is preferable is an approach which is concerned with exploring in great detail why and how people construct realities in the way that they do. Of course this doesn't preclude us from feeling that they may be wrong. However, it might prevent us from attempting to impose our reality on them when they don't want us to.

It might seem that we are a long way from our earlier discussion of ideas about socialization and role within feminist theory. But there are close links between what we've said about socialization and role and what we have said about positivism. The notions of socialization and role are structural ones; and structural accounts are premised on a positivist view of social reality. We feel that there are objections to feminism's adoption of this positivist view and we now summarize these.

Positivism describes social reality as objectively constituted, and so accepts that there is one true 'real' reality. It suggests that researchers can objectively find out this real reality – they can stand back from, remove themselves from emotional involvements in, what they study. It depicts social science as the search for social laws in order to predict and so control behaviour. And it argues that the techniques and procedures of the natural sciences are appropriately used within the social sciences. Basic to all of these is what we have already referred to as the 'subject/object' dichotomy. Positivism sees what is studied as an 'object'. The subject, the researcher, can stand back from this object, can look at it objectively, in a value-free and neutral way. And positivism maintains that the results of such study are factual in nature, hopefully capable of being formulated in terms of law or law-like generalizations.

Both as feminists and as social scientists we find each of these aspects of positivism objectionable. Few of our objections (if any) are unique to us – they derive from what is now a flourishing critique of positivism. But what we have tried to do so far, and will carry on doing in the rest of this book, is to point out that this critique says things which we feel have crucial implications for feminism and for feminist research.

We reject the idea that scientists, or feminists, are experts in other people's lives. And we reject the belief that there is one true reality to be experts about. Feminism's present renaissance has come about because many women have rejected other people's interpretations of our lives – the 'happy families' view of family life and the women's magazine picture of women's experiences. Feminism insists that *women* should define and interpret our experiences, and that women need to *re-define* and *re-name* what other people – experts, men – have previously defined and named for us. And so feminism argues that 'the personal', experience, is intensely political and immensely important politically. Each of these aspects of feminism stands in opposition to the basic tenets of positivism. For us, feminism either directly states or implies the following beliefs. The personal is the political. The personal and the everyday are both important and interesting and ought to be the subject of inquiry. It is important not to downgrade other people's realities. It is necessary to reject the 'scientist/person' dichotomy. It is essential to try to get away from the power relationship which exists between the researcher and the researched.

Positivism denies each of these beliefs, but we feel that each of them ought to be crucial to a feminist presence within the social sciences and within research. Each of these beliefs was important in feminist writings of the 1960s and early 1970s, but we feel that much current feminist research and theory now looks much more like our description of positivism. As we have tried to show, in our examination of 'the family' and socialization and role, this 'adds women in' to existing theory without subjecting this to any more critical examination than noting and deploring the absence of women from it. This is not enough.

We feel that it isn't enough for two reasons. The first is that feminism as we understand it demands that we take personal experience much more seriously. The second is that an examination of experience clearly demonstrates the inadequacies of a positivist approach. It does this because it shows us that we must get back into a detailed examination and analysis of 'the personal' if we are to understand more clearly 'oppression' and 'liberation'. 'The personal' has in many ways become a slogan often mouthed but rarely more closely looked at. We believe that 'feminist consciousness', our understandings of ourselves as women who are feminists, provides us with a focus for unpacking this idea of 'the personal'. And so it is to a discussion of this that we now turn in the following chapter.

Chapter 5

Feminist consciousness

Feminism hasn't sprung into existence fully formed and without origins. At least part of its message is the contemporary expression of a practical and intellectual debate which has occurred in many guises, and over a very long period of time. This has been a debate between 'science' and 'reason' on the one hand, and 'emotion' and 'intuition' on the other. But, as we've previously suggested, this debate occurs within feminism, as well as between feminism and 'science', feminism and 'reason' and so on. We have already hinted something of this in our discussion of feminist theory and its variations, and also in our outline of feminism's differing reactions to 'the personal'. In doing this we allied ourselves with feminism's earlier rejection of the terms in which this debate has been conducted, and its insistence that the dichotomies which are at the centre of it – the means by which it is conceptualized – rely on an artificial (an indeed man-made) distinction.

Having said that feminism is part of a wider intellectual debate, we are none the less aware that many feminists will reject this, will see it as a 'male' takeover, will insist that feminism has invented itself and everything contained within it. Nevertheless we stick to our interpretation while, at the same time, also insisting that feminism offers something new to this debate.

In this chapter we shall suggest that, although feminism has derived much of its style of argument and mode of analysis from elsewhere, nevertheless contemporary feminism offers to this debate something which is both crucial and, because it is centred upon *women*, which is really original. This 'original' contribution is, we shall argue, the proposal that women's experiences constitute a different view of reality, an entirely different 'ontology' or way of going about making sense of the world. In other words, we shall suggest, 'feminist consciousness' makes available to us a previously untapped store of knowledge about what it is to be a woman, what the social world looks like to women, how it is constructed and negotiated by women. However, this knowledge is made available to us through feminism's insistence on the importance of 'the personal' – precisely that phenomenon which many feminists are so concerned with 'getting beyond'.

'Feminist consciousness' is one expression of women's unique view of social reality, and we see it as 'unique' in the sense that it is concerned with, and can see, different aspects of conventional, sexist, reality. Women sometimes construct and inhabit what is in effect an entirely different social reality. In chapter 1 we argued that there were three themes which were basic to our understanding of feminism and its approach to women's oppression and the requirements of women's liberation. In this chapter we return to the third of these themes and look at the existence of a distinct 'feminist consciousness'.

FEMINIST CONSCIOUSNESS AND CONSCIOUSNESS-RAISING

Feminism's concern with consciousness, and with changing states of consciousness, is easily apparent in any collection of feminist writings, any discussion of feminist practice. The main expression of both its theoretical and its practical concern is, of course, through the existence of 'consciousness-raising' activities.

Our interpretation of material on consciousness-raising, and people's experiences in consciousness-raising groups, is that implicit (and sometimes quite explicit) in this is a three stage model of consciousness. These three stages are sometimes differently named: false consciousness, partial consciousness (which includes feminist consciousness) and revolutionary consciousness by marxist-feminists; and false consciousness, consciousness-raising and feminist consciousness by other feminists. This sequential, and temporal, model of consciousness has explicit within it the idea of change, of movement, and of development, but also the idea of stasis. The movement is from false consciousness through consciousness-raising to true consciousness; but then the model suggests nothing further. It doesn't concern itself with what, if anything, might lie beyond this, or even whether any changes in this form of consciousness are to be expected.

These 'stages' in consciousness aren't seen as discrete, mutually exclusive, like the rungs on a ladder. There is an acceptance that false consciousness is expressed within, and is confronted by, the process of consciousness-raising; and that feminist consciousness or true consciousness comes slowly and hesitantly out of consciousness-raising. And there is also an acceptance that hints of the third stage in consciousness are contained within the first, false consciousness. Indeed, without this there would be no attempt to become involved in the process of consciousness-raising – there would be no impetus for change, and no basis for this change to occur around.

The idea of a pre-revolutionary or pre-feminist consciousness, and a sequential and developmental change, is explicit in the term 'raising' used in feminist discussions of consciousness. It implies a movement from something less desirable to something more desirable, from something lower to something higher, from something which doesn't see and understand truly to something which does. The notions of a 'false' and a 'revolutionary' form of consciousness obviously owe much to marxist discussions. This link is apparent in much feminist work on consciousness. For example, Marsha Rowe argues that the WLM uses the processes of consciousness-raising in order to help feminists 'expose false consciousness'. And within her discussion of false consciousness is the idea of movement and of change from a lower to a higher stage:

> Consciousness raising is essentially a wider consciousness. It lifts the mysterious veils of womanhood . . . it wriggles away from the notion that we have been free to become what we will . . . we can understand the way our lives have been determined by our class and our sex (Rowe, 1975, p.6).

This idea of false consciousness isn't simply one which sees a movement from a lower to a higher plane of consciousness. It also sees this higher consciousness as one which enables people to escape from confinement within the purely subjective and the 'false' into a more *objective* state of consciousness. They can then see truly rather than falsely their objective position within the objective social world.

It will already be apparent that we find the idea that there is *one* true objective social reality, existing for all people, quite unacceptable. We are perfectly ready to accept that all people operate on the *assumption* that there is an objective social reality. What we reject is that this 'reality' is the same for everybody – or should be the same for everybody if only they weren't falsely conscious. The idea of 'false' and 'true' consciousness, with 'true consciousness' being what revolutionaries have, is offensively patronizing. It denies the validity of people's own interpretation and understandings. If these don't match the interpretations of revolutionaries then they are false. 'If you agree with me then you're right, if you disagree then you're wrong', is implied but not openly stated.

The idea that revolutionaries and revolutionary groups are 'the vanguard', the possessors of that consciousness which is closest to truth, and which enables them to see real reality as it truly is, sits uneasily among feminist principles. The principle of egalitarianism implies an acceptance of the validity of all women's experiences. But the idea of 'the vanguard' is grossly elitist and is based on a belief in the invalidity of the 'subjective' compared with the 'objective'.

Similarly the idea that 'revolutionary consciousness' or feminist consciousness is true, objective and right, is unacceptable to us. The notion that feminism and feminists occupy a higher plane of understanding about the true nature of social reality must be exposed. In the past feminism has adopted an accepting attitude towards women, all women, and has had an immediate sympathy with and understanding of the problems and contradictions involved in simply being a woman in sexist society. Its insistence on the validity of each woman's personal experience has been one of its most appealing facets. But the sequential model of consciousness, the insistence that feminist consciousness is 'true' and other consciousnesses are 'false', is in direct confrontation with this.

Now when we say that feminist consciousness isn't 'true', isn't 'objective', we don't mean that we don't find it preferable and in some sense better than any other consciousness. Also we're perfectly well aware, from our experience, that there is a 'before feminist consciousness' experience of the world, a 'discovering feminism' experience of the world and, for us, a 'post discovering feminism' experience of the world as well. It might seem from this that we too agree that a three stage sequential model of consciousness is the best means of conceptualizing it. But we don't; our experience suggests something much less tidy and much more complex than this.

The processes of consciousness tend to be described in terms of a spectrum, going from a *beginning* (false consciousness) to an *end* (true consciousness). But we prefer to think of the processes of consciousness in terms of a circle or spiral – there are no beginnings and no ends, merely a continual flow. As we've previously said, there's no such creature as a 'sorted-out feminist'. When we go into new situations, in a sense we go into them 'falsely conscious' – we have to make some kind of sense of them, whether we're feminists or not. We also feel that the terms 'false consciousness' and 'feminist consciousness' imply a unity of experience which doesn't exist. Within each of these 'states' is an infinite variety of interpretation and understanding which is simply glossed over by using such terms. Stand in any local shop anywhere and listen to 'falsely conscious' women knowing and talking about the fact that they live in a man's world, and that they're badly done to. To call such women 'falsely conscious' is to write-off them and their awareness in a quite unjustifiable way. Instead of doing this feminists need to go back into women's experiences and explore such complexities, not ignore them.

And as with 'false consciousness' so with 'feminist consciousness'. By this we mean that our experience demonstrates to us that feminist consciousness isn't the 'end' of changes in consciousness. But then, 'feminist consciousness' isn't something we see as monolithic, nor would we want it to be so. We don't believe it is something which should be experienced in the same way by all women who call themselves feminists. The merest glance at contemporary feminism easily demonstrates that feminists *don't* experience feminism in the same way, given the great diversity of opinion and approach among us. Unless, of course, we say that this 'diversity' is really false consciousness, and that most of us are wrong.

We suggest that the 'feminist consciousness' of every individual feminist will inevitably change. For all of us, and perhaps even for each of us, there will be many 'feminist consciousnesses'. So then, we reject the idea of true and false consciousness, while retaining as basic to our thinking the idea of consciousness and of changes in consciousness. In the rest of this chapter we shall explore some ideas about feminist consciousness, but without using what we see as an inherently stratified means of conceptualizing it. We shall discuss some of the differences and some of the changes which take place in consciousness, and some of the reactions to 'doing' feminist consciousness, without trying to attach to this any assessment of validity, any evaluation of 'higher' or 'lower'.

We have come across few formal analytic attempts to chart the nature and content of feminist consciousness. The most interesting, for us, is Sandra Bartky's discussion of the phenomenology of feminist consciousness (1977). Bartky suggests that the processes of 'becoming feminist' involve a profound personal transformation for us all; and this transformation involves both changes in behaviour and changes in consciousness. And so she sees it as a transformation of people's *physical involvements in* as well as their *interpretations of*, events within everyday life.

Bartky describes four key facets of the whole consciousness. These are the consciousness of 'anguish', of 'victimization', of 'constant exposure', and of 'the double ontological shock'. And also she argues that 'Feminism is something like paranoia' (1977, p. 19), because feminist consciousness involves an interpretation of social reality which may be radically different from that commonly provided by others. Within the transformed consciousness inhabited by feminists, the same behaviours and states come to be interpreted differently. They come to *mean* something different from what they previously meant; and because of this they are *experienced* as something different. They are no longer the same events, behaviours, ideas and beliefs – because they are now *constructed* differently.

SEXISM AND CHANGING CONSCIOUSNESS

Bartky's pioneering attempt to chart feminist consciousness is one which we have found exciting, insightful and useful. It has enabled us to grasp and put names to experiences and states of mind for which we previously had no names. We originally came across and used her work in relation to our attempts to understand our experiences of sexism in the form of the obscene phone calls which we received, and our changing consciousness of these and of ourselves as feminists (Stanley and Wise, 1979).

This earlier work of ours was concerned with changes in the content and nature of our 'feminist consciousness'. These changes occurred because of our experiences of sexism and our attempts to research these. We were concerned with how, why, and in what ways, consciousness changes; and how this might best be conceptualized and understood. We found that Bartky's analysis gave us a basis for our own work, and by doing so it also gave us a basis to define our feelings around, and also against.

Without her work we couldn't have done and thought as we did; but our experiences led us to feel that some aspects of it were inappropriate for us. We feel that the process of 'becoming feminists', the development of feminist consciousness, isn't an 'end state'. It isn't a situation of stasis within the individual. But at the same time we are well aware that consciousness can be, and usually is, construed as a 'state', and also as 'a' or 'the' consciousness. We all of us act on the assumption that *our* state of consciousness has some objective and fixed reality, as a 'social fact' in our lives (Coulter, 1977). But, while accepting this, we also feel that consciousness should be conceptualized as a 'process' *at the same time* that it is seen as a 'state'. It should be construed as a process because differently situated and changing understandings underpin any 'state' of consciousness. At any one point in time we may be able to point to our particular state of consciousness. And in months or years later we may be able to point again at our state of consciousness. But what we point to may well be a quite different state of consciousness. Change has occurred, although we may not have been aware of this happening at the time. And we may look back on 'ourself' as though at a stranger.

It is because of our belief that consciousness is both a state and a process that we insist that there isn't just *one* feminist consciousness. We believe that there is instead a multiplicity of these; and that they are derived from different involvements in, and constructions of, differently situated and contextually grounded experiences. And so we believe that many feminists may experience subtle or dramatic changes in consciousness after 'becoming feminist', because life and experience go on within feminism.

What we mean here by 'contextually grounded' is that the precise context in which something (a word, object, event) is located will provide a meaning or series of meanings for it. This 'meaning' is tied to the context, it cannot be 'transplanted'. An example of this concerns how we both feel about owning a washing machine. Ownership of this particular object says to us that we have grown up, become adults, in a way that no other possession does. But our washing machine was bought second-hand, broke down within days, involved patronizing remarks from sexist salesmen and threats from us about court actions. All of these things are involved in its 'meaning *for us*'. It isn't simply a material object; it is also a part of our *social* reality, and it won't have the same 'meaning' for other people who haven't been involved in this 'context'.

The obscene phone calls we received were centrally involved in the changes in our feminist consciousness. And so we now briefly discuss some of these changes, after briefly outlining the two 'states' of consciousness which we found ourselves in before and after these experiences. We call these 'consciousness 1' and 'consciousness 2'.

'Consciousness 1' could be described as a complete idealism. It involved us understanding patriarchy as an *ideology* reflected in institutions and negotiated through interaction. While not opposed to structural analyses, whether phenomenologically or conventionally based, we construed women's oppression as essentially ideological rather than material in basis.

'Consciousness 2', however, involved us in adopting a 'materialistic' theory of women's oppression, as used by the obscene phone callers, and an analysis of women's oppression in terms of 'phallocentrism'. The obscene phone callers identified power and the penis as synonymous. They screamed and shouted at us that those without penises, those who are penetrated by penises, are without power and therefore are the legitimate objects of contempt.

In consciousness 2 we 'adopted' this theory as it was presented to us by the callers. It appeared, and appears, reasonable to assume that people's stated understandings and interpretations are often the basis for their attitudes and actions. And so we argue that sexist males are a good source of information about their sexism and their daily oppression of women. And so consciousness 2 involves us in accepting as valid what the callers said their 'state of consciousness' was.

It is extremely difficult (probably impossible) to say exactly how, and in what order, different parts of consciousness changed as a result of our experiences. And so we shan't attempt to do this. Instead we shall simply describe some of the differences between consciousness 1 and consciousness 2 around Bartky's four facets of feminist consciousness: 'anguish', 'victimization', 'constant exposure' and the 'double ontological shock'.

Changes in feminist consciousness

Involved in 'anguish' is the realization of exactly how intolerable women's oppression is, both for the individual woman experiencing particular aspects of it, and also for all other women too. However, 'anguish' acquired an additional dimension for us in consciousness 2. We experienced it as an intolerable, and essentially *unchanging*, interaction with sexist males. Its central feature was that, however we presented ourselves, our entire being was interpreted in sexually objectified ways. We were related to as merely sexual objects there for the callers' sexual use. Each and every of our statements and responses was interpreted in the light of this view of us; and we experienced this as a complete powerlessness. There was no way in which we seemed able to affect their one-dimensional interpretations of us. *Their* reactions and interactions with us appeared to occur almost independently of *our* reactions. What occurred in the interaction between us seemed to be governed almost entirely by the callers' intentions.

'Victimization' is described by Bartky as an awareness of sexism as both a hostile force and also as an offence against all women. And so it involves a total rejection of the 'naturalness' of the sexual political system. She also argues that an integral part of the experience of victimization is the presence within it of two sets of dichotomies. The first of these is victimization as a diminishment of being and, at the same time, an awareness of strength from the new consciousness; and the second is victimization as a double awareness of how we are victimized as women but privileged as white, middle class, and so on. But we experienced it differently.

In both consciousness 1 and consciousness 2 we rejected the idea that there could be any valid legitimation of sexism. But in consciousness 2 we were faced by the dilemma faced by all feminists who argue that there is a physiological or other material basis to women's oppression. This dilemma concerns whether our particular analysis compels us to advocate men without penises (or no men at all) as the requirement of women's liberation. But we feel that, unlike many other such analyses, ours rejects the idea that physiological or any other structures have inherent meaning. For us, physiological experience is itself a social construction. The synonymity of the penis and phallocentrism is not something which is necessary or determined – the penis doesn't have inherent meaning, just like the rest of social reality.

We certainly experienced a 'diminishment of being' as Bartky describes this, but in consciousness 2 this appeared more total and more destructive than was at all comfortable. However, the dichotomy between victimization and privilege which she describes was something we failed to experience. Our exposure to phallocentrism, both in the obscene phone calls and in the rest of our lives as women, seemed to leave little that wasn't open to sexual objectification and degradation by phallocentric males. Whether they were working class or middle class, black or white, under-privileged or privileged was irrelevant to our experience of the interaction between us. We insist that lack of privilege doesn't absolve anyone from taking responsibility for their actions. Sexist men are sexist men; and who could possibly prefer to be insulted or raped by an under-privileged man compared with a privileged one? And, anyway, for us all men are 'privileged' because they are men.

The term 'complexity of reality' is used to describe the 'double ontological shock'. Bartky argues that this involves an awareness that events may be different from their appearance, but also not knowing when these are 'actually' different and when such differences are 'merely imagined'. Expressed somewhat differently, for Bartky this is the problem of distinguishing between 'valid paranoia' and 'invalid paranoia'.

For Bartky, the feminist view of social reality involves a valid paranoia; but she also accepts that there are views of social reality which involve invalid paranoia. We can't accept this. The belief that experience and consciousness can in some sense be 'invalid' is one we don't share, although obviously we recognize that such assessments are commonly made within everyday life. We believe that if something is real in its consequences then it is real to the person experiencing these consequences. As we have said several times before, obviously everyday life depends upon the assumption that an objective reality exists which is shared between people. And because of this we all assume that it is possible to make assessments about the validity and invalidity of people's experiences – we have recourse to our ideas about 'objective reality' and test them against this.

However, *everybody* believes that *their* objective reality is the true objective reality. And it has been our experience that most of the reactions to our discussions of the obscene phone calls have taken place on this basis. Many people remarking on our reactions to the calls have made it plain to us that there are valid and invalid reactions to obscene phone calls, and ours were somehow out of touch with the 'real objective reality'. We were seen as invalidly paranoid about them. This was the response that we received from feminists and non-feminists alike. The only people who immediately accepted our reactions as valid-for-us were other women who had similarly experienced such reactions from men; and these were mainly other lesbians. If other women have shared similar experiences then they're willing to accept ours as valid; and if they haven't then they are much less willing to do so.

As time passes, and more women speak and write about their experiences as feminists, so it becomes apparent that all of us experience feminism as something which changes. One indication of this is the changing kinds and forms of argument, changing expressions of language, used by individual feminists in a series of their writings.

The work of Mary Daly is a good example of this (1973; 1975; 1978). Another example is the written work of Robin Morgan, especially her collection of essays and articles *Going Too Far* (1977). This collection charts in a very direct and personal way Robin Morgan's own changing states of consciousness, and her retrospective analysis and conceptualization of such changes. And so, for us, it provides a personal and immediately assessable insight into another feminist's experience of change. And that this change is retrospectively apparent is indicated in her discussion of 'going too far', that perennial response to feminist behaviours, analyses and actions.

She suggests that the point at which we 'go too far' is something which changes, according to our ideas and also the climate of opinion around us. What was 'going too far', both for her and for non-feminist people, at one time is no longer so. Morgan's own change is from marxist to marxist-feminist to radical feminist, via many degrees of confusion, anger and doubt. And another facet of this work of great interest to us is her feeling that it is possible to conceptualize and understand such changes only in retrospect. At the time of writing each of these essays she experienced herself as in stasis, as in a 'state of consciousness'. Only afterwards was it possible for her to see that what was occurring was a *process*, was a continual although gradual change in consciousness.

Real and unreal realities

We have rejected the idea that there are 'real realities' which are experienced by some people, and 'unreal realities' experienced by others. We'd now like to explain a little further what we mean by this. We do so around a brief discussion of Karl Popper's three 'worlds' (1972), because Popper takes a particularly clear-cut view of the relationship between consciousness and 'knowledge'.

Popper refers to the objective world of material and physical things as 'World 1'. In this is included all the material 'kickable' world of chairs, tables, toilet paper, mountains, bodies, and so on. 'World 2' is what he calls the subjective world of minds, and it includes both interactions between people and also the subjective world inside of our own heads. 'World 3', however, is what Popper calls the world of objective structures which are the products (although not necessarily the intentional products) of the minds of people or the activities of other living creatures which, once produced, exist independently of them.

Some of the objective structures of 'World 3' are material, some are abstract, and it includes our 'culture' in so far as this is encoded in the material objects of 'World 1' and so accessible to others. And so the structures of 'World 3' include not only libraries, books, films, and so forth, but also human minds. However, it includes human minds only to the degree that the products of these are materially available to others – in other words, only when encoded. So then, for Popper knowledge is a 'World 3' phenomenon – that is, knowledge is 'knowledge' for him only when it is objectified in writing and other similar material forms which are materially accessible to other people.

It will come as little surprise to find that we object to this typification of 'Worlds' and understanding of what constitutes 'knowledge'. In our approach these three 'Worlds' overlap and are inextricably interwoven; and even for analytic purposes we feel that there is little justification for so separating them. We believe that what are material things, what is subjectivity, what is knowledge, all overlap; and what these are seen to be will differ. The notion that only 'encoded knowledge' is knowledge, and that anything which isn't encoded doesn't count, we reject.

We do so on experiential grounds. We all of us treat as 'knowledge' a great many things, a great many of which aren't
'encoded', in Popper's use of this term. But this doesn't mean that
they aren't encoded and treated as having objective and material
existence by people in our everyday lives.

We feel that such a suggestion is at the heart of many sociological understandings of the social world. This can be illustrated by
reference to the idea of a 'social fact'. Social facts are those bodies
of belief, those ways of seeing and understanding the world,
which have factual status and which count as 'objective knowledge' or truth for people. 'Social facts' embody people's understandings of what is factual and, because factual, what constrains
them.

If we believe that our every movement is being followed by
CIA agents who wish to kidnap us for nefarious purposes of their
own, then this will have the status of 'social fact', of 'objective
knowledge', in our lives. It will have this status because it will
be *consequential*. We will be extremely wary and observant of
other people; we will avoid situations in which we might be
kidnapped. And whether there are actual, materially present, CIA
agents is in a way irrelevant.

It is irrelevant because it is irrelevant for the person experiencing the fears of being kidnapped by CIA agents. If they experience
these fears as real, as objective, as social facts in their lives, then
they are, for all practical purposes, real. Of course, the point at
which the actual material presence of CIA agents becomes more
relevant is the point at which this person's reality meets with the
reality of others. If other people don't recognize the material
reality of the CIA agent then assessments of 'illness' or 'deviancy'
may be attached to the 'delusions' of the person who claims their
material existence.

So then, what is it that we're trying to get at in this discussion?
What we're trying to do is point out that 'scientific knowledge',
'objective knowledge', are social constructs, and as such are
exactly similar to all other forms of knowledge-held-in-common.
They all derive from the subjective world of minds, from what
Popper refers to as 'World 2'. Popper may feel that 'knowledge'
as he sees it is in important ways different from mere subjectivity;
and in this belief he would be joined by many other people, but,
and an important 'but' at that, in terms of how we live our
lives we all of us construct everyday knowledge as 'encoded

knowledge'. We treat a whole range of things as 'facts', as 'scientifically proven', as 'what everyone knows to be true', and these become constraining upon us. And yet another 'but' – nevertheless most of these things wouldn't be admitted to the select gathering of 'World 3' products as Popper sees them.

Now this may appear as something of a diversion from the subject of this chapter, consciousness. But we don't see it as such, because what we have been arguing is that 'consciousness' isn't something which exists inside of our own heads, inaccessible to others and only partly accessible to ourselves. What we believe about consciousness is what we have already hinted at – that we experience consciousness as a 'state' which enables us to interpret the facticity, the 'factual and objective nature' of the social, as well as the material, world. Our state/process of consciousness provides us with an ontological system for acting within the social world, in the sense of involving 'a set of assumptions about the nature of being or existence' (Roberts, 1976, p. 6).

Different states of consciousness aren't just different ways of *interpreting* the social world. We don't accept that there is something 'really' there for these to be interpretations of. Our differing states of consciousness lead us into *constructing* different social worlds. We may manage to negotiate, through interaction, these differences, but we *have* to negotiate them because their existence is something we daily experience. As we go on to show, this point may be more readily understood by feminists than by many other people, because feminists daily come into contact with different (and sexist) constructions of reality.

Doing feminist consciousness

Charting feminist consciousness in an analytic way is of course important and necessary. But it is only through *doing* feminist consciousness that we can really understand its dimensions, content and parameters. It is only when we find ourselves doing certain kinds of things that we can really see what, for us, are the consequences of our own state of consciousness at any point in time.

What we mean by 'doing' feminist consciousness encompasses all products of human action and interaction, whether these are physical objects or interactions between people. And an additional dimension is added to our understanding of our own consciousness through such behaviours, because these make available to us the reactions of others to us, and of us to them.

It is this, as well as our rejection of the idea of 'invalid paranoia', which leads our own work to differ in some respects from Bartky's. When any discussion of feminist consciousness is *grounded*, is placed within a particular time-period and a specific context, then it will differ because different women inhabit different realities and such differences are material in nature. In other words, we argue that 'feminist consciousness' is specific and unique to each feminist. Although the *form* of feminist consciousness may be similar for all women who call themselves feminist (and perhaps for many other women as well), the exact *content*, and so its exact expression, will differ. This is because we all go through unique, specific, and contextually grounded, experiences.

At this point we'd like to look briefly at some of the implications of considering feminism as a different construction of reality, and a different view of sexist reality. Alternative constructions of reality, we've suggested, lead to differences, to conflicts, in negotiating everyday life. But feminism as an alternative construction of reality doesn't inevitably do this because feminists always have the opportunity to 'pass'. 'Passing' is a term usually applied to 'white' black people or gay men and lesbians who behave as though they were heterosexual. It is the idea that we can pretend to be something which, if other people knew about our 'real' selves, they wouldn't see us as. Unlike some other groups of oppressed people, feminists are always faced with the choice of whether to 'pass' or not. We can always choose to behave in 'non-feminist' ways. We can pass-up the opportunity to challenge expressions of sexism, we can take an easier way out, a way that involves us in less effort or stress. We can present ourselves in such a way that people will see us as 'ordinary women', not feminists, because 'being feminist' would involve us in *behaving differently*.

If we aren't feminists then we experience expressions of sexism as mundane and routine – they aren't 'expressions of sexism' unless we construct them as such. They are instead part of the ordinary ongoing activities of our everyday experience. An example concerns opening doors for other people. This might be simple politeness or an expression of sexism. Which it is will depend on a number of things, including who opens the door for whom, and how we attribute their motives for doing so. In other words what this behaviour 'is' depends on our construction of it. However, the presence of 'doing feminism' in a situation disturbs its taken-for-granted quality. It renders the 'mundane and routine' problematic and extraordinary, and it disturbs what is otherwise undisturbed. It does this because it challenges the validity of a whole range of phenomena – from the way that people dress, move their bodies, conduct wars, have sex, to the hiring and firing of staff, and to the opening of doors.

In effect, feminism is something which brings people up short, because it challenges the routine and mundane, the taken-for-granted nature of everyday life, by denying particular facets of it. It says 'no, this won't do', 'no, this mustn't occur', 'no, what you say isn't so', and so on.

We have emphasized that we all live our everyday lives around the assumption that an objective social reality, shared in common with others, exists 'out there'. What feminism does is point out that this one 'real' reality isn't *the, one*, real reality at all. It says that the 'objective' reality is subjective and it is merely one reality which co-exists with many others. And, for most of us, such a challenge to what we take-for-granted, what we experience as routine and unproblematic, is threatening. We reject it, we push it away from us. We deny the validity of this view of reality. We suggest that the people proposing it are mistaken, wrong, neurotic or mad.

FEMINISM AND 'THE OTHER'

Feminists are frequently confronted by arguments which state that feminism is merely the expression of paranoia, and that we are hysterical, or man-hating, or screwed-up; and that because of this, what we say can be rejected out of hand. The strength of the reaction to feminism will be quite apparent to most feminists. Threats, physical assaults, verbal assaults, death threats, rapes, bombs, murders are all examples of male reactions to feminism and individual feminists. The strength of this reaction, the extent of the threat experienced by many people, we believe is something which derives from precisely feminism's challenge to what is seen as mundane and routine, what is considered to be unquestionably and inevitably factual. Feminism questions this, says it isn't inevitable, and can and must be changed. It involves the intrusion of a quite different reality which disturbs and threatens what is taken-for-granted as the one real objective reality which we all share – unless there is something wrong with us.

By challenging 'typical' assumptions and views about everyday reality, feminism involves the confrontation of people (people who are competent in managing their own lives and in interacting with others) with a group of women who, while themselves claiming to be competent members, behave as people do who are disturbed, mad or deviant. Of course, people could accept this 'other' view of reality as valid and true. But this is difficult to do, because it involves changes in one's life, including changes in how we see ourselves. Feminists, of course, are familiar with these painful, difficult and far-reaching changes; other people may be less so.

What feminism hints at is the problematic nature of 'objective reality', its artful construction by people who are competent because they are seen to be so by others. And by 'competent' we mean competent in knowing what to do, how to behave 'appropriately' in particular situations and surroundings. 'Doing feminism' is behaving 'incompetently', 'inappropriately', in the same way that other 'deviances' involve 'inappropriate' behaviours.

Men generally react in a rejecting way to feminism's different view of reality. But we also argue that most women, and not just feminists, have a 'different' view of reality – different from the sexist one which doesn't recognize that women are oppressed or that men are oppressors. And so we believe that an exploration of reactions to feminism's 'different reality' will tell us a great deal about the reactions of men to *all* women. We see such an exploration as of crucial importance to feminism – *this*, everyday life, is where we see oppression and liberation. However, we believe that feminism as it is presently constituted doesn't have the resources for such a detailed exploration of everyday behaviours. Its original insights here have been lost in the search for 'feminist science'. And so what we now turn to is a consideration of how feminism might recover and extend its ability to analyse 'the personal' and the everyday.

Recovering the personal

We argue that all existing systems of thought, without any exception, have treated women's everyday experiences and understandings of social reality as peripheral or unimportant: they've generally failed to notice that such a thing as 'women's experience' exists. Our understandings of the world have been consistently downgraded, individual women and groups of women have been persecuted for daring to suggest that this is so, and there is no evidence that any wholehearted wish to reconceptualize sexist realities exists – except among women ourselves.

We have characterized existing approaches to women's experience as positivist and structural and involved in 'adding women in'. We have suggested that these not only make unacceptable assumptions about the nature of 'reality', they also sanctify a power relationship between researcher and researched because they see the researcher/theoretician as more competent, because more objective, than the researched.

These structural approaches have at their heart the belief that experience is frequently wrong or not objectively true. For them, social reality can be conceptualized and researched in much the same way that physical reality can – for them it exists 'out there' as objectively constituted and discernible as such by the competent researcher. From the perspective of women and women's realities, this is disastrous. This is precisely what we have been on the receiving end of for too long: other people, 'experts', telling us how it is and how we *should* be experiencing it, if only we weren't failures, neurotics, stupid, *women*. But the essence of feminism, for us, is its ideas about the *personal*, its insistence on the validity of women's experiences, and its argument that an understanding of women's oppression can be gained only through understanding and analysing everyday life, where oppression as well as everything else is grounded.

Because of this we prefer to look at those approaches, whether social science or any other, which *start* from people's experiences and which treat these seriously. By 'seriously' we mean they accept them as entirely valid in relation to the view of reality adopted by the person experiencing them. We are not claiming that such approaches don't include their share of sexism. They most certainly do. But their basic assumptions are concerned with the validity, the paramount importance, of the everyday. And because of this we feel that they have much more in common with *our* kind of feminism, with its insistence that 'the personal is the political', than structural and other positivist approaches.

Feminists have often claimed marxism as the sole ally, because many feel that only marxism hasn't disgraced itself in its treatment of women. Unfortunately, we feel, feminism's pink-misted alliance with marxism has led it to throw out the baby with the bath water in its wholesale rejection of the rest of the social sciences. What is of interest and of explanatory use has been discarded along with what is dross, what is confining and sexist, in the belief that marxism alone can provide feminism with whatever it needs in the way of theory.

Feminism isn't alone in attempting to produce a system of thought which grants all people some measure of competence and self-determination, while at the same time recognizing that oppression exists in everyday life. And one of the things that has been thrown away, we feel, is the possible contribution of these perspectives which focus on the personal, which accept the essential validity of experience and the need to concentrate substantive work on the everyday. The view we have put forward has been at the heart of contemporary debates within the philosophy of the social sciences for many years now, but feminism appears more or less oblivious to this.

An 'alliance' between feminism and any other perspective is fraught with danger, particularly the danger of 'take over', of the colonization of feminism. And so we are not suggesting that we should replace feminism's 'special relationship' with marxism with a similar link between feminism and anything else. Instead we believe that feminism should borrow, and change, any and everything from anywhere which would be of interest and of use to it – but that we should do this *critically*. We ought to know by now that we should *never* take anything at its face value. All feminists who are involved in writing and research should be more adventurous, more daring, and less concerned with being respectable – and publishable. And so we must be more concerned with being feminists *and* being members of our particular disciplines. For too long academic feminists have been mediocre feminists and mediocre academics as well – and we include ourselves in this.

Both of us arrived at 'recovering the personal' by using various ideas and approaches from ethnomethodology through our initial interest in interactionism (Schutz, 1972; Mead, 1934; Blumer, 1969; Goffman, 1959; Garfinkel, 1967). So what we'll now do is briefly outline some of the ideas we've culled from this. Interactionism is concerned with everyday life, with face-to-face relationships of

all kinds, whether these are street interactions or those within
institutions or families. It also adopts a non-deterministic attitude
towards both the person and to inter-personal interaction. Interactionism rejects the belief that people's behaviour is the result of
any 'imprinting', any deterministic socialization which lays down
the basis for all future behaviours. Instead it sees these as the result
of *interaction*, in which beliefs, expectations and a variety of other
factors are used to construct 'society'. Another key feature of
interactionism is that it insists that 'structures' don't exist as some
meccano-like thing hovering in the sky, but are to be found within
everyday behaviours and events. Structures are constructed from
within interactions and events – they do not exist outside of these
to be 'released' within them.

For us, interactionism was the means of sensitizing us to a
view of reality we'd never come across before. And this is one
in which 'oppression' isn't seen as a once and for all event, located
'back there' in infancy. In it people are seen as actively involved
in constructing and negotiating and interacting, not just passively
'enacting'. But later we came to realize that many, most, versions
of interactionism retain a positivist adherence to science, objectivity, and insist on a clear distinction between the objective
researcher and 'people'. Another closely associated approach
seemed to avoid these grosser aspects of interactionism, and this
was 'there' and available to both of us at precisely the moment
that we were both searching for an alternative. This was ethnomethodology.

Frequently ethnomethodology is seen as over jargonized and
forbidding or just simplistic and irrelevant. Sometimes it is downgraded as 'fag sociology', the kind of sociology that only homosexuals would concern themselves with. 'Sociology without
balls', in other words. For this reason alone it is attractive to us.
Something which so arouses the ire, the scorn, the disgust, of
social scientists because of its 'effeminacy' is an obvious candidate
for feminism's interest and support. We believe that what arouses
this reaction is exactly that which is of prime importance to
feminism – a concern with the everyday and 'the personal'. As
to why other social scientists should feel so threatened by this,
we can only hazard guesses. But our guess is that such a concern
with the everyday brings social science a bit too close to home
for many people. As long as it is about structures and other
people, then it is a job like any other. But when it focuses on

more personal concerns then it promises to turn some attention towards social scientists themselves.

Ethnomethodology takes the everyday and the personal as both a topic of its research and also the resource with which it works. It uses the everyday in order to find out about and understand the everyday. It doesn't lay claim to special expertise over other people's lives, and nor does it attempt to falsify experience. We agree with the criticism that it is often overimbued with jargon and badly written. Nevertheless we find it interesting and useful because of this concern with the everyday.

Ethnomethodology sees itself as very different from what it calls 'conventional sociology'. This is because it argues that conventional sociology has confused 'topic' and 'resource' in its study of social phenomena. Conventional sociology, it insists, uses 'data' provided by members of society as a resource for building theories. In most instances, however, this resource data is seen by conventional sociology as a competing account of the same social reality which the researcher seeks to describe and account for.

Ethnomethodology argues that sociology uses a whole variety of data provided for it by members of society in order to do its work. But any one provider of data might have their account described as valid or invalid, faulty or correct, as an interpretation of the reality which it is provided out of. These assessments are made by the researcher, who lays claim to special warrant in the interpretation of other people's realities. This 'special warrant' derives from their use of special techniques and procedures and from social science professional-ideological understandings about 'truth'.

'Truth' is seen to lie within, and be produced out of, aggregates interpreted by the objective and removed observer – the sociologist – and compared with and assessed against theoretical understandings. The upshot of all of this is that sociologists (and this description could equally well be applied to all other disciplines within the social sciences, let us not forget) frequently describe people's accounts as invalid or inadequate interpretations of the social reality which they experience and live in.

But ethnomethodology rejects such an approach. Instead it argues that 'data' should be used as a 'topic', and not as a resource. The idea of using data as a topic is one which suggests that we shouldn't use people's accounts as unexplicated data. We should instead explicate them. We should examine in close detail how people provide us, themselves and others, with the accounts that they do. The emphasis is on understanding how people construct and describe reality. In other words it is on understanding how we 'do' everyday life.

The next thing for discussion, then, is how the researcher should go about this 'explication' of data, and how we should attempt to understand what is going on in the accounts provided for us. Of crucial importance here is the term 'members'. Ethnomethodology argues that the term 'member' is preferable to 'subject' or 'actor' or any other term which stands for 'person-in-society'. This is because 'membership' involves the idea of a shared body of facts about the social world, shared in common between the people who are party to such knowledge. As members of society we have knowledge of how to behave as competent members of that society, and believe (and have confirmed to us every day) that other competent members also share this.

The idea of 'membership' stems from one of the basic propositions about social behaviour held by ethnomethodology. This is that the social world is seen and experienced by all of us as a 'factual reality', as an objective reality which exists outside of us and which constrains our behaviour because of this. Ethnomethodology doesn't mean by this that we hold a set of concepts and beliefs which are simply 'released' in situations we find ourselves in. It goes beyond this, to argue that these concepts and beliefs are used by us and others in appropriate ways in specific settings, and that by 'doing' these we both give accounts of them and so construct the reality that they describe.

How researchers go about understanding the data that is everyday life is, suggests ethnomethodology, precisely the same way that all other members of society go about knowing what they know and doing what they do. We use what it calls the 'documentary method of interpretation'. Ethnomethodology insists that documentary method of interpretation is a *members'* method, one that is used by all of us in our everyday lives, although it may, perhaps, be used more consciously and deliberately by us-as-social-scientists than it is by us-as-members.

The idea of the documentary method suggests that, in new or problematic situations, we look for 'evidence' of what is going on, of what the events in hand are, and what our own behaviours and responses to these should be. We use events, speech, ways

of looking and a whole variety of other evidence, as precisely
evidence, and this is interpreted as 'evidence which stands on behalf
of . . .' a whole body of knowledge which we deduce from it.
We use it as something which points to an underlying pattern,
of which the evidence is but a small part. This pattern is used to
organize the evidence *at the same time* as the evidence is used as
the basis for abstracting the pattern. We go about 'doing life',
suggests ethnomethodology, in much the same way that detec-
tives go about solving crimes.

To suggest that social science methods are 'merely' members'
methods is, of course, a quite unacceptable suggestion for many,
perhaps most, social scientists. Most social scientists have an enormous amount invested in their 'professional expertise', including
their competence in a range of technical procedures which they
see as far superior to anything which mere people possess. This
claim to expertise, then, is one which is seen by social scientists
as setting them apart, as different in kind from the people they
'do research on'. People 'do' life, but social scientists understand
and interpret it. However, the egalitarian impetus within ethnomethodology, which rejects the belief that there is any sharp
distinction between members' and social science approaches, is
one which we view very sympathetically. We feel that it accords
well with the egalitarian ethos of feminism itself.

The idea of 'membership' is one which argues that we all
assume the existence of common and shared views about the
'facticity' of social reality. What goes on within social life appears
to us as factual; and we experience these social facts as constraining – as constraining as any other material facts. In other words,
it is the consequential nature of social facts which constitutes their
'factness'. We believe that they have consequences; we act on the
basis of this; and so they *do* have consequences. And closely
related to this is ethnomethodology's understanding of social
structure.

'Social structure' is something which it sees as occurring within,
and as constructed out of, everyday life; and not as something
which exists only in the form of 'ideologies' which shape our
behaviour. In a sense, ethnomethodology rejects the distinction
between 'beliefs and values', on the one hand, and 'behaviours',
on the other. It argues that there is a symbiotic relationship
between the two. We know what we believe because we do it
or don't do it, not because it exists purely in our heads.

That there isn't any necessary 'fit' between everyday experience and social science structures has traditionally been responded to by pointing the finger at the subjective, involved, stance of people within their everyday lives, contrasting this with the objective and removed (and so more scientific) stance of the social scientist. The implication – the insistence even – is that the stance of the social scientist yields results which are preferable because more objectively true. But ethnomethodology says, instead, that we should see the product of 'social science reasoning' and the product of 'members's reasoning' as *both* the products of *members'* reasonings. The 'scientific, factual' nature of social science accounts is rather to be seen as yet one more interpretation of what goes on. These accounts aren't 'the' truth, or even necessarily preferable to the accounts provided by members. And this really leads us into the next aspect of ethnomethodology of relevance here.

While recognizing that objective social reality exists, at the same time ethnomethodology suggests that what this 'objective reality' is will be contextually grounded and specific. It won't be something which is objectively true for all people at all times, but is instead the result of specific sets of encounters, events, behaviours. So it recognizes that many competing objective realities coexist and that we all of us, as members, have methods for producing accounts-held-in-common-between-us. Members have a variety of 'tools' with which to prevent our slightly different viewpoints, our slightly different constructions of events, from becoming so different that it becomes obvious that 'reality' is not shared-in-common at all.

We are ordinarily competent in doing this. But sometimes we find ourselves constructing events differently from other people, and 'differently' in such a way that it becomes apparent that these differences are potentially unreconcilable. When this happens, then, to use an ethnomethodological concept to describe it, an 'interpretive asymmetry' will exist (Coulter, 1975).

But potentially significant differences in constructing reality are usually managed by participants. There are procedures held-in-common which we all know about as competent members, and use in such situations. But sometimes these differences can't, or won't, be reconciled; and the situation then, to use another ethnomethodological concept, becomes a 'reality disjuncture'. Interpretive asymmetries are potential 'reality disjunctures' which are defused or dissolved. Reality disjunctures themselves are situations in which participants become fully aware that the very existence of phenomenon claimed by one is denied by the other/s.

We can respond in various ways. We may assign 'special motives' to people for doing and saying what they do. We may provide motives for them which discredit either the account and/ or the person/s providing it. The effect is, of course, the same – we impute its validity. But such asymmetries are frequently prevented from turning into reality disjunctures by one of the people involved agreeing to the existence of *something* which needs to be explained, and finding alternative explanations for the 'fact' which is thereby recognized as existing. Each of these procedures are available to all members. And we might note in passing that they are all responses which are made to feminists and feminist interpretations of social reality, and we shall discuss this point again later in this chapter.

The use of 'fault categories', such as the term 'delusion' or 'hallucination', to discredit other people's accounts denies the validity of both the account offered and also the character of the person providing it. The description of people's realities as illusory, unreal, is something which we have mentioned earlier in our reference to the idea of 'invalid paranoia'. When we describe people as paranoid we thereby deny that they can competently describe and interpret their own cognitive processes, and the events and objects these are used in relation to. And, again in passing, this too is a frequently used means of discrediting feminist views of reality. Feminists are seen as women suffering from delusions, women who are paranoid, and thereby women whose beliefs and understandings are to be discounted.

When we come across conflicting or asymmetrical accounts we do our best to account for these in a variety of ways, some of which we have briefly outlined. And typically, of course, it is *other people's* accounts which we treat as producing the asymmetry, and not our own. We retain the sense of our own correctness, the facticity of our own view of reality as 'the' valid one.

The anatomy of reality disjunctures is the subject of discussion by Melvin Pollner (1975). As he argues, 'some people see what others don't.' Seeing what other people do not, or knowing that other people see what we do not, is what constitutes a 'reality disjuncture'. It is a disagreement about the existence or non-existence of something. The experience of disjunctures is often puzzling, given our understanding that the world is 'out there' and shared in common with others as an objectively constituted phenomenon. The availability of a variety of common-sense explanations of these, such as jokes, lies, or other deliberate provision of 'unreal' accounts doesn't, however, enable all disjunctures to be resolved. In some disjunctures exactly who is the 'deficient witness' of reality is as problematic as the nature of the deficiency.

Reality disjunctures arise in situations in which the common assumption of an objective social reality produces a situation in which *each* of two or more competing explanations is capable of undercutting the contesting claim to facticity. Attempts to resolve the situation are concerned to demonstrate that the competing version of reality is the product of exceptional circumstances, faulty description, incompetence, and so on. And so these focus on three dimensions: the experience itself, the method of observation, and the reportage of experience by any given person.

However, these explanations are available to each of the conflicting parties. *Each* presumes themselves to be in possession of 'the truth' and has available to them what Pollner calls the 'rhetoric of mundane reasoning'. In other words, we all have the means to explain away the 'truthfulness' or the 'adequacy' of other people's conflicting experiences of situations, characters and events. What this looks like in less abstract terms can perhaps best be seen through an example used by Pollner.

This example concerns an encounter between two people, one a psychologist and the other a mental patient. Leon, the patient, claimed that he had the ability to make objects levitate. In his interaction with Milton, the psychologist, he volunteered to levitate a table for Milton, who disbelieved his ability to do so. Leon stood near a table and commanded it to lift. Milton said that he couldn't see the table levitating. Leon's response was that this was because Milton was unable to see 'cosmic reality'.

Leon's command to the table was the empirical test of the validity of his claim. But the result of the test merely restates the very problem it was intended to resolve, because Leon lays claim to see a reality which Milton is excluded from. As Pollner says, this disjuncture:

cannot be reconciled by simply examining whether the table is

on the ground or floating above it . . . each of the
disputants . . . finds the experiential claims of the other to be
the product of an inadequate procedure for perceiving the world
(Pollner, 1975, p. 418).

Each of the people involved believes their version, their view of
reality, to be the true one. And this belief renders their own
accounts quite unassailable by what the other person regards as
'irrefutable evidence'. What we see as 'irrefutable evidence' is
what is constructed to be such within our own view of reality.
What lies outside of it will be seen as refutable and non-factual.

Women as 'the other'

We find these two closely related concepts, 'reality disjuncture'
and 'interpretive asymmetry', extremely useful in understanding
the reactions of other people to the existence of feminism as a
world view. As we have already suggested, feminism incorporates
a view of reality which may frequently be in conflict with other
'ontological systems'. Sometimes these differences in perceptual
accounts can be 'managed' by the people involved. But sometimes
it becomes quite apparent that a reality disjuncture exists – that
quite different views of 'the facts' have come into conflict with
each other.

We feel that such a state of conflict between different realities
helped to produce the obscene phone calls we have already discussed. We also feel that many other reactions to feminism derives
from its threat to other people's realities. The perception of feminist views as threatening, as in conflict with the 'true facts', leads
people into using various means of handling the discrepancies
between these views and their own. And, of course, feminists
too use the same ways of attempting to discount or manage such
situations.

In the light of what we have said about feminist consciousness
constituting a different view of reality, Simone de Beauvoir's
view of women as 'the other' becomes extremely pertinent (1949).
We have said, in effect, that feminist consciousness constitutes
'the other' in grand terms. It disputes what most people take to
be 'facts' and 'objective truths' about the world. The world is
defined and constructed in male terms through male eyes. The
resultant 'reality' is at best partial, propounded by one group of

people and almost necessarily accepted by others as 'the truth' about and for everyone. We say 'almost necessarily accepted' because without feminism and a feminist consciousness, there is no coherent organized alternative means of conceptualizing reality in non-sexist terms.

But, simply by existing, women give the lie to this view of 'reality'. It isn't necessary to be feminist to be found threatening by men. Women *do* experience reality differently, just by having 'different' bodies, 'different' physical experiences, to name no others (and we put 'different' in quotation marks because using the word 'different' means using male bodies and experience as the norm, from which women differ).

Women are bound to be experienced as threatening, are bound to be reacted to with frequent violence and even more frequent scorn, puzzlement and dismissal. Our very existence suggests that reality isn't as it is said to be. What *our* reality might be like, what it might consist of, how we might express it, we cannot say. As Mary Daly has said many times, women have had the power of 'naming' our experience of the world taken from us (1978). These experiences have been named for us by men; but men have used what Sheila Rowbotham has called the 'language of theory' and not the 'language of experience' (1973). Our experience has been named by men, but not even in a language derived from *their* experience. Even this is too direct and too personal. And so it is removed from experience altogether by being cast in abstract and theoretical terms. We need a woman's language, a language of experience. And this must necessarily come from our exploration of the personal, the everyday, and what we experience – women's lived experiences.

A language which can conceptualize feminism's concern with providing a view of social reality as inhabited, shared and experienced by women, need not be one language. Social science, art, literature, science must all be involved; and no one of them should be seen as 'standing on behalf of' feminism and feminist consciousness. Feminist consciousness mustn't become the prerogative of only some women; and feminism must come to terms with the presence within it of many, and many conflicting, views of social reality. We must not do what we recently heard one feminist academic do – apologize for providing more than one possible explanation for something instead of 'the truth' about it.

The 'explaining away' of alternative views of reality as spurious or inadequate occurs frequently within the social sciences. 'Deviant' views of reality are treated as eminently refutable simply because 'deviants' usually don't have the power to dispute these interpretations. People who argue that they have the legitimate ability to name other people's experiences say that they have access to transcendental knowledge, to 'the truth'. Alternative accounts are measured against this 'truth' – they are 'predicated upon' it rather than seen as autonomous and valid in themselves.

However, we feel that social science or other 'expert' versions of reality (including feminism as an expertise) should have no privileged status *vis-à-vis* those of the people who live in the 'situations' which are being researched. Those people with less power, those people without power – the oppressed – are more likely than those with power to find their accounts of reality discredited by others, especially by social scientists. Women have been on the receiving end of this process. We must resist enacting it on others. And we have argued that ethnomethodology provides us with insights into this process which feminism can make good use of.

Ethnomethodology rejects claims to privileged status as an interpretation of reality. It also insists on the epistemological validity of all interpretations of reality or realities. And it is aware that the labelling of people as 'mentally ill', 'paranoid', 'deviant' and so on, is the result of a *political* process which takes place within the events and experiences of everyday life. In other words, by locating 'the political' and the construction of reality *within* the everyday, ethnomethodology implies that we are all involved in our own oppressions and, conversely, can be equally involved in our own liberations. Individually we can effect many small changes. Together we can revolutionize all interactions, all constructions of 'reality, for all practical purposes'.

The ethnomethodology approach implies that 'oppression' isn't a once and for all phenomenon. It isn't the result of processes which occurred in 'primary socialization', or any other hypothetical 'stage' in which we have 'internalized' oppression and then for evermore blindly enact it. It looks to the processes involved in our construction of an objectively defined social reality as the scene in which oppression *daily* occurs. And as feminists this is something which we are ever aware of – the rapes, insults, sexist assumptions and actions, all of the everyday experiences of sexism as an ongoing and continual oppression of women. This is a *material* oppression dependent on force and the threat of force, not some magic internalization by women of a 'system' which we accept as a 'natural order'.

This, then, is the reason why we must be particularly concerned with a detailed examination and analysis of 'feminist consciousness'. It is through an examination of how we experience ourselves as feminists as we 'do feminism' within the everyday, and how other people experience themselves, that we can best understand *how* oppression and liberation are constructed. Unless we fully understand the mechanisms by which we are daily oppressed we can't know how we can construct a 'liberated' reality of any kind.

But we shouldn't be interested in other people's views of reality purely in order to render them invalid. We can find no better way of expressing this than by repeating Robin Morgan's account of life as a radical feminist. She suggests that the more outrageous, in conventional terms, she becomes (in the sense of inhabiting a different 'radical feminist reality'), the more tolerant she becomes of what is conventional, and the greater her willingness to accept the validity of an entire spectrum of other realities. This isn't because she thinks these are 'better' or right in any sense, but because she knows that attacking other women's ideas about themselves and the world alienates them from feminism. And it of course alienates feminists from them.

In many ways we see 'feminist consciousness' as the most fundamental and important aspect of feminist theory and feminist practice – it both underlies everything else and at the same time includes this 'everything else' within it. Because of this we believe that the exploration and analysis of consciousness is the key to everything else about feminism. It is the constant dialectic between consciousness and interaction that constitutes 'the personal'. Moreover, it is also that aspect of feminism and feminist practice most available to any feminist researcher. What we mean by this is that the particular 'the personal' that is more available to us than any other is *our own*.

If what we are interested in and are concerned with analysing is 'the personal', and the events and practices of people within their everyday lives, then what could be more obvious than to examine our involvements and our knowledge? We too are people; we too inhabit and help to construct 'society'. And so, in the next chapter, we explore some of these issues and possibilities by looking at 'consciousness' within the research process by examining the relationship between 'the researcher' and her research.

Chapter 6

The research process

The 'research process' we describe in this chapter isn't our account of what happens when people do research and at what point it happens. Such mechanistic descriptions can certainly be found, but we believe that these are misleading and simplistic. 'What happens' is idiosyncratic and redolent with 'mistakes' and 'confusions' and almost invariably differs from such descriptions. And we believe that these personal idiosyncrasies, 'confusions' and 'mistakes' are, as Virginia Johnson has suggested, at the *heart* of the research process (1975, quoted in Bell and Newby 1977, p. 9). In effect these *aren't* confusions or mistakes, but an inevitable aspect of research.

What we discuss in this chapter, therefore, are some important ideas about the place of the personal within research. We insist that the presence of the researcher, as an ordinary human being with the usual complement of human attributes, can't be avoided. Because of this we must devise research of a kind which can utilize this presence, rather than pretend it doesn't happen. We argue that the kind of feminist social science we describe can do this better than most of the alternatives that so far exist. We feel that a positivist interpretation of reality is embedded within most 'alternatives', as well as within what is more usually seen as positivism – and thus our stress on the importance of ethnomethodology's contribution. We feel that ethnomethodology attempts to use the personal in ways which are in sympathy with feminism, and so feminist social science should pay careful attention to it.

Much feminist academic research seems to cling to conventional ideas about research even though these systematically downgrade the importance of the personal and of experience. This may derive in part from a desire for respectability and prestige. But we believe that the power and pervasiveness of positivist world views is the most important factor in this, and we shall attempt to show exactly how pervasive these are in chapter 7. However, the point at which we begin our discussion of the 'research process' is with an outline of two characterizations of it. The first of these we refer to as a 'positivist' model, the second as a 'naturalist' one.

POSITIVISM AND NATURALISM

The models . . .

The 'positivist' model argues that the first stage in research is involvement with theoretical concerns. These may involve general 'problems' for a particular discipline or the theoretical interests of a researcher. This leads to the formulation of hypotheses which express the nature of the problem or interest to be investigated. The second stage involves the use of a set of technical procedures to collect information or 'data' from the chosen research population (which may be people or documentary sources of various kinds). The third stage is one in which the results of this data collection are analysed and interpreted.

What we have just described is the deductivist version of positivism. This is because it is this version of it, and not inductivism, which appears in research texts. Or rather, as we shall go on to argue, it is deductivist positivism which is presented to us as 'positivism', and inductivist positivism which is presented to us as 'naturalism'.

The 'naturalist' model of the research process similarly describes a linear movement, but one in which 'theory' comes out of research rather than preceding it. It suggests that a researcher enters a natural setting and then 'lives' in this for a period of time. This 'living' may be as a member or as someone with a recognized 'research role' within it. Out of this involvement, the researcher then goes away to produce both a description of the natural setting and also a theoretical interpretation of what has occurred within it.

We have described naturalism in terms of a linear movement from research to theory, although other accounts see it as less tidy and more complex than this. We don't accept this view of naturalism. Instead we see it as a re-casting, in superficially more radical terms, of the inductivist version of positivism we briefly described in chapter 4. Inductivist positivism sees research proceeding from theory-untainted data, just as naturalism does. We feel that naturalist research texts (Glaser and Strauss, 1968; Lofland, 1971; Johnson, 1977) end up describing and promoting inductivism while at the same time rejecting 'positivism' on various grounds.

Within these linear descriptive models of the research process 'data' are provided by research populations, and discussions of these data are organized around a schema implicit in each. In other words, the nature of each of the models structures the way in which descriptions and accounts are presented within them. The organization of this isn't 'realistic' in the sense that it doesn't attempt to describe what happened, when it happened, how it happened, and how people felt about it. Instead, research reports within both of these models utilize abstractions from reality organized and presented within a pre-chosen framework. This framework organizes material for us, the readers, in a 'logico-temporal' manner. We aren't given information about the *temporal* occurrence of events, but a form based upon the *logical* development of an argument.

So far we have written as though all research is based upon one or other of these two models. This isn't inevitably so; and at least some research conducted within the naturalistic approach does make an attempt to present material in a different way. What are described as more realistic accounts certainly exist (Fletcher, 1974; Platt, 1976; Johnson, 1977; Bell and Newby 1977). However, these should perhaps be seen as revised non-naturalistic accounts, as non-naturalistic as the original research reports themselves (Halfpenny, 1979). Nevertheless, even revisions like these are exceptional; they are even more rare outside of naturalistic social science; and a very large body of research, whether positivist or naturalist in emphasis, makes no attempt either to revise its products or to present us with more realistic descriptions of research.

. . . and research 'problems'

Presenting the research process as orderly, coherent and logically organized has consequences. One of these is that most social science researchers start off by believing that what is presented in these descriptions is a reasonable representation of the reality of research. Most of us get a nasty shock when we come to do research ourselves. However, the point at which we begin to realize that this 'hygienic research' in which no problems occur, no emotions are involved, is 'research as it is described' and not 'research as it is experienced', is frequently a crucial one. It tends to be the point at which we are required to present our research products to academic colleagues, supervisors, publishers and so forth. And so it is precisely the point at which we are most vulnerable, most likely to find pressures to conform to 'normal science' most difficult to resist, should we want to.

One problem all researchers have to cope with is their actual experiences of the research process. If these fail to correspond to textbook descriptions, then we have to face the possibility that this is because we are inadequate researchers. That these descriptions are over-simplistic and misleading isn't usually the first possibility that occurs to us. This problem is generally 'solved' because most of us fail to confront the contradiction between consciousness and research ideology. Our research simply gets written up in exactly the same way that previous researchers have written up theirs. By doing so, of course, we help to perpetuate the research ideology of 'hygienic research'. We become a part of the research community by enacting the same rituals that others have done before us.

We aren't suggesting that this is deliberate, usually. Nor are we suggesting that it is some kind of con trick. Instead we feel that social science researchers are taught to mistrust experience, to regard it as inferior to theory, and to believe that the use of 'research techniques' can provide data unclouded by values, beliefs and involvements. Researchers work within a 'normal science paradigm' and the world view embodied within this provides us with the categories through which experience is gained. In other words, frequently we fail to report or discuss the contradictions between experience, consciousness and theory, because the paradigm we work within tells us that these are unimportant or non-existent.

By 'paradigm' we mean not so much a theory, more a theoretically derived world view which provides the categories and concepts through and by which we construct and understand the world. Our paradigm tells us what is there and what isn't, what is to be taken seriously and what isn't, what are data and what aren't, what is research and what isn't. Kuhn argues that there are *no* 'facts' which are 'paradigm-free', theory-independent, because what we regard as 'fact' differs according to the world view or paradigm we live and work within (Kuhn, 1962). He also suggests that, because of this, talking about 'truth', in terms of theoretical constructions of social reality, makes no sense at all. And this is the position that we too advance. How researchers see and present research isn't a product of pure, uncontaminated, factual occurrences. All occurrences are a product of our consciousness because they derive from our interpretation and construction of them. And so 'research' is a product of whatever is 'normal science' for us. Whether we are more 'positivistic' or more 'naturalistic' in our research inclinations will affect the basic structure of our presentation of 'research findings' because it also affects all other aspects of 'doing research'. Some people argue that they don't work within any particular theoretical stance. In a sense this may be so. But this does *not* mean that, because their work isn't marxist, feminist, functionalist, or whatever, it is somehow paradigm-free, because of course 'paradigms' can be both explicitly and implicitly present.

People who work within a particular paradigm use its descriptions of research as a means of structuring their own. And regardless of which of the basic research models we adopt, we present our research as 'scientific' in whatever way 'normal science' is regarded in the paradigm we work within. By 'scientific' we mean that we fit our research into current concerns and relevancies, and also we adopt the ways of writing and discussing which are current too. We address ourselves to 'the issues' as these are seen by our colleagues. We present our data and our arguments so as to address these, we omit what are seen as irrelevancies. Another way of describing this is to say that we present *our* science as courageous, radical even, but not outrageous. We attempt to say something new and exciting, but not threatening. To do this would mean that our credibility would be impugned, we would not be taken seriously, our membership of that particular scientific community perhaps even withdrawn – excommunication!

As part of this we also attempt to be 'objective'. Within both positivism and naturalism this usually means that we present our work as scholarly and detached from what we have conducted research on. It may now be all right to be involved, committed even, but we must necessarily preserve 'scholarly detachment'. We must present our research in such a way that we strip 'ourselves' from descriptions, or describe our involvements in particular kinds of ways – as somehow 'removed' rather than full-blown members of the events and processes we describe.

All of this is a 'reconstructed logic', not a 'logic in use' (Kaplan, 1964). It isn't a realistic description of what occurs, but an idealized and wishful set of statements and prescriptions which we construct after the event and around our account of this. In other words what we present is a 'doctored' account, in the sense that we fit it into the normal presentation of research of the kind we are doing. To do otherwise, even to *say* otherwise, is to invite sanctions, as we are beginning to find in terms of our own work. What we mean by this is that feminism is now producing its own 'normal science', and so generating its own view of what is 'theory', what is 'research', what are proper questions for analysis and proper modes of analysis. We view this with alarm because the 'feminist normal science' that is coming into existence bears much more resemblance to what already exists in the social sciences than it does to anything more radically and uniquely feminist. For those of us who don't produce this kind of work there are problems – we seem to be no more 'conventional feminist academics' than we are 'conventional academics'. We've mentioned being sanctioned by non-feminist academic colleagues; and now sanctions are coming from sisters too.

To present research in a reconstructed form is, of course, inevitable and necessary. If we were to simply describe all events as they happened (assuming this could be done), what we described would be chaotic, boring and extremely lengthy. It would, in practical terms, be impossible to do and few people would be interested in the result anyway. However, we don't accept that recognizing that there are problems in presenting research means that the 'scientific' and 'objective' mode of presentation must be adopted as the answer. This, we believe, raises more problems than it solves.

One of these problems is how we recognize 'data' when they occur, and another is how we tell when we are 'doing research properly'. How we know that particular behaviours constitute 'gender', 'class', 'race', 'industrial disputes' and so on is, however, largely a theoretical rather than experiential problem. This is because theoretical categories in the social sciences are only rarely everyday ways of categorizing the world. Even where the words are the same the meaning rarely is. We search out data with which to examine theoretical ideas; and so experiential problems – like whether we are justified in fitting other people's lives into our categories, whether our interpretations are in any way like those of members – are lost sight of. Or rather, as we've said before, they are often seen as irrelevant. When we notice discrepancies between what we theoretically know and what we practically experience we tend to simply ignore the problem or resolve it by the researcher deciding her experience is in some way defective.

These problems are compounded by a further difficulty, one which occurs particularly for people involved in more naturalistic research. This is how we can tell 'when we are experiencing things as a researcher' and 'when we are experiencing them as a person.' We are encouraged to believe that there is a difference between these two states of being – that we do different things, conduct ourselves differently, in each of them. If we fail to recognize our research experiences as suitably 'objective', 'scholarly', 'non-directive', then we may fail to recognize when the research has 'begun'. Frequently research students doing ethnographic work report that none of the expected events and stages that they have read about have occurred to them while many that are taboo have (Georges and Jones, 1980). 'Rapport' does not occur, 'over-involvement' does, 'detachment' is lost sight of. And after this comes the problem of coping with yourself as a 'failed researcher' – usually at the point when your research has to be written up and presented in such a way that your credibility is maintained.

Central in all of this is how, and to what extent, researchers can be uninvolved to the extent that they do not 'disturb' what is going on. But what is *not* discussed is what kind of effect a researcher who behaves in textbook ways might have. We feel that such behaviour would render them immediately noticeable because it would be so unnatural. Reasonable people behave in ordinary and everyday ways – unless they are odd or peculiar in some way. The 'ideal' stance recommended for researchers is that of the odd or peculiar person. To our minds this is not a 'role' to be recommended to anyone who does not wish to 'disturb' situations. In our experience of trying to behave like this, the researcher is treated as deficient in some way. Indeed, in one instance, one of us was accused of behaving like a sociologist!

Another major problem concerns what we should do with our experiences of involvement within the research process. Whether we like it or not, researchers remain human beings complete with the usual human assembly of feelings, failings and moods. And all of these things influence how we feel and understand what is going on. Our consciousness is *always* the medium through which research occurs; there is no method or technique of doing research other than through the medium of the researcher. This is so no matter what style of research we are involved in – whether we are interpreting results produced by computers out of data collected by government or other agencies, whether we're involved in ethnographic research, or whether we're doing any other kind of research, including 'just reading' – like you reading this.

Basic to feminism is that 'the personal is the political'. We suggest that this insistence on the crucial importance of the personal must also include an insistence on the importance, and also the presence, of the personal *within research experiences* as much as within any other experiences. But, more than this, the personal is not only the political, it is also the crucial variable which is absolutely present in each and every attempt to 'do research', although it is frequently invisible in terms of the presentation of this research. It mustn't be absent from presentations of feminist research, because this is to deny the importance of the personal elsewhere. In other words, academic feminism must take feminist beliefs seriously, by integrating these within our research.

Of course most people working within the social sciences are well aware of the idiosyncracies, quirks and problems of research. As we've already said, one-off revised accounts of research which deal with some of these experiences exist. This pretend-naturalism has become popular as a more gossipy, lighter and less 'academic' way of wringing yet one more publishable paper out of research gone by. It seems that feminist researchers too are beginning to adopt a similar way of writing about past research. We view this development with some dismay and see it as a cop-out from attempting to do and write about research in ways which try to combine feminist theory and practice more closely.

Paradoxically enough, it often appears to be feminist social scientists more than most who argue in favour of a value-free, and a truly 'scientific' social science. We have already outlined some of these arguments in our first chapter, and looked at the idea that feminism is the means by which the bias of sexism can be eradicated, leaving the pure and uncontaminated truth. We say paradoxically because we believe that feminism embodies a set of positive values and isn't just the absence of sexism.

Earlier, in chapter 1, we outlined some feminist responses to the criticism that positivist approaches are 'hard science', male, and innately sexist. In a sense we agreed with these because we feel that methods in themselves aren't innately anything. We also feel that a positivist world view which insists on the validity of only one reality, 'the' objective reality, is at odds with the kind of feminism we ally ourselves with. And so while we wouldn't reject the contention that positivist methods and world views are objectionable, sexist even, we feel that what should be objected to about them isn't quantification or their use of statistical techniques. It is their assumptions about the nature of reality, and about the relationship between researcher and researched, which should be rejected. The alternative often proposed is 'naturalism' – 'soft science' as an alternative to the sexism of 'hard science'. But we have already pointed out that positivist assumptions can equally well form the basis of 'soft science' approaches – and frequently do. We believe that 'naturalism' is a false alternative, no real alternative at all and this can be illustrated through a brief discussion of the 'ethnographic method'.

Ethnography, living in a natural setting of some kind as a means of deriving data, seems quite different from the quantified, frequently statistical, approach usually associated with positivism. But even in ethnographic accounts 'the researcher' only rarely appears. Bland 'objective' description follows bland description follows bland analysis. This is how it was, this is what life here is like, we are told or it is implied.

But life wasn't 'like this', this wasn't 'how it was'. What we have, instead, is one person's construction of this. And this person is usually not a natural member of the setting, can't speak the 'natural language' except as a 'foreigner' does (and we place these words in quotation marks because they apply equally to settings 'at home' as well as those conventionally 'abroad'), and is concerned to demonstrate research 'competence' by firmly and deliberately remaining an outsider. 'Scientific detachment', 'truth', 'non-involvement', all rear their heads here too. And despite all the controversies and debates about the place of 'values' in ethnographic research, detachment, truth, non-involvement and all their bedfellows are still alive and well and frequently to be met.

What we are arguing is this. 'Naturalism' is essentially 'dishonest', in the sense that it too denies the involvement, the contaminating and disturbing presence, of the researcher. Here too, not just in conventionally positivist research, we necessarily look at events *through* the researcher; but, in spite of this, such research is presented to us in such a way as to deny this, to suggest that what we have instead is 'truth'.

INVOLVEMENT AND EMOTION

Feminist reliance on 'naturalism' and 'soft science' is insufficient. It stems from insufficient feminist criticism of positivism, insufficient attempts by feminists to find better alternatives. And so we argue, as we have earlier argued, that it is necessary to go back to the basics of feminist theory. It is this which should be used to produce a critique of social science theory, research methods and techniques, and descriptions of the research process itself.

We feel that few feminist discussions of research do anything other than choose between the alternatives already available. They seize upon existing models of research and depictions of research methods: naturalistic or positivistic, qualitative or quantitative, hard or soft. We not only see this as no *answer* to the kind of problems we have outlined (and the problems raised by feminism itself), but we also feel that the identification of values as a 'problem' by feminist researchers doesn't even lead to the identification of the right kind of *question*.

Something which *our* experience of research has demonstrated very clearly is that 'theory' always and inevitably comes before research, if we use this word to mean the formulation of ideas which attempt to understand and explain something. All people derive 'theory' or 'second order constructs' from their experiences or 'first order constructs' (Schutz, 1962). It isn't only social scientists who produce general accounts of reality in this way, in spite of what we are frequently told (Denzin, 1972). Everyone constructs explanations of what they experience in their everyday lives.

And so we believe that all research is 'grounded' in consciousness, because it isn't possible to do research (or life) in such a way that we can separate ourselves from experiencing what we experience as people (and researchers) involved in a situation. There is no way we can avoid deriving theoretical constructs from experience, because we necessarily attempt to understand what is going on *as* we experience it. The research experience itself, like all other experiences, is necessarily subject to on-going 'theorizing', on-going attempts to understand, explain, re-explain, what is going on. This is what consciousness is all about; this is what people do in new situations and researchers do no differently from anyone else.

Our research on, and experiences of, obscene phone calls emphasizes this. We found that our experience of this affected our lives outside of the research, including our 'theoretical understandings and perceptions' of the nature of women's oppression. This, in its turn, influenced how we saw previous and current events connected with the obscene calls and the men who made them. And then our experiences of the research, as our theoretical perceptions changed, changed too. All of this had consequences for our consciousness throughout the entire process. Everything fed into everything else.

It isn't possible for feminists to do research on sexism in such a way as to leave 'us' untouched by this. But the kind of experiences we had, which we suggest are inevitable wherever feminism encounters sexism, are something which researchers are generally counselled to prevent. Often, indeed, it is suggested that the point at which such involvements begin is the point at which research should be terminated (Whyte, 1955).

'Emotional involvement', the presence of emotions, is taboo; and an ideology exists which states that it is *possible*, not just preferable, to prevent this from happening. But we say that this is mere mythology. Emotions can't be controlled by mere effort of will, nor can adherence to any set of techniques or beliefs act as an emotional prophylactic. And of course emotional involvement isn't something which occurs only to researchers. However much we might be able to prevent our own feelings from showing (if not from occurring), we cannot control those of other people. 'The researched' will have feelings about us as much as we will about them, and also feelings (and theories) about the research itself. This isn't, however, often discussed in research literature, which tends to describe people as simply the repositories of 'data' which can be emptied into questionnaires, interviews, ethnographies and so on.

Our experiences suggest that 'hygienic research' is a reconstructed logic, a mythology which presents an oversimplistic account of research. It is also extremely misleading, in that it emphasizes the 'objective' presence of the researcher and suggests that she can be 'there' without having any greater involvement than simple presence. In contrast we emphasize that all research involves, as its basis, an interaction, a relationship, between researcher and researched. We also believe that such a relationship exists whether 'the researched' are books, secondary data, other objects, or people. Because the basis of all research is a relationship, this necessarily involves the presence of the researcher *as a person*. Personhood cannot be left behind, cannot be left out of the research process. And so we insist that it must be capitalized upon, it must be made full use of. If we can't do research in any other way than by using ourselves as the medium through which research is carried out, then we must fully explore this.

We see the presence of the researcher's self as central in all research. One's self can't be left behind, it can only be omitted from discussions and written accounts of the research process. But it *is* an omission, a failure to discuss something which has been present within the research itself. The researcher may be unwilling to admit this, or unable to see its importance, but it nevertheless remains so. If nothing else, we would insist on the absolute reality of this: that being alive involves us in having emotions and involvements; and in doing research we cannot leave behind what it is to be a person alive in the world.

So how – and why – should we use consciousness within the research process as a resource and topic in our exploration of feminism and social reality? This question has been tackled by Dorothy Smith, who argues that 'women's perspective' on and in social reality makes available to us, women, a radical critique of sociology (1974). We feel that this critique can to a large extent be extended to other social sciences too.

Feminism, Smith argues, has given women a sense that our interests must be represented within sociology. It is possible, as we've seen, merely to add women in to what already exists, but if the social sciences *begin* from the point of view of women's reality then this will have far-reaching consequences. It isn't enough for us to supplement what already exists, and to add women into fundamentally sexist social science. Doing this not only isn't enough, it also leaves us unable to account for the important disjunctions that exist between women's experiences within the world, and the concepts and theoretical schemes available to conceptualize these.

The social sciences don't merely justify and rationalize the power relationships which oppress women. They also provide the concepts, models and methods by which experience can be translated and transformed. Theoretical terms take over experience and reformulate it. And sociology is the main means by which this process occurs, argues Smith, because it is centrally involved in the provision of this conceptual language. What people actually say and do is transformed into the 'abstract mode'. And, through their involvement in this, the social sciences contribute to a systematic process by which what are examined are social science problems, not social problems, not the issues and concerns of our everyday experiences.

In a sense we could say that women's lives involve a continual reality disjuncture, as we discussed this idea in the previous chapter. There is a continual contradiction between women's involvement in everyday experience and the 'language of theory'. The language of theory exerts a conceptual imperialism over experience. In effect, there is a power relationship between theory and experience, and one consequence is that women are not only alienated from theory but also experience itself.

The dislocation that exists between social science theory and women's experience is crucial for those of us working in the social sciences. If we choose theory as opposed to experience then we necessarily deny the validity of our experiences as women. But if we choose to stand by the validity of experience, and deny the validity of theory, then we risk definition as incompetent and we may become failed members of our profession.

The view of social reality contained within the social sciences is an inadequate representation of what we experience; this is immediately obvious to women, especially to feminists. Feminist consciousness emphasizes that the social sciences present a partial, a specific and an androcentric view of social reality. But, the more successful we are in academic terms, the more likely we are to experience alienation from our *selves* because we have learned to value theory above such experiences.

The separation of theory and experience is, argues Smith, a

condition of the androcentric presence of men within the discipline. Men, as men, tend to be alienated from the physical facts of their existence, from the world of concrete practical activities, including domestic labour and child-rearing. For many, perhaps most, women these are inescapable social and physical facts; but they aren't features of most men's experience at all. Because women do their shit work for them, male social scientists can more easily become absorbed into the world of theory and divorced from the everyday.

It is sometimes claimed that male social scientists are involved in a 'transcendental realm' (Bierstedt, 1966). This piece of professional ideology says academic work 'transcends' the specifics of person, time and location. 'Transcendence' is a state supposedly achieved through use of specific practices and adherence to a body of knowledge known as 'objectivity'. But Smith argues that the male practice of objectivity is primarily concerned with the 'separation of the knower from what he knows'. In particular it is concerned with the separation of what is known from any interests, and any 'biases', which the researcher may have. And thus are the products of social science 'liberated' from time and place.

In other words, the social sciences claim to provide us with objective knowledge independent of the personal situation of the social scientist. But, of course, women's perspective, women's knowledge, and women's experience, provide an irrefutable critique of such claims. Within such products of social science research women's lives are omitted, distorted, misunderstood, and in doing this men's lives too are similarly distorted.

If the social sciences cannot avoid being situated, being located within a particular time, space and place, and formed by the experiences specific to these, then Smith argues that they must make full use of this. Indeed, she argues that the situated nature of the researcher should form the very beginning and basis of social science work. This would require a thorough examination of where the social scientist is actually situated; and then making her direct experience of the world, and the research process, the basis of her knowledge as a social scientist.

FEMINIST SOCIAL SCIENCE RESEARCH

A feminist social science

We believe that a feminist social science should begin with the recognition that 'the personal', direct experience, underlies all behaviours and actions. We need to find out what it is that we know and what it is that we experience. We need to reclaim, name and rename our experiences and our knowledge of the social world we live in and daily construct. We conceptualize this world through a language provided for us by sexist society, and by a thoroughly androcentric social science. We need to reject this imposed language and to construct our own social science, a social science which starts from women's experience of women's reality. Without doing this we can have no truly feminist social science; we can only have a social science in which women's experiences are researched and analysed using the conceptual procedures, the methods of research, and the research models provided by sexism.

The kind of feminist social science and research we envisage is not one which is concerned only with what goes on in our heads, with a psychology of inner thoughts and feelings. Women, like all other people, are *social* beings. We live in a social world with other social beings; and merely living requires that we behave in social ways. We interact with other people at all times, either physically or in our minds. It is all of these *social* actions and reactions which should properly be the concern of feminist social science.

Much contemporary social science appears to us over-concerned with predicting the motives and feelings of the researched. However, social scientists frequently cannot or will not enter into the world as it is experienced by the people who are its subjects. Virginia Woolf has expressed something of our feelings about this (1931). Discussing her attempt to understand the experiences of guildswomen at a conference of co-operative working women, she wrote that, however hard she attempted to participate in these women's emotions, she continued to feel that she was a benevolent spectator, irretrievably cut-off from them. She goes on to argue that 'fictitious sympathy' differs from 'real sympathy' and is defective because it isn't based upon *sharing* the same important emotions; and the only way to share emotions is to share experiences.

The basis of our objections to social science attempts to deduce or predict feelings and emotions is that these derive from the 'fictitious sympathy' of people who remain outside of the experiences they write about and claim competence in. Instead of writing about how they know what they claim to know (which would necessitate locating the social scientist *within* the research process) they write about the experiences of others as though these were directly available to them. That these are necessarily transformed in a researcher's construction of them is ignored.

Feminist research as we envisage it wouldn't take this false sympathy as its basis. It would instead explore the basis of our everyday knowledge as women, as feminists, *and* as social scientists. As we do this we must make available to other people the reasoning procedures which underlie the knowledge produced out of research. We must tap our experiences of 'being a researcher', and as feminist researchers with feminist consciousness this involves tapping our experiences as *feminists* in any social situation.

This kind of research is necessary and even crucial to the feminist enterprise. We see it as crucial to an understanding of both women's oppression and women's liberation; and we insist that feminist social science should be concerned with everyday life because of this. But there is another reason for doing so as well. 'Everyday life' is what we spend our lives doing; is what we are involved in all of our waking, and a large part of our sleeping, hours. What all people spend most of their time doing must obviously be the subject of research. What women spend most of their time doing must obviously be the subject of feminist research.

We need to know how, in minute detail, all facets of the oppressions of all women occur. To talk blithely of 'the family', 'capitalism' or 'men' as the reasons for women's oppressions may in a sense be true. But this merely re-states the problem. It doesn't tell us the mechanisms, the experiences, the behaviours, the looks, conversations, which are involved. Nor does 'the abolition of the family', 'the over-throw of capitalism' or 'no more men' give us any answer, any solution to these problems.

If we are to resist oppression, then we need the *means* to do so. The means to resist oppression, we believe, are to be found where all of our oppressions are themselves to be found. Without knowing *how* oppression occurs we cannot possibly know *why* it occurs; and without knowing how and why it occurs we cannot find out how to avoid its occurrence, how it is that liberation might be achieved. Liberation has to start somewhere; we cannot leap into a liberated world overnight. We must necessarily effect many small liberations in many small and apparently insignificant aspects of our lives, or we shall never begin 'the revolution'.

'Be true to the phenomenon' is an axiom often stated within the naturalistic approach. It suggests that we should attempt to represent reality as it is experienced and lived by the people that we carry out research on. But the only way that it is really possible to do this is for those people themselves to present their own analytic accounts of their own experiences. The best alternative is that researchers should present analytic accounts of how and why we think we know what we do about research situations and the people in them. The only way we can avoid overriding other people's understandings as 'deficient' in some way is not to attempt to present these within research. Instead we should be much more concerned with presenting *ourselves* and *our* understandings of what is going on, by examining these in their context. We must make ourselves vulnerable, not hide behind what 'they' are supposed to think and feel, say and do.

Some objections

In the remainder of this chapter we discuss three major problems which people have suggested exist with the kind of research we're proposing. The first is that it deals with only a 'sample of one' and therefore it is of extremely limited use or interest. The second suggests that frequently researchers want to find out things which cannot be discovered using the kind of approach we advocate. And the third is that this research produces exactly what is to be found in novels, poems, and other works of literature. It may be therapeutic but it isn't 'science'.

1 A sample of one?

The researcher, whether woman or man, white or black, heterosexual or homosexual, feminist or not, is usually only *one* person. And an obvious objection to the kind of research we are proposing is that it would simply use a sample of one. Such a 'sample' would of course be 'unrepresentative' – social scientists almost invariably come from a white, middle-class background, almost never admit to anything other than heterosexuality. The kind of research we are proposing, therefore, would not permit us to say anything about the experiences of people unlike us. Because of this most minority groups would be absent from it because their members only rarely become social scientists. And so, however interesting (or uninteresting) the research that we might carry out, it would not permit generalizations from the person carrying it out to the people who form the 'research situation'. It would apply to the researcher and the researcher only. And a further and associated problem is that this kind of research could not be replicated. No other person could repeat it – it would be unique to the original researcher.

It is most certainly true that social scientists tend to come from a section of society not noted for being oppressed or exploited. More often than not social scientists *are* white, male, middle-class, heterosexual. But this is precisely the point that we have been arguing – to look at the kind of research that's produced and published you'd never know this. The kind of research we advocate would point up how dishonest existing research is, dishonest in the sense that it *pretends*; it is based upon an ideology which legitimates the pretence of being 'representative'. It claims to be able to represent the experiences and understandings of the people who are its object.

As women we know that this claim is false, is empty. Those of us who are lesbians know it doubly. We know that what is represented to us as 'truth' about women, about lesbians, is no such thing, is unrecognizable to those of us it claims to be about. And we also know that our awareness of this gap between experience and theory is written-off as the product of our 'emotions', 'involvements', as though these disqualified us from knowing what we know.

The time has come to reject such posturings, such arrogance, and to name it for what it is. Recently we were told that to reject 'objectivity' is only an excuse for 'sloppy work'. We turn this on its head and say that it is 'objectivity' itself which is the excuse for sloppy work. And it is also an excuse for a power relationship every bit as obscene as the power relationship that leads women to be sexually assaulted, murdered, and otherwise treated as mere objects. The assault on our minds, the removal from existence of our experiences as valid and true, is every bit as objectionable.

It will be quite obvious from what we have just said that we view the power relationship between researcher and researched very seriously. As women, as lesbians, as working class, we both have bitter experience of it. It is obscene because it treats people as mere objects, there for the researcher to do research 'on'. Treating people as objects – sex objects or research objects – is morally unjustifiable. Some feminists have sought an answer to this very serious problem by rejecting 'research on' in favour of 'research with', and we have earlier outlined one interesting and heartening attempt to do this within ideas about 'interactive methodology'. But we find this no answer for us. We do not want people, 'the researched', to have more involvement in designing questionnaires, interpreting statistical or other results. This is partly because we reject the underlying philosophy of positivism. It is also because we reject a feminist research which is concerned only with women. We've already asked whether this approach would work satisfactorily with rapists, obscene phone callers, and other sexist men. Our answer is still 'no'.

We look to the kind of research which approaches this *inevitable* power relationship in a different way. Its 'different way' is to lay open, to make vulnerable, the researcher. It therefore involves displaying her actions, reasonings, deductions and evidence to other people. We're not arguing that 'vulnerability' is the magic key that enables us to enter other people's experiences and emotions. 'Fictitious sympathy' must be rejected in favour of us honestly saying that we don't, can't, possibly know how it is, for example, to live as a paraplegic person. But we *do* construct a view of what this is from how we feel about what this experience might be like for the other person. It is *this* construction which is made accessible to us through our vulnerability. And it also makes quite apparent the part played by the researcher in constructing what goes on. This is much more honest, because it portrays as central what *is* central anyway. Social events and behaviours can only be interpreted and constructed by the person who is describing their experiences of them. In essence, of course, this is what research is – it relates research experiences to an audience as these are interpreted by the researcher. Nothing else is possible, so we must say this and make it central to what we say about research. What we are proposing would make this quite explicit in its analysis of the reasoning procedures utilized by the researcher in carrying out her research. It might not be 'representative', but at least it has a chance of being honestly representative of the researcher herself.

But at least a few researchers are not male, white, heterosexual or middle class in origin. Those who aren't should make good use of this by examining, as research, our experiences as female, black, lesbian, working class and so on. Few such accounts find their way into research of any kind. Frequently, indeed, membership of such groups is in itself taken as proof of 'subjective involvement' and thus of disqualification from research competence. How many other professions, we wonder, make such a fetish out of *ignorance*, elevate it into the only possible claim to professional competence? Members of such groups have a unique opportunity to represent directly the experiences and understandings of oppressed people of various kinds, and this opportunity should not be passed up because we are too busy trying to fit ourselves into the social sciences as they are, too concerned with respectability and conformity.

Making use of these experiences is necessary for feminist social science, partly because the experiences of oppressed people ought to be represented within it, and partly because oppressed people of all kinds see and experience social reality in uniquely different and interesting ways. Reality *is* contradictory, realities do co-exist and over-lap, and conflict; and people who are in some sense excluded from 'the reality' of dominant groups *live* such contradictions and conflicts. As women, as lesbians, as black, as working class, as disabled, as otherwise 'deviant', we see the world in a different way, different experiences happen to us, people relate to us differently, we relate to them differently.

2 Too limited?

Another suggested criticism is that ours is a very limited kind of research because it focuses only on what is directly experienced by the researcher. It would not enable many, perhaps most, feminists to find out the kinds of things that feminism needs to know. What we need to find out is not knowledge for its own sake. Moreover, we do not need an exploration of the everyday – we already know about this because we directly experience it. What we need to find out are the answers to problems which are of greater concern to feminists, such as why women do not seek promotion, why marriage and childbirth is seen as an alternative to a career, why girls do not study scientific and engineering subjects, how rapes can be prevented, where job discrimination occurs.

These criticisms seem to us to be based on a very limited and narrow idea of what is useful and practical, and of what research might be about. 'Knowledge' for its own sake we believe to be as 'useful' as what appears to be directly practical. Without properly understanding what is going on, without subjecting experience to analysis, then 'experience', even our own, is *not* something we already know about. Most of what we do, we do in a routine fashion. Because it is part of everyday life we tend to treat it as unproblematic and uninteresting.

Although all women share oppression, we absolutely reject the idea that women who aren't lesbians, aren't working class, aren't black (and also of course who are not heterosexual, not middle class, not white) can know what it is to be oppressed as such. Women don't share the same experience – *the material forms of our oppressions differ*. We feel that an enormous amount of very basic research remains to be done on the varying natures of women's oppressions. And this is research to which a more phenomeno-logically based approach is ideally suited.

We also feel that this criticism implies that 'right answers' to social questions can be found – that there is one right answer to every problem that exists. Many feminists claim to know already what 'the problem' is, in the sense that much feminist theory has identified 'the problem', the basis of women's oppression, in terms of structures of various kinds. But we see this as merely restatement of the problem; it isn't an examination of what occurs, nor an analysis of how it occurs.

We remain absolutely unconvinced that feminism yet knows how and why women are oppressed. To find this out we need to know *how* oppression occurs *where* it occurs: in the context of our differing everyday experiences. Feminist research of the kind that we are interested in would take this as its subject matter. The positivist research style, and the belief in one social reality, appears to be useful because it seemingly enables us to find things out. But what positivist research finds out is what the researcher already knows, in terms of knowledge already existing within particular disciplines; and it might better be seen as an efficient means of 'proving' to others that what the researcher already knows is really 'true'.

Of course we accept that everyone, us included, sees and experiences 'reality' through the framework of our paradigmatic preconceptions and understandings. Our 'truth' is as partial and contextually grounded as anyone else's. However, we believe that our view of reality is *preferable*, in feminist terms, because we believe it flows out of our feminist understandings and beliefs more directly and explicitly than most other approaches utilized within feminist social science. In addition, it is not a view which would be imposed on other people's experiences during the conduct of research. Having at its heart the belief that many 'objective realities' exist, it takes as its task the exploration of these, not their obliteration, their dismissal, as 'false' or 'inadequate'.

3 Just like literature?

We've already rejected the idea that research concerned with consciousness and with the everyday will be a psychology of our inner thoughts, because human experience is unavoidably social. We are none the less well aware that many people will see what we are arguing for in these terms. And it has been suggested to us, as a criticism, that what we are proposing is something very similar to the production of literature. This kind of research, we've been told, is 'fiction' in the sense that it is one person's view, one person's attempt to account for and describe 'society, as it is experienced'. This is the stuff of literature, we are told, of novels and poetry, and not of science. Science is concerned with rational explanation, based on facts derived through research.

We both accept and reject this criticism. We reject it because we don't believe that 'science' exists in the way that many people still claim it does. We don't see it as the single-minded and objective pursuit of truth. 'Truth' is a social construct, in the same way that 'objectivity' is; and both are constructed out of experiences which are, for all practical purposes, the same as 'lies' and 'subjectivity'. And so we see all research as 'fiction' in the sense that it views and so constructs 'reality' through the eyes of one person. We accept it because much literature is concerned with such an exploration of 'society' through the eyes of particular characters, but ultimately and frequently explicitly through the eyes of the writer. If this is the kind of literature that our kind of research is compared with then we accept the comparison and feel flattered. We view this kind of literature much more highly than to regard any comparison with it as down-grading. If this kind of research can open people's eyes, can influence them and change them, to the extent that literature has done, then it will do better than any other social science research that has appeared to date.

Throughout this book we've attempted to reject using dichotomies to categorize and divide people's experiences within everyday life; and we see the dichotomy between science and literature as yet another of these. We hope it is apparent from everything that has gone before that the kind of feminist social science we envisage would mean that such distinctions cease to have the significance they now have.

Obviously we haven't produced an exhaustive series of criticisms. We aren't primarily interested in appeasing those people who would seek to deny the validity of what we're proposing, its right to existence among other approaches within feminist social science. We feel that if people don't like what we're proposing then they should simply not do it. We aren't attempting to persuade every feminist researcher or academic to interpret her feminism in the way that we do. What we are trying to put across is our feeling that feminism can and should be understood in the way we have described, not for everyone, but at least for some women. And those of us who do so must be seen as understanding and living our feminism in absolutely acceptable and valid ways, and not treated by some other feminists as falsely conscious, stupid and less than competent in understanding what is going on in the world. And of course we also feel this about feminist research of the kind we have outlined, because we believe that this flows directly out of our understanding of feminism and so our approach to feminist theory and practice.

Chapter 7

'And so, dear reader . . .'

And so, dear reader, in this last chapter we give you no easy answers to the problems and issues we've raised, and no recipe for doing feminist research of the kind we'd like to see. We have no latterday equivalent to '. . . I married him' because we have no 'end' to this book in any traditional sense. Ends are usually the point of revelation, of pronouncement, the place where untidy loose strands are tidied away and the answers to all questions given. But if we were to provide an 'end' of this sort we feel that it would come in one of three possible forms (or perhaps a combination of these).

We might provide a summary of what we have written about in this book. But it would be difficult, and tedious, to pick out of some hundreds of pages the pure essence of our ideas (supposing that there is any pure essence there to pick out). And doing this would necessarily involve repetition and restatement of what has already been said. You, and we, would be likely to find this boring.

We might provide some guide as to how we see 'feminist research' by critically discussing various pieces of research which are an approximation to this. But we don't know of any ready-made examples which we could use as 'ideal types'; and critically discussing approximations would lead us into doing something we don't really want to. And this is saying that other women have got it wrong, have gone about it in the wrong way. We're of course aware that, in a sense, we've already done this in parts of this book, and we do it again later in this chapter. However, we have tried to make it clear that the grounds on which we've said what we have aren't those of 'scholarship' or 'correctness', but 'feeling' and 'experience'. We are simply saying that in our experience these things don't 'fit', don't make sense to us.

We might provide a series of pointers and exemplars for 'doing feminist research' which would add up to a recipe for other women to follow. But we're suspicious of other people's attempts to specify what, exactly, 'research' should be, and feel that other people should rightly be suspicious of any similar attempt by us. We also reject the idea of telling other women exactly how things should be, although in a sense writing a book about feminist research is doing precisely this in a grand way. But we'd like to think that what we've done in it is to highlight principles and relate them to *our* kind of feminism, not making nitpicking and querulous points purely for the satisfaction of doing so. For people who share in our view of feminism, this might make some kind of sense to you. If you don't, no doubt you'll find it all rubbish anyway. We most certainly don't want to be seen to be telling other feminists how things are and should be, for a start because we don't know anyway, but also because we really don't want there to be a, one, feminist 'line' on research or anything else.

So then, we've said that these are the three main possible endings to this book, and that we aren't going to provide any of them. So what are we going to do? We have tried to emphasize, and to make absolutely clear, that this book is about (and, in a way, is *for*) *us*, not other women. Our warrant for writing what we have isn't that we have any 'truth' to give people, any message that is better than can be found in a multitude of other books. Having rejected 'truth', and 'better' and 'worse', our warrant is our feelings, our experience, and our consciousness of ourselves as women and as feminists. All of what we have said, including our reservations about other people's work, has derived from these same sources: that this work in some sense doesn't *feel* right to us, and this feeling occurs because what they say is belied by our *experience*.

One of our main arguments has been that the analytic use of feeling and experience in an examination of 'the personal' should be the main principle on which feminist research is based. To this extent, at least, we're willing to provide a recipe and tell other women what they should be doing. This may be a contradiction at the heart of what we believe and what we've written, but neither of us minds being contradictory.

However, apart from this, there is little that we can say for other people. We can write about feminist research only in so far as we do so around what this looks like for us, at this point in time, by looking at how we see the analytic use of feeling, experience and consciousness within the research process. The 'ending' that we go on to outline, then, is one in which we discuss some rather disparate ideas connected to how we see the use of feeling, experience and consciousness in feminist research – for us. How it might be for other women is for you to work out, not for us to say. But we insist on having our cake and eating it too, because we refuse to be bound by what we go on to say. In a few months or a year or so it may look very different. We hope so because we hope that our future experience of life and research will help change us as much as what's past has done.

RESEARCH AND US

Using feeling and experience as the basis for explicating the personal and the everyday ought to be the guiding principle of feminist research, we have argued. In a sense what this might look like could be expressed in the phrase 'telling it like it was'. This grand cliché of the hip 1960s, crass and simplistic though it may be, nevertheless does capture something of the approach we're advocating. 'Telling it like it was' doesn't, for us, mean that the researcher is some sort of omnipotent oracle-like figure mouthing truths about past, present and future. It does mean saying why and how particular research came to be carried out, why and how the researcher came to know what she knows about that research. And it also means leaving behind such devices for achieving objectivity/omnipotence as 'it is felt that . . .', and descriptions of people, events and behaviours which are presented as non-problematic and indisputably 'true'.

'Research' is a process which occurs through the medium of a person – the researcher is always and inevitably present *in* the research. This exists whether openly stated or not; and feminist research ought to make this an open presence. To paraphrase a slogan once current in the gay movement, researchers must 'come out' in their writings. And so, for example, Dorothy Smith, in discussing an interview which documents the processes by which K comes to be seen as mentally ill, notes that a multiplicity of people are involved in the production of 'sociological data':

not just the sociologist, the interviewer and the respondent, but also those who brought about the original events and those who tried to reach a decision about what they were . . . I have accordingly also stressed throughout, the fact that we all recognize but normally bracket, namely that the sociologist is and must be an active participant in constructing the events she treats as data (Smith, 1978, p.24).

And to this she later adds-in yet another level of data construction: 'You, as reader of what I now write, may also wish to add the penultimate if not the ultimate level, namely my analysis of the document' (1978, p. 32). What *we*, researchers, write is an artful construction – the penultimate level of construction; and of course how *you* read and understand it is yet another (and different) artful construction – the ultimate (perhaps) level of construction.

John Lee's account of the interpretation of newspaper headlines dealing with rape, around categories such as 'innocent victim' and 'evil doer', locates himself as absolutely central within the processes by which sense is assembled out of these:

From the heading I was able to anticipate that the story was probably a rape story. But more than that: I was able to anticipate that it was not *just* a rape story but a story that had a certain 'angle' or 'slant' and that this 'angle' or 'slant' was related to its tellability as a story. The discussion in this paper is concerned to analyse the informative content of that headline to see how I and presumably others could come to such expectations (Lee, 1984, pp. 69).

What both Smith and Lee are pointing up for us is the tangible presence of researchers in what they research and what they write (even if this is, as Smith says, normally 'bracketed'), and the necessary assembly of 'research' out of 'experience' or 'consciousness'. Of course writing research in this way makes us vulnerable or, to emphasize this in a rather different way, it makes *us* vulnerable. If we appear 'in person' in our research then we are open to personal attack – people can and frequently do attack our work by attacking us. Inextricably bound up in the 'scientific' approach and its firm removal of the subjective from research is a large measure of fear: fear of what other people might say, and what they might think. If we aren't 'there' in our research then they can't say it, or they will say it in a 'scientific' and removed way rather than directly and personally, so we don't have to feel so frightened.

Undoubtedly to locate oneself within research and writing *is* a hazardous and frightening business. Vulnerability is always frightening because it can be, and often is, abused or countered by bland invulnerability. Women know this perhaps better than men. But to be vulnerable is an everyday hazard for 'the researched', for little research is done on those people powerful enough to force the non-publication or recantation of results they don't like. The researched are vulnerable in the sense that their lives, feelings, understandings, become grist to the research mill and may appear, in goodness knows what mangled form, at the end of the research process. And, whatever mangled form it is, its form is unlikely to be subject to control by them. We cite, as but one of the thousands of possible examples we might use, research by liberals and illiberals alike which purports to present 'the truth' about lesbians and lesbian communities. Where is the research that has been changed, withdrawn, because its 'subjects' have objected here?

We don't feel that any of the attempts to tackle this problem made by feminists go far enough in trying to dissolve the power divisions that exist between researchers and researched. We also believe that even the most radical of these attempts is likely to work only when 'the researched' are women – and perhaps only when they're also feminists. But surely we owe some responsibility to 'the researched' of all kinds, whether we morally approve of them or not? We believe so, and feel that placing 'us' in the research as well as 'them' does something to even up the imbalance of power between researchers and researched, though it obviously can't remove it. If *they* are vulnerable, then *we* must be prepared to show ourselves as vulnerable too.

Vulnerability isn't all altruism, however; self-interest is also involved. The greater the impact of feminism on the social sciences and the greater the revolt against positivism, the greater will be the emphasis on personal experience. But perhaps of even greater importance than this is the communicative power of direct experience directly related to us, in comparison with 'abstract discourse'. Compare, for example, the two following passages:

> Unfortunately I found it impossible to learn to behave in every respect like a Utkuhiksalingmiut daughter. Inuttiaq lectured me in general terms on the subject of filial obedience, and once in

a while I think he tried to shame me into good behaviour by offering himself as a model of virtue – volunteering, for example, to make bannock for me if I was slow in making it for him. But to little avail . . . I found it hard sometimes to be simultaneously a docile and helpful daughter and a conscientious anthropologist . . . A number of times, when I could have helped to gut fish or to carry in snow to repair the sleeping platform or floor or could have offered to fetch water or make tea, I sat and wrote instead or sorted vocabulary – tiny slips of paper spread precariously over my sleeping bag and lap. It was sometimes professional anxiety that prompted me to disobey Inuttiaq, too, and I am sure that on such occasions, as on others, he must have found my insubordination not only 'bad', but completely incomprehensible (Briggs, 1970, pp. 24–5).

Frequently researchers are counselled not to allow the occurrence of the kind of involvement we have just outlined. That is, emotional involvement is seen to detract from a professionally correct detachment for sociologists as it is for prostitutes and for social workers (Stanley and Wise, 1979, p. 361).

Both of these quotations are saying exactly the same thing – except that they aren't! What we mean by this is that Briggs shows us, because she tries to reconstruct for us, the clash between professional social science ideology and (research) experience. But our own statement is precisely that – it states, but it doesn't show, because it presents *what* we know without demonstrating *how* we know it. To say this slightly differently – 'theory' means something rather different when shown in relation to, and as a construction out of, 'substantive work', because to locate it within a context enables us to see how and why it was constructed, not just that it was constructed.

To be fair to ourselves, we try to do this by tying our statements to a substantive analysis. However, we can't help but feel that there must be alternative ways of writing and analysing that help us to approach experience and research in quite different ways. Writing of Simone de Beauvoir's *The Second Sex*, Patricia Meyer Spacks says this:

She demonstrates her logic, her grasp of reality, her capacity to deal with the abstract as well as the concrete; demonstrates thus her intellectual identity with those beings who have attempted to separate her into a special category (Spacks, 1976, p. 16).

And later on she adds: 'Despite Mlle de Beauvoir's penetrating criticism of male writers' "myths" of women, her own standards of accomplishment are masculine' (1976, p. 19). We are uncomfortably aware that similar remarks can – and should – be levelled at our own style of presentation and mode of argument, as well as that of many other feminist writers.

Words, sentences, writing styles, ways of presenting arguments, arguments themselves, criticism, all these are part and parcel of masculinist culture. They are among the artefacts of sexism, and their use structures our experience before we can even begin to examine it, because they provide us with how we *think* as well as how we *write*. We are in a circle, a circle vicious in its eradication of feminist culture. Sexism isn't discriminatory practices in employment and education, nor even the domestic division of labour. At its root sexism is a set of practices, contextually located and daily enacted, which fix us within them. This 'circle' we refer to is one in which sexism provides us not only with a vocabulary but also the structures through which we think, through which we conceptualize and enact 'society'. We can't break out of the circle until we can conceptualize 'outside of the circle'; and to do this requires new ways of conceptualizing; but to do this requires a different 'language', a different set of ways of structuring the world; but this requires . . .

Of course it isn't quite like this. The social world is neither so determinate nor so relentlessly sexist as this – but that it is presented as such is an important feature of the means by which sexism is perpetuated. To see that it *can* be changed, and that anyway people aren't so stereotyped as we're told that they are, is to begin to change it. But *how* we change it, how we break out of the circle – as well as whether we recognize that it is there to be broken out of – matters. Few feminists, even fewer academic feminists, dare to be very different, and dare to do anything other than sit within the circle, pointing the finger at other parts of it. Again, this can perhaps be illustrated by comparing two quite different, but both interesting and useful, approaches.

SITTING INSIDE THE CIRCLE . . .

We have argued that oppression and liberation are to be found within the everyday, within all facets of our involvements and interactions. Nancy Henley's *Body Politics* focuses on an aspect of this that few other feminists have taken note of – non-verbal communication of all kinds. As she suggests:

> If you care about power, if you care about how power is wielded over you, this book is for you. It describes the way we sit, smile, take up space, stare, cock our heads, or touch others is bound to our power relationships. Body language is not composed only of messages about friendship and sex; it is body politics also . . . And it is also especially for those who have been fighting the oppression of power over their own lives, while ignoring the meaning of much of their day-to-day interaction with the powerful (Henley, 1977, p. vii).

While in absolute agreement with her concerning the crucial importance of non-verbal communication, and finding much of interest and excitement in her book, we also find some aspects of it rather off-putting. The first and last chapters of it, we feel, add much to feminist understanding, and promise much for the future development of feminist theory. But what lies between doesn't come directly out of Nancy Henley's insights to us, as the first and last chapters do. In what lies between her insights are imposed on a veritable morass of 'scientific psychological research' and so legitimated by this as 'proper academic work'.

By this we mean that endless pieces of research on miniscule numbers of captive psychology students and the like are cited as 'proper evidence', as proof, as 'solid research findings and clearly traced logical argument' (Henley, 1977, p. viii). And the extension of such research, although in non-sexist ways and including the examination of things of interest and relevance to women, is seen as one of the prime tasks of future work. Henley makes it quite clear that this work must consist of academically respectable, scientifically proper, research.

However, this style of research, and this idea of what 'research' and 'science' is, begs a lot of questions – indeed, all the questions we have addressed in this book. Consider, for example the following statement of one important finding in a study concerned with the relationship between different facets of interaction: 'black male interactions involving touch or physical conduct with white class-mates decreased from 63 percent to 61 percent to 53 percent from primary to intermediate to junior high grades' (Henley, 1977, p. 38). On one quick reading this, and many other similar statements in this book, seems plausible enough. But, once we think about it, how many doubts arise and problems appear: is such a percentage decrease in any way significant in relation to the size of the samples used? how was 'interaction' defined? and why? who measured it and in what context? What was the role of the researchers and their interaction, if any, with the 'subjects'? could any features of this research be termed 'sexist' or 'racist'? and what difference might this make to our interpretation of it? These, of course, are the sort of problems an even half-way awake positivist might make; to them we also add all of the doubts and criticisms that can and should be made of positivism itself.

But we also believe that a further set of difficulties arise in relation to its style of approach, its mode of argument and presentation. Of course, the critique of positivism is closely related to these, but we feel that these particular aspects are too infrequently singled out for scrutiny. Positivism is a paradigm which is part and parcel of the *construction*, not just the interpretation, of social reality. And similarly the 'mode of presentation' we refer to here isn't *just* a presentation – it is itself part of the process by which we come to construct the world as it is.

There's little point in rejecting sexism and machismo ways of relating to people as masculinist if we then replicate perhaps more subtle (perhaps not) aspects of sexism and machismo ourselves. And this, we suggest, is in effect what most of us do. We attack (note the aggressive phraseology, and try to find a non-aggressive alternative) sexism but use sexism's weapons: objectivity not subjectivity, rationality not emotionality, experiments not experience.

. . . AND BREAKING OUT

Alternatives undoubtedly do exist, or can be brought into existence; the circle can be broken. The circle *must* be broken because, if it lies anywhere, 'women's liberation' lies outside of our encapsulement by sexist language, sexist ways of thinking, sexist styles of writing, sexist forms of argument, sexist ideas about criticism. All these construct women's oppressions only. To use these to find liberation is a bit like trying to construct a bicycle out of water. Water doesn't make bicycles, and you can't use sexism to construct living feminism.

But 'breaking out of the circle' isn't to be done by merely wanting to, otherwise few problems would withstand solution. To break out of our ways of thinking, writing and speaking is, in effect, to break out of how we presently live in all of its infinite aspects. No easy matter then. We see it as synonymous with the achievement of liberation, not a stage on the road. And we see it so because it is something which has to be grown into, constructed piecemeal, just as sexism has to be grown out of, dismantled piecemeal within our everyday experiences. To express this slightly differently, we might say that the infinity of experience is bounded and transversed by sexism. The world we inhabit is marked out by its sexism – in an almost literal sense social reality is constructed by and through sexism. If all aspects of sexism could be immediately destroyed, this would also destroy the social world and us with it.

This is a bit flowery perhaps. But one hopefully crystal-clear aspect of it is our insistence on the importance of language and its uses, of forms of discussion, and uses of other people's ideas. Verbal and written language isn't everything, but it is enormously important. And particularly so, of course, for those of us concerned with the conduct of research and its presentation to others. More than anything else the researcher and the teacher are people who wheel and deal in words.

This last chapter, indeed all of what we've written and a lot that we haven't, owes much to Mary Daly's Gyn/Ecology (1978). We both read it just before beginning to write this book; its style and its approach have influenced us greatly. Most of this influence, we feel, is as yet undetectable – food for thought but only as yet partially for action. However, what has appealed to us so immensely about Gyn/Ecology has been its attempt – its generally successful attempt we believe – to combine scholarship (and not in the sense of standing back from) with a heady mixture of word-weaving and word-unravelling, and an intense appreciation of how language constructs thought and action and so all aspects of experience.

Confronting Mary Daly's revelling-in and revolting-from language, and her use of gynomorphic and Gyn/ecological Hagography, is to flinch and to recoil in embarrassment. Why can't this woman write sensibly, in ordinarily constructed sentences? was how one of us initially reacted to it. Why can't she stop behaving like this, can't she see that she's giving feminism a bad name? Of course she can – for 'bad' read 'hag' read harpy, fury, evil, frightening, ugly old woman. And, as she says:

> this, considering the source, may be considered a compliment. For the beauty of strong, creative women is 'ugly' by misogynistic standards of 'beauty'. The look of female-identified women is 'evil' to those who fear us. As for 'old', ageism is a feature of phallic society (Daly, 1978, p. 15).

It is useful, we have found it useful for us, to look our embarrassment in the face and try and see it – and name it – for what it is. And this is what we now try and do.

Earlier we wrote about women as 'the other' and the idea that women's oppressions lie within the everyday, as well as within women's-differences-from-men-within-men's-constructions-of-us. Women's existence, we suggested, gives the lie to 'the truth' of sexist and positivist views of social reality. Women's lives, women's bodies, women's experiences, demonstrate that the social (and physical) world is complicated. 'Reality' is shown to be multi-dimensional and multi-faceted. But 'reality' is constructed as one reality, simple and unseamed. And thus the necessity to suppress, distort, use, oppress, women's differences. Women's lives demonstrate that 'the circle' is a collection of gaps and broken links, not iron-clad and inviolate at all.

Part and parcel of the positivist view of one true material reality, one true social reality, are positivist ideas about argument, logic, evidence and criticism. But these are not only 'scientific' ideas, they are also 'commonsense' ones as well. Positivist world views are those we all of us ordinarily use to construct and interpret social reality. To use a piece of ethnomethodological jargon here, 'competent members' speak, write, argue, in particular and accepted ways. It is only 'incompetent members' who infringe such rules of conduct – and 'incompetence' can be assigned to people on various grounds. These include stupidity, wilfulness, criminality, mental illness, physical incapacity, and a host of other 'deviancies'. And among them is not only being a woman who behaves in 'unwomanly' or 'unfeminine' ways, but also being a woman who dares to be different, who loudly and stridently proclaims her difference. The effect of Mary Daly's combination of difference, daring, anger and (from a positivist point of view) incoherence is of thumbing her nose to 'the world' as we ordinarily construct it. Many people's response is anger and a summary rejection of what-she-writes-and-how-she-writes-it. Many other people's response is embarrassment, in the same way that we would be embarrassed with someone who behaved 'inappropriately' in a rule-governed situation – farting loudly and unrepentantly at a posh tea-party perhaps.

Again we may seem to be a fair way from the major topic of this chapter. But these two styles of approach, 'sitting inside the circle' and 'breaking out' as we have called them, illustrate clearly for us the limitations of sitting inside the circle of the world as constructed by sexism while also thumbing our noses at it. They also clearly demonstrate the complications and the trials of trying to break through and out of the circle. If we stop within it then we may never see the circle, never see it for the snare and cage that it is, nor for the charade that it is too. If we try to break out of it, and especially if we succeed, we risk the almost certain alienation and rejection of those women who do not.

The choice is ours, individually and together. How we make these choices, and why, is of crucial importance for us all. Feminism is not a finished structure but a living process; and how and why we choose what way forward will influence not only the future but will also lead us to reinterpret and so rewrite the past. As this will inevitably happen, as it is happening now, we must – now – go back to the basics of feminist theory to see what 'feminism' means for each of us. We have tried to do this, imperfectly and only partially, for *us* in the early part of this book. And we have tried to see in what kinds of directions our understanding of feminism takes us when we use it to examine 'feminist consciousness' and 'feminist research'.

Something of the result (but not all of it, because books can't encompass lives) appears in the rest of it. We have tried to say that as we are women and people so will we be researchers; that research and life are not separate and divisible but one and the same and must be shown to be so. And we have also tried to show how and why, from some of our experiences, 'the personal' is involved in the construction and assessment of theory and so consciousness. 'Consciousness' is, in a sense, all we have. It is the entirety of what we know and do and how we know and do it. And so it must be, visibly rather than invisibly, not only the focus of feminist research, but also the medium through which *all* research is conducted.

Chapter 8

Breaking out again

Afterword

INTRODUCTION

The contours of feminist social science in 1990s Britain are very different from those of the 1970s and 1980s (Spender, 1981; Kramarae and Spender, 1992). There are large active groups of feminists working at all levels in disciplines ranging from sociology, accounting and economics, to politics, anthropology and development, to law, to economic and social history. Mainstream social science journals, such as *Sociology*, are considerably more sympathetic to feminist material than such journals were in the late 1970s and early 1980s, while a range of specialist academic feminist journals, such as *Gender, Gender & History, Women's History Review, Gender and Education*, and *Feminism & Psychology*, now stand alongside *Women's Studies International Forum* and *Feminist Review*. The academic job market is tighter and considerably more depressed (and depressing); and, although jobs still go mainly to the boys, these days many more people, departments and institutions are embarrassed about it. There is a wider recognition of the limitations, as well as the strengths, of feminist systems of thought as of others. Structuralist approaches – particularly functionalism, marxism and conjunctions between the two – are no longer in the vanguard, and feminist versions of postmodernism, deconstructionism and post-structuralism confidently stalk our intellectual landscape.

These changes can clearly be discerned within feminist sociology (Stanley, 1992d). Within sociology, feminism has had an impact on particular subject-areas such that fundamental changes have occurred in the way the topic of investigation is conceptualized. In particular, 'work', 'the family' and 'crime' (especially violence towards women and children) have taken on new, gendered and sexually politically aware meanings which are directly ascribable to the influence of feminism within the discipline. In other areas of sociology not so fundamentally marked by feminist thinking, there is none the less a widespread recognition that gender now has to be considered for work to be taken seriously. This is of course not to say that either the treatment of gender or the motivation of those involved will necessarily be acceptable in feminist terms. But it does mean that the status quo 'before feminism' no longer exists even if the long-term consequences of such changes are difficult to gauge.[1]

Feminist ideas addressed through the sociology of knowledge and concerned with women's 'double vision' of reality, the complexity of human consciousness, the rejection of Cartesian binary or dichotomous categories as supposed descriptions of social life, criticisms of abstract deductivist 'grand theory' approaches and the reflexivity of research as of all other intellectual processes were once at the forefront of feminist thinking (e.g. Hochschild, 1975). However, the perceived importance of these sociologically influenced ways of thinking has been overtaken by theoretical and epistemological developments elsewhere: what is thought of as 'the action' in feminist theory has largely moved on, although we continue to think that these themes remain fundamental and should be of abiding feminist concern.

Some of the issues and questions dealt with in *Breaking Out* and in our subsequent writing (particularly Stanley and Wise, 1990) continue to be at the centre of contemporary feminist thinking; these include:

1 debates concerning a 'feminist method', and the emergence of ideas concerning a distinct feminist epistemology;
2 the related development of a feminist ontology, and its theorizing of body, mind and emotions;
3 the perceived need for a feminist ethic which guides research conduct and feminist social interaction more generally;
4 ideas concerning the fracturing of the category 'Women', and thus deconstructionist influences on feminist theory;
5 related debates concerning essentialist versus constructionist positions regarding the binaries 'Women'/'Men' and the categories 'the homosexual' and 'the lesbian';
6 awareness of the power of 'representations', including in

relation to history, that is, representations of the past and their relationship to feminist theorizing of women's oppression;

7 promotion of the concept of 'difference' around race/ethnicity, sexuality and other sites of experiential difference between women, and the deconstructionist notion of 'différance' as a signifier of discordancies and controversies;

8 discussions concerning the 'epistemological privilege of the oppressed' and, relatedly, whether distinct black and lesbian feminist epistemologies exist.

All of these debates raise epistemological questions, not just the ones which come bearing this title; and most of them also raise questions and issues concerning substantive research processes. In what follows we develop our ideas regarding these aspects of contemporary feminist thought in relation to the broad concerns discussed in *Breaking Out* and summarized in the Introduction to this second edition, and particularly in relation to our feminist 'fractured foundationalist' epistemology.

'FEMINIST METHOD' AND FEMINIST EPISTEMOLOGY

Is there a distinct feminist method, in the sense of a technique of data collection and analysis that is specific and unique to feminist social science? Very few feminists (primarily Reinharz, 1979; Reinharz, 1983) have argued so; and certainly neither of us, either now or in *Breaking Out*, have argued in favour of there being a 'feminist method'. This has rather been a charge levelled by critics, who mistakenly interpreted our discussion of 'methodology' in this way rather than as an intervention at the level of epistemology concerned with remaking what is seen as 'knowledge' in feminist terms. In contradistinction, our work throughout has been concerned with epistemological questions and issues.

An 'epistemology' is a framework or theory for specifying the constitution and generation of knowledge about the social world; that is, it concerns how to understand the nature of 'reality'. A given epistemological framework specifies not only what 'knowledge' is and how to recognize it, but who are 'knowers' and by what means someone becomes one, and also the means by which competing knowledge-claims are adjudicated and some rejected in favour of another/others. The question of epistemology, then, is crucial, precisely *fundamental*, for feminism, for it is around the constitution of a feminist epistemology that feminism can most directly and far-reachingly challenge non-feminist frameworks and ways of working.

There are a number of key areas of the research process in which we think precepts drawn from feminist epistemology need to be integrated: in the researcher/researched relationship; in emotion as an aspect of the research process which, like any other aspect, can be analytically interrogated; in critically unpacking conceptualizations of 'objectivity' and 'subjectivity' as binaries or dichotomies; in the 'intellectual autobiography' of researchers, that is, in the processes by which 'understanding' and 'conclusions' are reached; in the existence and management of the different 'realities' or versions held by researchers and researched; and in issues surrounding authority and power in research, but also and perhaps more crucially in written representations of research. Existing feminist epistemologies do this in varied ways.

The two dominant coexistent feminist epistemologies are identified by Sandra Harding (1987) as 'successor science' in their assumptions and operations. However, we see both the earlier 'feminist empiricism' and the later 'feminist standpoint' approaches as, in our terms, grounded in the Cartesian assumption that a single and unseamed social as well as physical reality exists 'out there', and that particular kinds of persons (trained, experts, scientists) have a greater degree of access to knowledge of this. Feminist empiricism at basis aligns itself with other forms of empiricism – the feminist (social) scientist joins her male scientific peers; while feminist standpoint approaches both share and depart from traditional foundationalism by insisting that, while the feminist (social) scientist has a privileged access to *real* social reality, this is because the oppressed have epistemological privilege and can see people and events as they really are. However, a new feminist epistemology of feminist postmodernism, apparently rejecting foundationalism in all its forms, is being constituted, suggests Harding; and postmodernist feminists themselves say the same thing about the epistemological implications of their work. This feminist postmodernist epistemology (e.g. Weedon, 1987; Lather, 1991) rejects all 'grand narratives', including feminist grand theory explanations of women's condition and oppression. It also dismisses any notion of a representational, effectively one-to-one, relationship between reality and textually based (written, verbal, visual) accounts of it. Postmodernism claims to be the originator of these epistemological claims. However, we recognise most of them in the 1960s critiques of positivism in the social sciences, in the 1930s work of philosophers such as Wittgenstein and Collingwood, and indeed earlier still in strands of late nineteenth-century sociology influenced by German philosophy. We also recognize them in *Breaking Out* as well as in the work of other feminists influenced by interactionist ideas. We reject the colonizing activities of postmodernist intellectual imperialism, including by feminists, and lay claim to these ideas as instead the *common property* of a number of divergent intellectual traditions.

Marking out the attributes of different although related feminist epistemologies, such as feminist empiricism, feminist standpoint and feminist postmodernism, is useful as long as it is recognized that this produces a *model*, and is thus necessarily a simplified (not a literal–representational) account of only some few of the epistemological possibilities that exist. Typically feminists who are allocated to one of these positions actually encompass in their work elements of all three – and also of feminist epistemologies that are silenced in Sandra Harding's (1987), Alison Jaggar's (1983) and other socialist feminist accounts of epistemology, such as radical feminism and black and lesbian feminism. Sandra Harding's (1991) *Whose Science? Whose Knowledge?* was published in Britain as this book went to press, so we are unable to discuss in any depth her account of the contribution of black feminism to feminist epistemology and of the existence of a lesbian standpoint. However, we are concerned that each position is subordinated to the pre-existing framework and assumptions of the 'standpoint' approach as outlined in Harding's earlier writings. Our conviction is that both positions are distinct epistemologies, and they raise fundamental questions about the constitution and utility of the 'standpoint' categorization. A further reservation is that most of the elements Harding describes as definitional of a 'lesbian standpoint' (she has a separate chapter on this, although her account of black thinking is integrated in other chapters) are actually not epistemological in character. Our discussion of 'the epistemologies of the oppressed' later in this afterword adopts a very different approach, concentrating on the epistemological results of the ontological specifications of being, as well as knowing, within black feminism and lesbian feminism.

We find it useful to adopt five broad principles in discussing feminist epistemology. First, there is a spectrum of feminist epist-emological positions looked at abstractly, although in practice these shade into each other in people's actual work. Second, these different positions argue for sometimes conflicting ideas about the bases of knowledge, who generates it and under what conditions. Third, people often manage to combine elements of a number of these positions in their work, and this suggests not only the human ability to work within contradictions, but also that often we fail to think through the bases of what we do and what we claim for it – or, alternatively, that we do think it through and still work with 'contradictory' elements because this is what social reality is like. Fourth, there is no *a priori* right or correct feminist epistemology: each can be seen as plausible and sensible, given the particular political projects and purposes of those who hold it. Fifth, recognizing this does not mean that any of us has to agree with other people's positions, but it does suggest the need for mutual respect between different feminisms and the concomi-tant need for diversity rather than the hegemony of one form of feminism over all others.

The feminist critique of knowledges (Caine *et al.*, 1988) has moved away from simple accusations of 'bias' and the accompany-ing successor science supposition that feminist approaches are unbiased and that non-feminist knowledge is one, hegemonic and oppositional. Cartesian approaches assume the unproblematic generalizability of knowledge from its context of production (con-ventionally called a 'context of discovery')[2] to a variety of contexts of use. These also and relatedly see knowledge as existing inde-pendently (because 'out there' in social reality and merely 'dis-covered' by a knowledge-producer) of the person/s who produced it. That is, their 'science' claims are founded not only on notions of the generalizability and transferability of knowledge, but also its non-contamination by influences drawn from either the context of its 'discovery'/production or the social location and character-istics of those who produce it.

Cartesian approaches, including feminist ones, ignore or deny their grounding in ontology: that is, in the interests, competences, experiences and understandings of knowledge-producers. Our feminist critique of knowledges argues instead for a materialistic, but not a marxist, theory of knowledge, one irrevocably rooted in women's concrete and diverse practical and everyday experi-ences of oppressions; and it insists that these analytic knowledges are reflexive, indexical and local: they are epistemologically tied to their context of production and are ontologically grounded. This is what we have earlier referred to as our feminist fractured foundationalist epistemology.

More recent expressions of marxist feminist approaches (e.g. Barrett, 1991) are positioned as post-structuralist, an epistemological shift which we welcome; however, these still tend to be tied to scientistic claims for the research products of this position (e.g. Currie, 1988). Moreover, such shifts in the direction of anti-foundationalism still frequently resist any notion of an ontological basis for knowledge (e.g. Fuss, 1989). What this of course demonstrates is the complexity of foundationalism, which is less a unitary 'position' and more an overlapping set of somewhat different viewpoints, some aspects of which are 'classically' foundationalist and other aspects of which reject foundationalist formulations. This needs to be kept in mind in what follows – as indeed does a similar argument applied to anti-foundationalist approaches.

One consequence of acknowledging the social location and production of knowledge is that knowledge-claims are thereby positioned as part of a *political process* in which some knowledge-claims are seen and certified as superordinate in relation to others. Power is involved here, and of a very effective kind because apparently rooted in unseamed and incontrovertible kinds of knowledge about the world. 'Knowledge is power' has quite rightly been the watch-word of radical social movements since the eighteenth century, for knowledge-production is a crucial part of any apparatus of power, including within feminism.

The contrast for us is between feminist variants of Cartesian ideas and a feminist epistemology rooted instead in a feminist ontology; that is, a feminism rooted in the acknowledgement that all social knowledge is generated as a part and a product of human social experience. We think that there is nothing separate from social life and experience, nor which exists outside it, and reject ideologically derived theories of knowledge (including post/marxist ones) which seek to counter this materialist viewpoint. Thus, for us, the relationship between feminist epistemology and feminist ontology is one which positions ontology as the foundation: being or ontology is the seat of experience and thus of theory and knowledge. Nothing else is possible: there is no way of moving 'outside' experientially derived understandings/theories, whether derived from so-called first-, second- or third-hand knowledges of the social world; and nothing exists other than social life, our places within it and our understandings of all this.

Relatedly, an ontologically based theory of feminist intellectual knowledge, and a feminist ontologically based theory of emotionality, are crucially implicated in the development of a distinct feminist epistemology. 'The body' and its physical but also its intellectual, mindful experiences is a cultural text: its meaning and experience are irrevocably inscribed within a cultural (and thus political) frame, although its materiality exists in complex relation with this. Thus our feminist ontology does not seek to reify 'experience' as lying beyond culture, as some critics of *Breaking Out* suggested, but rather seeks analytically to come to grips with the cultural specificity of experience, and thus with the medium through which all experience is channelled – the body/mind/emotions.[3]

Within traditional epistemologies, emotions are perceived as disruptive and subversive of knowledge as a wild zone unamenable to reason and its scientific apparatus of investigation and control (Bordo, 1986). In contrast, our feminist fractured foundationalist epistemology rejects such Cartesian binary ways of polarizing reason and emotion (as does Jaggar, 1989). Instead it positions ontology, including emotionality, as the product of culture and thus as amenable to 'rational' analysis as much as any other culturally inscribed behavioural form. More than this, our feminist fractured foundationalism refuses to disparage emotion as a second-class (or worse) source of knowledge by treating it as an obfuscating layer between social reality and reasoned understanding. Instead it banishes the myth of the dispassionate and unemotional 'scientific observer', by locating an experiencing feeling subject at the centre of all intellectual endeavour, as we did in *Breaking Out*. In other words, it insists that emotion is vital to systematic knowledge about the social world (that is, to what we later called the 'intellectual autobiography' of researchers and analysts), and that any epistemology which fails to recognize this is deeply flawed.

Useful reading

Cain (1990); Harding (1986; 1987, pp. 1–14, 181–90; 1991); Heldke (1988); Jaggar (1983; 1989); Reinharz (1979; 1983); Ruth (1987); Sherwin (1989); Stanley and Wise (1983; 1990); Winnant (1987); Zita (1988).

A FEMINIST ONTOLOGY: THEORIZING BODY, MIND AND EMOTION

An 'ontology' is a theory of 'reality' or being; and within Cartesian systems of thought 'being' is seen to encompass the body and the mind, with body associated with women and mind with men. And there is a further dichotomizing here, of the rational aspects of mind seen as male and the irrational emotional aspects associated with women.

Our feminist ontology is concerned with theorizing being, and with rejecting Cartesian binary ways of understanding the relationship between the body, the mind and emotions.[4] The 'masculinist' ontology associated with Cartesian dualisms and foundationalism (Bordo, 1986; Bordo, 1989) sees all of reality as characterized by two opposing principles, those of masculinity and femininity (or rather maleness and femaleness) and their working out through science and nature, reason and emotion, objectivity and subjectivity and so on; the very grounds of reality are presupposed in binary and gendered terms. And these opposing principles are seen as both symbiotically related and necessary to each other *and* as existing in relations of super- and subordination, with the feminine supportive of the masculine. Reality is 'naturally' thus both stratified and heterosexual in its ordering within Cartesian thought systems.

Our feminist fractured foundationalism challenges the binary fundamentals of Cartesian ontology, for it recognizes differentiation but sees this as neither oppositional nor dualistic, and is also appreciative of, rather than antagonistic to, difference. Such a feminist ontology is not concerned merely to affirm and revalue those characteristics which masculinist Cartesian ontology associates with the feminine; its task is the more challenging and radical one marked out in *Breaking Out* – that of disputing the binary basis of Cartesian systems of thought altogether.

People experience their 'selves' neither as complete social constructions nor as essential and 'uncultured' sites of unchanging difference. Rather, 'the self' is the production of interaction and social construction and is irrevocably social and cultural in its basis. However, although dynamic in its constitution, ordinarily the 'self' is experienced as in stasis – 'this is me' – at any one point in time: nevertheless, looking back people can construe 'other' and rather different selves – 'I was that' – that once were them. 'The self' is positioned here in terms of 'mind', a composite of thoughts, understandings and emotions that exists in complex relationship to 'the body'. The supposed 'mind/body dualism' is one people in Western societies are familiar with, and it conditions although it does not predetermine how we think of 'our selves'. However, this dualism is one people multiply traverse: at one time we may define ourselves in terms of physicality, of looks, of the body and its face; at other times we may distance ourselves from our bodies, and see our selves more in terms of intellectuality or emotions or spirit. In other words, such dualisms operate at a *categorical* level: as such they considerably oversimplify the theorizing that people actually engage in, in going about the business of understanding social reality and their various places within it.

Our feminist ontology, then, rejects binary and oppositional notions of 'the self' and its relationship to 'the body' and 'mind' and 'emotions'. It also rejects a notion of 'self and Other' that the self supposedly defines itself *against* and *in opposition to*. Here 'the Other' is seen as a threat to the integrity of self, for, without an Other, self would not, *could not* in this ontology, exist. The feminist approach we adopt to the construction of self, in contrast, sees 'self' as relationally and interactionally composed, its construction being historically, culturally and contextually specific and also subtly changing in different interactional circumstances. Thus an alternative feminist way of understanding the dualisms of masculinist ontology – of self and other, individual and collectivity – is to treat these not as oppositions but rather as *co-operative endeavours* for constructing selves – *both* selves – through collective relational systems of action and interaction. As we argued in *Breaking Out*, the interactional and phenomenological sociologies offer a variety of conceptual means of exploring the social construction of self, and particularly of mind, and the work of George Herbert Mead and Alfred Schutz interestingly conceptualizes these processes in non-reductionist terms.

We do not think that our feminist ontology needs to assume a different pattern of 'psychological' development for women and men. Proponents of feminist developmental theories such as Nancy Chodorow (1978) and Carol Gilligan (1982) do assume this. However, unlike many critics, we read them as arguing that, although such differences may result in different moral and ontological 'voices', these are the product of *culture* and *social* construction, not biological or other 'essential' differences between the sexes. As might be expected from *Breaking Out*, our reservations about these developmental approaches focus instead on their reductionism, their elision of the social and political as the site for the construction of difference, and their slip into psychology as a 'sufficient explanation' of social life – all aspects we cannot accept.

Earlier we noted that our feminist fractured foundationalist epistemology positions the emotions as a legitimate source of knowledge, as minded and rational responses to given situations, and how different this is from Cartesian ideas, which position emotions as the antithesis of reason and thus as incapable of producing 'real' or 'true' knowledge. Emotions, the product of the mind, can be separated, at least at the level of theoretical discussion, from feelings, rooted in the responses of the body: cold and pain are feelings, love and envy are emotions. But of course, as Alison Jaggar (1989) has argued, in practice separating them is by no means so simple. The cultural specificity of feelings immediately alerts us to the fact that 'the body' and its 'feelings' are constructions located within particular historical and cultural circumstances and can differ considerably over time and between different cultural groups, as much interesting comparative work on illness symptoms demonstrates. And also people talk about – and experience – feelings and emotions in very similar ways: for instance, 'pain' exists as an emotion as well as a feeling, for physical pain is typically experienced as also emotionally distressing. Emotions and feelings, then, cannot be readily assigned across a supposed mind/body divide, yet another indicator of fundamental flaws in Cartesian ontology when looked at from a feminist viewpoint.

'The body' can be conceptualized in abstract, universal and essentialist terms, as a biologically constituted and determined organism which has real, essentially derived, differences in terms of sex – the position of classical Cartesian ontology. Alternatively, within our feminist ontology 'the body' is rather seen in terms of *embodiment*, a cultural process by which the physical body becomes a site of culturally ascribed and disputed meanings, experiences, feelings. Here 'the body' is positioned within culturally specific – and sometimes competing – discourses of meaning, authority and control. For us, 'the body' is rather to be conceptualized as a *becoming*, its meaning is never fixed to a particular type of person, but rather these different meanings have to be achieved and re-achieved in order to be seen as constituting a particular type of person. Certainly the body is continually invoked in terms of closure, fixture; but this is also continually undercut and fractured by knowledge of the processes of physical change, ageing, illness and death. 'The body' is thus both signified – the product of language and a set of institutions that define, classify, assign, order and control; and also one of the key signifiers in Western culture – 'the body' is actually different *bodies* around which different readings, significations and judgements can be made.

'The body' is the product of an elaborate system of production, through toilet manners, table manners, sexual manners; appropriate dress, posture, responses, demeanour, bodily indicators of health and well-being or of illness and dis-ease, and the giving and losing of face. Bodies are regulated, classified and normalized; and there is nothing to say about 'the body' outside of this process – beyond the social there is nothing. One product of this process is the marking out of unruly bodies and unruly minds, those which are 'disordered' by virtue of their resistance to the processes of regulation and normalization, which are classified and therefore normalized as exemplifying 'diseases' or 'perversions' or 'disorders'.

It has become *de rigueur* for feminists making claims to theoretical sophistication to eschew any invocation of 'the body' as anything other than discursively, textually and thus linguistically created, to insist that the body has no 'real' physical or material importance outside this. We do not accept this view, in spite of our constructionist position. Certainly our bodies seemingly have 'their' own rhythms and responses over which 'we' often feel we have little or no control: the experience of acute or terminal illness being a case in point. Nevertheless, we can understand such experiences and dislocations only through socially constructed frameworks of understanding. It is not that the experience is mediated by such frameworks: it is rather *constituted by means of* them. Thus, rather than travelling the 'strict' constructionist route, we feel the necessity of 'taking the body seriously' at a conceptual level. Consequently we ask the question whether it is possible within the kind of feminist ontology and epistemology we favour to speak, think and write of the body as not merely a linguistic creation but as also having a physical, material and consequential reality. And, a closely related question, can 'the body' and its biology be invoked and analysed in ways which are not essentialist?

For some feminists, 'l'écriture feminine', the 'parler femme' of French feminists such as Helene Cixous (1981a; 1981b), Julia Kristeva (1981; 1982) and especially Luce Irigaray (1980; 1981; 1985), provides precisely such a means. Irigaray's writing valorizes women's bodies, but in ways which deconstruct the phallic organization and ordering of sexuality and the bodies which perform it. For Irigaray, phallocentrism constitutes not only the social order, but also a male economy of desire in which women are the objects of, and currency of exchange between, men – or rather this currency is constituted by possession of women's bodies and sexualities. However, unlike for men, she argues that women's sexuality 'is not one', is rather a plurality based on the primacy of labial touch and pleasure. Irigaray thus positions women as sexual subjects, not as sexual objects of male desire. She uses the idea that women are 'other' to men to articulate an oppositional stance to phallocentrism, indeed to challenge it at the level of the symbolic order through the mis/use of language, by rewriting the meaning of language and what it inscribes about women's sexuality. Thus, through a 'linguistic turn' Irigaray deconstructs the binary oppositions of essentialism and constructionism, but from the side of and by means of essentialism itself. By speaking 'labial politics' Irigaray not only speaks the unspeakable, women's sexual autonomy, but also blurs the social and constructed and the biological and essential. Favourably inclined critics see this as a political strategy which speaks to a particular historical, cultural and sexual political moment, and which uses a textual politics of essence to place 'parler femme' into discourse and thus into culture and history. The less favourably inclined – among whom we are placed – accept the positive evaluation but also see this work as a refusal to recognize that life, politics and oppression are constituted by more than language alone. For us, the 'linguistic turn' of post-structuralism is not a sufficient basis for a feminist praxis.

Although Irigaray rejects much of the heritage of Lacan, she retains Lacanian ideas concerning the development of self in relation to an Other seen in oppositional terms, while our feminist ontology instead sees self in relational, collective and collaborative terms. Also, although on one level Irigaray denies the synonymity of the phallus and its place in the symbolic order with the actual common or garden penis that men have, none the less at every point her discussion collapses the two; her denial brackets thinking through the implications of retaining Lacanian phallacious ideas *at all*. And in addition, construing 'parler femme' as defined by the subject-position of the speaker, and thus as available to men as well as to women – that is, as constituted primarily through linguistic and indeed grammatical form – undercuts the more radical feature of Irigaray's work, which is to wrest language back from men, not to hand them the means to speak 'as women' as well as 'as men'.

This latter point links Irigaray's and our own conviction that women's bodies and the (constructions of) differences of these from men's are central to the category 'Women' and its sexually politically subordinate status. We think it crucially important for feminist social theory to continue to recognize two things. The first is that in Western Cartesian ontology only men are seen to have an essence: women are deemed flawed, partial, lacking, different. Thus to claim an essence for the category 'Women' continues to be a highly successful political strategy, not least because it provides women, real living and breathing women as well as the category, with an entry into subjecthood at the level of ideas, language, politics *and* at the level of the body and its rights as well as responsibilities. The second is that both women and men have a material physical existence, are *embodied*, and these embodiments *do* have differences between them. That is, there are some different experiences that cannot be communicated across gender divisions, which remain experientially the preserve of the category members men and women. This is not to claim that how we in Western culture understand such 'sexual' difference is immutable or somehow innately 'there' within physicality. It is however to recognize, indeed to insist, that positioning material physicality as a matter of language and discourse only, as Irigaray (and other feminist post-structuralists) seemingly does, is to condemn feminist social theory to the analysis of abstract categories alone. This may be seductive; however, it is also redundant as a means of *changing* as well as understanding social life. To effect change we need a feminist social theory capable of analysing everyday life, experiences, understanding and theorizing. We cannot just deconstruct binary categories as linguistically constituted; we rather need to change them at the level of *experience*, of *practice*; and here too the body has an indubitable experiential importance that cannot be reduced to the linguistic alone.

Useful reading

Bordo (1986; 1989); Butler (1988; 1989); Gatens (1988); Grosz (1986); Hochschild (1975); *Hypatia* (1991); Jaggar (1989); Lugones (1987); Martin (1987); Purdy (1986); Tuana (1983; 1986); Whitbeck (1989).

A FEMINIST ETHIC

An 'ethic' is a framework of thought concerned with morality and with moral choices between things and actions seen as good or bad. Our feminist fractured foundationalist epistemology specifies morally adequate means of knowing and understanding women's experiences, particularly through insisting that feminist theory should at some level be consonant with experience. This is an ethical, and thus we think also a political, choice; and it emphasizes that there are – or rather there should be – symbiotic links between feminist epistemology and a feminist ethic. That is, a feminist theory of knowledge must be morally adequate in feminist terms. Epistemology is not simply or merely a system of ideas, a theory; it is also constituted through the activities and codes of an *epistemic community*. The feminist research community takes organizational form, of however loose and fluid a kind, and has developed standards and procedures which mark out what constitutes a morally responsible epistemology that gives what is due to all parties in research contexts.

These epistemological precepts include: recognition of the reflexivity of the feminist researcher *in* her research as an active and busily constructing agent; insistence that the 'objects' of research are also subjects in their own right as much as researchers are subjects of theirs (and objects of other people's); acceptance that the researcher is on the same critical plane as those she researches and not somehow intellectually superior; and, most fundamental of all, no opinion, belief or other construction of events and persons, no matter from whom this derives, should be taken as a representation of 'reality' but rather treated as a motivated construction or version to be subject to critical feminist analytical inquiry. Of course these are not *exhaustive* precepts of a feminist epistemic ethic, but they are constitutive, and they point to the importance of treating feminist 'researching' and 'theorizing' as material labour processes which are as capable of investigation and analysis as any other labour process (Stanley, 1990b).

One fundamental difference between styles of feminist research is between those who think that the job of feminist research is to re-describe *post hoc* a slice of social reality (that is, a representational view) and those who think that there should be something more than re-describing research in writing (that is, an interpretational view). The interpretational view proceeds from the assumption that researchers deal with accounts or versions located in one epistemological frame, and use these to provide another account or version from the viewpoint of another epistemological position (e.g. Strathern, 1987). That is, it rejects representational views of research in favour of ironizing lay representations by placing them in subordinate position to scientific ones. Our feminist fractured foundationalist epistemology eschews representationality; but at the same time it also rejects an ironizing approach to everyday accounts, and instead seeks to provide theoretical accounts which are continuous with experience. As *Breaking Out* argues, we think these should be continuous with the experience of the conclusions, interpretations and analyses of *the researcher* as the agent involved in constructing them. We say this not as an affirmation of an actually outmoded élitism that seeks to ignore the world-views of 'the researched', as a reading of *Breaking Out* should confirm. It is rather to recognize and highlight the role of researchers in *constructing*, not reconstructing or reclaiming or reflecting, research situations and data. That is, if the academic feminist epistemological community accepts anti-representational arguments (and we feel strongly that it should), then we also and concomitantly need to adopt a different approach to how we present our research products and writings. Thus what drives our thinking here is neither individualism nor solipsism, but rather an insistence that feminist knowledge should be accountable knowledge, knowledge which acknowledges and reveals the labour processes of its own production (Stanley, 1990b), and which turns the scrutiny of readers towards writers and the texts they construct.

Of course, in the production of unalienated knowledge (Rose, 1983) one strand of what is ethically important for feminist researchers is the quality of research relationships and the preservation of trust within them. However, this is not all there is to the ethics of feminist research. Moreover, ethical issues and dilemmas are solved neither by 'being nice' nor by 'taking research back', because alongside ethical issues and dilemmas concerning the use and abuse of 'subjects' are epistemological issues; these concern *whose* knowledge, seen in *what* terms, around *whose* definitions and standards, and judged by *whose* as well as *what* criteria, should count as 'knowledge' itself.

Our feminist ethic is thus concerned with far more than behaviours and activities, for, as well as taking on board the issue of representationality, it also recognizes the rational and intentional basis of emotional and other rational responses to social situations and those involved in them. That is, recognizing research products as representations does not require anyone to deny that a real social world of action and interaction and of emotional and other responses to this actuality does exist. Moreover, within representations of research, emotion is as available to analytic scrutiny as any other mindful research behaviour, and is equally as capable of yielding 'knowledge' as conventionally 'rational' intellectual behaviour. This view of emotion construes it as socially constructed ways of responding in/appropriately in given contexts and times; and a part of this construction is the 'in/appropriate' expression of emotions, but also and contradictorily their assumed general unavailability to mindful control.

Emotion, then, is a social and cultural construction regulated in and through social engagement; and is seen as 'appropriately' conditioned by age, class, race/ethnicity, gender and indeed sexuality. That is, in Western society younger people are deemed to have a wider and more volatile range of emotional licence, women more than men, gay men more than heterosexual, black people more than white, working-class people more than middle and upper class. None the less, there is no reason to suppose that emotional range has any basis other than social construction, given the enormous cultural differences in the specification and distribution of emotionality. However, the notion of emotional control has definite sexual political ramifications: 'real men' can exert such control, women, children, black people and gay men cannot. Emotionality, then, is a socially constructed product of the supposedly different ontologies of different types of person; and different ethical positions are ascribed to these types of person as a consequence, because the boundaries between the behaviours and characteristics that people are seen as responsible for, and those seen as outside their control, are specified differently.

Many statements of ethics are made at the level of principles which should – *ought* – to govern conduct. In effect this is ethics as a deductivist approach to social behaviour, specifying a system of, for example, research morality. We do not find such an approach helpful, for its separates off a particular and distinct kind of behaviour – 'research' – and specifies a set of ethical principles which should govern it and which are different from those that govern other kinds of social relationships. Moreover, these are literally principles – trans-situational ethics seen as capable of regulating all research contexts – while we find preferable an approach which is concerned with a *contextual* approach to ethical ideals and practices. That is, while we need ethical principles, these should be constituted as 'recipes' (Heldke, 1988) which can and should be adapted to the relational parameters of different situations.

Our feminist ethic is thus at basis a feminist ontology which is not confined to any narrow definition of 'being', but rather adopts a panthesistic (not just womanistic) formulation of the ethical. It is thus an inclusive ethic which ties together the nature of feminism, the practical conduct of human social relationships, and the relationship between humankind and the animal and 'natural' world. Moreover, this feminist ethic is also concerned with the moral adequacy of a feminist epistemology. The framework and basis of 'knowledge', theoretical accounts which investigate or generate such knowledge, and practical uses to which such knowledge and theory are put, should each be morally adequate in our feminist terms. Indeed, we think that distinguishing between moral adequacy and feminist epistemology is a contradiction in terms, for the one is synonymous with the other.

Useful reading

Bell (1989); Code (1989); Cohen (1986); Curtin (1991); Govier (1992); Hoagland (1988a; 1988b); Holmes (1989); Nye (1986); Rose (1983); Sherwin (1989); Walker (1989).

'WOMEN' AND DECONSTRUCTIONISM

A major feminist deconstructionist argument has been that the fractured and divergent experiences of actual women have been subsumed within the category 'Women'. 'Women' is treated as an absolute, a binary category in a hierarchical relationship to 'Men', with these two defined against each other in inappropriately dichotomous terms. We think that analysing experience – or rather subsuming its complexities – in binary terms constitutes a form of deductivism, for here theory – treated as a description – acts in an imperialistic relationship to life, which is then 'read off' from the binary categories. Thus the binary categories come to constitute a grand narrative of social life, prescribing and proscribing the behaviours of men and women, and also providing a measure of the correctness and thus the adequacy of analytic as well as everyday accounts of gender and sexual politics.

Feminist causal theories of women's oppression of the early and middle 1970s are in these terms plausible causal analyses of the relationship of super-and subordination existing between the two poles of the binary categories 'Women'/'Men'. What is perhaps most interesting here is the extent to which so many women (and indeed men), at a particular point in their political lives, were and are able to identify with these categorical statements about sexual politics. However, as Schutzian phenomenology suggests, people think through category terms, using typifications of the social world as a means of comparing and contrasting 'similar' experiences, and this is a basic feature of people's sense-making procedures. And in Cartesian frameworks, a hierarchy also exists between the category or typification and the experience that the category is supposedly 'of'. That is, the tendency is to assume, when experience and category are unsynchronized, that it is experience which is somehow faulty. It is because conventionally the category 'Women' and the experience of women are seen as synonymous that in research terms any particular woman can be seen as a repository of information about 'Women', about the category, which, when added to that of others, can be treated as generalizable to all. Foundationalist approaches to research are thus not only premised on representational principles but also, at a fundamental level, on deductivist ones. That is, the category acts as a grand theory as well as a grand narrative, and life's events are treated as a series of hypotheses which need to be checked and indeed measured against the theory.

Deconstructionist arguments about the category 'Women' and the binary gender system propose (e.g. Lather, 1991) that such binaries should be identified, the dependent category reversed or displaced, and then a more fluid conceptual organization should replace the binary one. It works, then, in part by deconstructing the content of the category, in part by ironizing 'essentialist' invocations of it. Our feminist fractured foundationalist epistemology, in contrast, retains its foundation upon the category 'Women' and upon recognition of its binary relationship to the category 'Men'. Without this, a distinctively *feminist* philosophy and praxis would no longer exist, would be dissolved into an apparently ungendered deconstructionist position. Jane Wolff (1990) suggests that it is only by non-epistemological means that we can close the deconstructionist dynamic destructive of feminism. She herself advocates either political considerations or 'self-reflexive provisionality' as her means of doing so, while our own grounds – as we argue later – are clearly and irrevocably ontological. That is, we proceed from theorizing women's experiences in feminist terms. Moreover, there are considerably more than sentimental reasons for the retention of the category; in particular there remains the political and ethical necessity to use 'Women' in its own right and its own terms rather than as derivative of and 'other' to 'Men'. Doing so is necessary for as long as women – as well as 'Women' – are in any sense unequal, exploited or oppressed in relation to men as well as to 'Men'; that is, for as long as 'gender' exists as a meaningful way to categorize aspects of social life and people's behaviours within it. Deconstructionist, like post-structuralist, approaches imply change at the level of language and texts and categories alone; but, as part of a world-wide political movement, academic feminism necessarily retains a praxis firmly concerned with more than a 'linguistic turn'.

Additionally, humanist arguments that women should be treated as fully part of humanity, with the same ontological constitution and the same rights and responsibilities as men, remain very powerful in political terms, for rejecting such arguments is increasingly accepted, on a world-scale and on a micro-scale, as discriminatory and morally unjustifiable. Thus any approach which militates against the possibility of fully utilizing these and related humanist arguments must, realistically, be seen as gendered and masculinist in its consequence. Moreover, at this point in time and for the foreseeable future there is no such thing as 'ungender'; and any argument that feminism should become subsumed within a more general deconstructionist impulse in intellectual life must be seen as not only anti-feminist but also, whether intended or not, as promoting the interests of the category 'Men'. There are, however, other possibilities which focus on 'Women' as a category but do not deny or ignore the analytic and practical importance of the complex relationship between category and experience.

One such possibility for feminism is to analyse the category binaries of both 'Women' *and* 'Men' (and the related poles of binaries such as masculine and feminine, self and other, subject and object, active and passive, and mind and body) as representations which act as *oughts* rather than as *descriptions* of how women and men actually are. That is, this is to focus upon the processes by which such representations are constructed, used or rejected, reconstructed, and to reject any notion that somehow 'behind' these lies a 'real' level of social reality.

Another possibility, the one we favour, is for feminism to become explicitly concerned with the multiple and continual fractures that occur between experience and categories. This is partly because of the need to break the hierarchical relationship of super- and subordination between them, that when the two clash it is experience which is seen as wrong. It is also and perhaps more importantly because the 'ontological jolts' (Riley, 1987; Stanley, 1988) which occur when events constrain by bringing women back into being 'a woman' rather than a person are crucial to the processes by which an explicit feminist analysis comes into being. Being 'a woman', someone who is in some sense part of the category 'Women', is ontologically little like the category 'descriptions' or theoretical accounts. 'A woman' is not a 'socialized' stasis but is rather composed by a series of ruptures or jolts when we stop being 'just me' and are constrained to behave as or to be seen as 'a woman'. It is rarely possible to '*be* a woman', for to be such is to become the category only, to surrender, or to be parted from, self so totally that the slips, confusions, resentments, puzzles and jolts that typically result when category expectations meet everyday behaviour never occur.

Neither bodies nor minds are innately gendered; however, both body and mind experience and play their part in the construction of gender. A theory of mind, of human consciousness, is crucial to our feminist ontologically based epistemology. Earlier feminist accounts – including structuralist and materialist ones – advanced an actually idealist and ideological view of mind and of gender: women's minds filled with partriarchal lies through a process – socialization – akin to brainwashing, with feminist consciousness being a higher stage, one in which reality was seen and understood more truly. This crude specification of a hierarchy of consciousness that we criticized in *Breaking Out*, with feminism unproblematically at its apex as an *a priori* true account of reality, is no longer so evident in feminist theorizing. However, feminism still has no proper theory of mind, whether structuralist, post-structuralist, interactionist, materialist or any other. This is a major gap in its epistemological armory; and deconstructionism is certainly unable to supply the conceptual means to repair its absence, given its displacement of feminism.

Our embryonic feminist theory of mind sees this as ontologically and materially based. It recognizes that 'mind' and 'body' are only analytically, and not experientially, separable – and only then to the impoverishment of the analysis. Equally, it proceeds from the recognition that 'mind' does not exist in some kind of intellectual ether, but is rather to be seen – and only to be seen – through the *material products* of mind, in statements about its constitution and workings, in behaviours and decisions and justifications for these, in retrospect on past behaviours, and so on. Thus our feminist theory of mind, proceeding from such a materialist interactionist basis, also rejects any conceptual analytical separations between mind and emotion, for the rhetorical means through which emotions are invoked, displayed, questioned and justified are precisely those which show the mind in action, at points of comparative stasis: 'I felt and thought *this*, and then *that*'.

This is mind seen as the constructions and invocations of mind: its everyday representation in all manner of situations, persons and events, and not as any kind of essence. Our feminist theory of mind thus eschews any psychologistic or psychoanalytic reduction of mind to 'inner' processes and states, and instead insists upon its social and so analytic availability as well as its socially constructed being. 'Mind' becomes available for analytic scrutiny through the accounts given of its workings as typical features of social interaction in all times, places and circumstances.

The place to proceed from in further constructing a feminist theory of mind, we argue, is constituted by everyday accounts of mind and its relationship to the body and emotions.

Useful reading

Alcoff (1988); Butler (1990); Hekman (1991); Kittay (1988); Lather (1991); de Lauretis (1986); Morris (1988, pp. 1–16); Poovey (1988); Riley (1987); Stanley (1988).

ESSENTIALISM AND CONSTRUCTIONISM

'Essentialism' indicates a belief in the existence of fixed and essential properties which often invokes 'biology' or more loosely 'human nature' as the supposed basis of these. The subject is seen here as located within, indeed defined by, a fixed set of attributes treated as innately physical, intellectual or emotional, and thus deriving from the essential properties of body, mind or emotions. The term 'essentialist', however, is now frequently used within feminism and associated intellectual movements less in this definitional sense and more as a rhetorical signal of deviance, legitimating criticism of or even attack on theoretical pariahs; those dubbed 'conservatives' associated (or seen to be associated) with the taint of essentialism in their ideas or organizational practice. 'Essentialism' here indicates something old-fashioned, outmoded, unsophisticated and irrevocably conservative. Within feminism it is also often used as a covert way of marking out and criticizing varieties of radical feminism, for critics continue to reify radical feminism from the work of a few supposedly 'essentialist' writers (Firestone and Millett, Daly and Dworkin), when we think it actually has no theoretical hegemonic internal structure in the way that, for example, marxist feminism has had.

'Essentialists' are criticized for: their supposed rejection of the social constructionist base of properties or characteristics deemed to be fixed; their claimed ahistorical view that these characteristics have been fixed across time and different cultures; and their supposed positioning of gender in binary terms as strict divisions of attributes which contain no internal fracturing. In relation to essentialisms connected with the binary categories 'Women'/ 'Men', essentialists are also supposed to embrace a particular ontological position in which actual women and men as well as the categories 'Women'/'Men' are seen as ontologically stable, unitary, coherent and fixed. The litany of criticisms also links essentialism with separatism – and thus, covertly, without admitting the direct link, with lesbianism, also tacitly condemned as a political analytical position if not as a behavioural practice.

One major problem with these criticisms is that they treat 'essentialism' *in essentialist terms* as pre-dating its naming and intellectual origins at a particular time. That is, the criticisms imply the people condemned were always essentialist, even before the term was invented. Our view is that 'essentialism' is precisely an *invention*, the construction of a site of 'différance' (a notion we discuss later) and thus of competing forces jockeying for control, and not the *discovery* of something innately 'there'. Imposing the charge of essentialism *post hoc* on work produced before its invention is as inappropriate as imposing the nineteenth-century invention of sado-masochism as an explanation of the conduct of St Sebastian, and of homophobia onto those who killed him, and constitutes temporal chauvinism. Moreover, the ideas and positions these criticisms fix upon, and ironically *essentialize* by treating as unitary, coherent and fixed, are more complex and certainly far less essentialist than allowed. There are a number of overlapping discourses within feminism which have essentialist features, although each of these actually pivots on what we see as constructionist principles.

One such discourse coheres around the view that there are 'womanist' qualities untainted by the patriarchal order, which lie beneath or behind the levels of falsity and deformation. However, this 'cultural feminist'[5] position is closely related to the earlier widely held adherence to a 'stages of consciousness' view of the relationship between feminism and contrary thought-systems and was largely a product of the influence of marxism on feminism. And as with marxist feminism, radical feminism actually turns on a strong social constructionist conviction that the self, the subject, can change from stage to stage precisely because *not* unitary, coherent or stable. Critics might object that once the higher stage of consciousness is reached then change is presumed to stop, that the real coherence and stability of the true inner self is then revealed; and certainly earlier rhetorical accounts from both marxist feminism and radical feminism may well have promulgated this view. However, more autobiographically expressed writing from both positions suggests that the rhetoric of coherence contained in 'theory' goes hand in hand in practice with a narrative of continued and complex change (e.g. Morgan, 1977; Wilson, 1982).

A second supposedly essentialist discourse within feminism turns on the notion of 'women's oppression', which is taken to indicate that all women are subjugated for the same reason/s by the same means to the same extent across all cultures and history within patriarchy. Certainly feminists – and for as long as they *are* feminists – take the view that there *is* something which binds together all women. However, we see this as the viewpoint that, although the specifics of subjugation will certainly differ in particular times, places and circumstances, nevertheless the result is always to position women in relationships of subordination to men. Moreover, all varieties of feminism take the view that 'oppression' is precisely *not* fixed, can be changed by changing the behaviours and attributes of actual women and men, as well as by the changing of structures and systems. Here too supposed essentialism actually rests on strong constructionism. However, a more telling criticism of this position for us is that it conflates analyses and statements about the *binaries* 'Women' and 'Men' with analyses and statements about *actual* women and men. Feminist grand theoretical narratives of all varieties or 'types' (such as liberal feminism, marxist and socialist feminism, cultural feminism, radical feminism, psychoanalytic feminism and so on) pinpoint elements of the relationship of super- and subordination between the category members 'Women' and 'Men'; but in our opinion they all consistently minimize the complexities of actual relationships between women and men, which may, in particular times, places and situations undermine or even reverse elements of 'oppression' and the supposed powerlessness of women (Wise and Stanley, 1987).

The third possibly essentialist feminist discourse is that which perceives unity in its object of inquiry, women. Seeing 'Women'/ women as united by certain characteristics is treated as essentialist because supposedly deriving from perceiving a fixed coherent set of properties as constituting women. However, there is no necessity for what unites women to be physiological or psychological or anything other than that 'women are oppressed': that is, characteristics resulting from a particular distribution of sexual political power at a micro- as well as at a macro-level between women and men. In addition, actual women and men do indeed exist and do in practice display certain differences from each other along (fairly) constant lines at any one point in time, including both differences perceived as physiological and also as behavioural. But there is absolutely no need within feminist thinking to treat either the 'behavioural' *or* the 'physiological'/'psychological' as having any fixed essential properties, as existing outside of cultural and thus of socially constructed patterns of meaning, as we have already proposed.

Moreover, at this point in time in Western culture, women *do* share certain kinds of socially constructed attributes and are subjugated to and by men; and to be convinced that this is a legitimate object of inquiry is neither outmoded nor unsophisticated. It is and remains crucially, fundamentally, important. Nor is there anything about this conviction that necessarily indicates any measure of 'essentialism'. Additionally, whether 'essentialism' is conservative is not inscribed 'within' as a fixed property of it, but rather depends upon the who, how and where of its use. Certainly there are feminists who do adopt essentialist positions around one of these three discourses (or others), but equally so there is a good deal of conservative essentialism in the position advanced by feminist deconstructionism, in ascribing essences to others no matter how much these others protest that doing so misrepresents their ideas and political programmes.

The discourses that constitute present-day feminism – by no means confined to the 'grand theory' variants referred to above – are more appropriately conceptualized by interpreting 'discourse' in the Foucauldian sense of divergent voices competing to name a position. Like other broad social movements, feminism has a large measure of internal fracturing, although externally it may appear otherwise by virtue of rhetorics of unity and stability advanced by particular proponents – or more usually by opponents. Constructionism, there should be no doubt about it, is fundamentally inscribed within feminism; and a defining element in all feminist theorizing is its treatment of gender as socially constructed and of feminism as the remaking of a changeable and non-essentialist gender order. All feminisms are by definition constructionist, but necessarily retain essentialist elements in the ways the categories 'Women'/'Men' are inscribed within them by virtue of positioning these categories, particularly that of 'Women', as fundamental to both their style and their focus of analysis.

There is moreover no such thing as a deconstructionist position 'untainted' by essentialism. Deconstructionist ideas are predicated upon the existence of essentialism: essentialism has to be detected and criticized or a deconstructionist grouping within intellectual life would have no legitimacy, indeed no existence. And at the basis of deconstructionist theorizing are essentialisms – remember here Derrida's 'what is woman?' and his essentializing answer that 'woman' is a symbol of undecidability, as well as the more general deconstructionist ascribing of definite, coherent and fixed properties to people and work labelled essentialist. We continue to be convinced that 'deconstructionism' in practice operates as a source of would-be hegemonic control through the specification, by a particular epistemic community-in-the-making, of what it is permitted to think and, through this, what is theoretically and politically acceptable. The career of deconstructionism is a troubling one, for at least some of its proponents operate as a latter-day inquisition within intellectual life; however, many intellectual and political movements go through zealot phases but are gradually remade over time, and we hope deconstructionism will do likewise.

Within *Breaking Out* we were concerned to argue that 'Women' is internally fractured, including around sexualities, but that part of the totalizing claims of much feminist theory (our particular target was feminist writing on socialization) was its implicit heterosexual chauvinism. More recent analytic writing has considerably shifted feminist thinking concerning sexuality, with influences including Foucauldian-influenced debate concerning the category 'the (male) homosexual', and feminist debate concerning 'the lesbian continuum', including by Adrienne Rich (1980) and Lillian Faderman (1979). Both debates have been concerned with essentialism and constructionism. The 'essentialist v. constructionist' debate has taken a particular twist in relation to 'the homosexual' as explored by gay male historians and other academics. However, the same political issues and problematics arise for 'the homosexual' as for 'Women': how – and if – to relate experience to the category and how and in what directions to remake the category. These debates about the cultural making of the category 'the homosexual', and the different meanings ascribed to it in different times, places and circumstances, bear upon what has come to be called – and criticized as – 'identity politics'.

Within the first debate the charge of 'essentialism' has been levelled against any hint that something comparable to contemporary (male) homosexual behaviour and/or relationships existed in pre-modern times. Different turns of the debate have focused on the Graeco-Romano period, the Renaissance, the seventeenth century and the nineteenth century, with constructionists searching for a temporal point of origin for the category 'the homosexual' and denying its existence outside the modern period. Here constructionists invoke superior facticity against perceived opponents: their view of a slice of the past is deemed to be more true, more real, in relation to how meanings actually were. Outsiders like ourselves are left wondering at the rich ironies of such a thoroughly representational and foundationalist view of 'the past' enshrined in the work of supposed constructionists, and at the undoubtedly political purposes of this marking out and condemnation of deviation from the 'correct' line of thought.

'The lesbian' as a category has been an absence here, for the conduct of this first debate has been largely irrelevant to the predominantly feminist line that academic lesbian work has taken. However, the second debate has been concerned with essentialism and constructionism via feminist theorizing of the 'lesbian continuum' of relationships between women and of 'romantic friendships' of the past. This discussion originated in recognition that close relationships between women of the past existed on a continuum from the familial bonds of mothers and daughters and of sisters, through 'everyday friendships', to romantic friendships which were love relationships in everything other than genital expression, to sexual relationships between lovers. The discussion has recognized that a very thin dividing line indeed can exist between romantic friendships and sexual relationships, but also argued that until comparatively recently lesbianism as a sexual engagement between women was typically subsumed by lover-like but non-sexual friendships. The conclusion has been that 'lesbianism' as we currently know it did not exist until, in the late nineteenth century, the 'sexologists' 'sexualized' romantic friendships by defining these around a stereotype which brought together romantic friendship and what was actually transvestism with no necessary sexual content. However, the argument goes on, the stereotype *was* a sexualized one, and offered the new and deviant role of the 'mannish lesbian'.

It is at this point that this feminist debate has touched the 'essentialist v. constructionist' debate among gay male academics, for the feminist 'romantic friendship' position has a strong constructionist argument as its pivot: 'the lesbian' was not only made rather than a given, but was made at a particular point in time as constituting a part of the changing patriarchal order of the late nineteenth century (and see particularly Faderman 1979; 1991). The focus has thus been upon the category or stereotype of 'the lesbian', although there is again a repeated slide between category and experience, reading off how women actually behaved from the constitution and properties of the category, rather than recognizing and studying the highly complex dialectic between the two (and in relation to this latter approach see Stanley, 1992a; 1992b; 1992c).

These debates bear upon 'identity politics' in the gay (once mixed but now largely if not exclusively male) movement and in the 'lesbian community' in a number of ways. 'Identity politics' is seen to consist in the belief that being gay is innately political, and that as only 'the personal' is political therefore the oppression of gay people can be removed through life-style politics. Its advocation is treated as irrevocably essentialist because it purportedly inscribes fixed inherent properties to being gay. In addition, the notion of 'identity' is positioned by critics as the search for the real, true gay identity that lies beneath the layers of misrepresentation, and thus as also essentialist.

However, as with other deconstructionist accounts, it must be remembered that these are *critics'* mis/constructions, not those of proponents; and the positions actually held are more complex, less one-dimensional and certainly less 'essentialist' than represented. That is, the critics are attempting to fix and essentialize as a unitary position what are in fact a variety of different and indeed competing positions. There is nothing inherent in the notion of 'identity' which requires an essentialist definition: and indeed the strong present-day tendency is both to treat identity as completely constructionist in everyday practice, *and* to inscribe essential features to it in political arguments and debates, in very similar terms to those we outlined in relation to feminist approaches to 'Women'. Moreover, among both gay men and lesbians, 'identity politics' actually encompasses highly consequential differences and disagreements. Certainly there are enormous differences between the British gay 'identity politics' of the period of the 1890s to the First World War, of the post-Second World War 1950s and 1960s gay rights movement, of the early 1970s, and of now; and equally certainly these varieties of identity politics depart in significant ways from the construction of 'identity politics' criticized by deconstructionists. Moreover, we cannot accept that there is something 'wrong' or 'misguided' in the twin claims, first, that there are indeed truer versions of homosexuality/lesbianism than 'theirs' promulgated in 'their' representations, in the sense of better fitting the common experiences of lesbian women and gay men; and, second, that there should be lesbian/gay male identities of self-construction, with sets of political practices organized around and in support of these.

A coda here on 'the heterosexual'. Etymologically speaking, 'the heterosexual' was invented synonymously with 'the homosexual'; but, by whatever name or none that heterosexuality was known in past times, the more interesting question is whether in particular times, places and circumstances something existed as a hegemonic sexual political formation which specified behaviour and feelings for category members placed in a superordinate relationship to sexualities treated as deviant. Some lesbian feminist theorizing, such as that of Monique Wittig (e.g. 1980a; 1980b; 1992), has argued that heterosexuality is *the* dominant narrative and is a product of the construction of 'Men', constituting the means by which 'Women' comes to be subordinate to its binary; and this approach constitutes one of the few sustained feminist attempts to theorize both 'Men' and 'heterosexuality'. One of its more problematic features is that it sees the existence of 'the lesbian' effectively as having nothing to do with women's feelings for and relationships with *other women*, and everything to do with the control of 'Women' *by men*. Behind this lies another collapsing of category and actuality, for the category may be thus constituted without this necessarily saying anything about how and why women behaved and felt, and behave and feel, as they did, and do, towards other women. Doubtless proponents of this position would reject our evaluation as denying the liberating possibilities of treating 'the lesbian' as an empty category which can be filled in any way chosen, as a 'free space' to which are consigned women who are (seen to be) deviant from the heterosexual order. However, whatever the attractions of this approach, we think it misguided to read off the behaviours, feelings, responses of women (and men) from those assigned to 'Women' (and 'Men'); and we prefer to develop an ontologically based feminist epistemology which proposes a materialist analysis of representation and categorization and does not treat actual people and their behavioural vagaries as mere ciphers filled by representational and categorical content. Representation is certainly important, but, unlike some postmodernist arguments imply, it is not all.

Useful reading

Altman *et al.* (1989); Bunch (1989/1975); Duberman *et al.* (1989, pp. 17–36, 37–53, 54–64); Faderman (1979; 1991, pp. 11–61); Fuss (1989, pp. 1–21, 97–113, 113–19); Grosz (1990a); Rich (1980b); Spelman (1988); Stanley (1992b; 1992c); Vicinus (1989); Wittig (1980a; 1980b; 1992).

REPRESENTATION AND THE QUESTION OF HISTORY

In discussing contemporary currents in feminist social thought, again and again we return to the power and importance of representation. Representations may be everywhere but they are not everything, and we reject a Baudrillardian – representation is all – approach to them in favour of a materialist one. This sees ideology, and thus representation, not only as crucial but also to be conceptualized and analysed as sets of concrete *material* ideological *practices*. The categories and binaries which are the concern of deconstructionism are a key element in the operations of such practices, for they constitute representations of types of persons and attributes as ready-made classificatory packages which are used as short-cuts to reading social situations and the persons which constitute them. Representations provide both the framework and also a large part of the content of accounts – typically but not exclusively *verbal* – of social action and social situations. Deconstructionists may reject the supposed paramountcy of the spoken word, while just as certainly we reject insistence on the paramountcy of the *written* word in deconstructionist and other basically literary views of social life. Social life is not 'a text' in the strict sense of the word, something fixed and inscribed, but is rather both dynamic and interactional, and in it the 'texts' of social action are always available to be 're-written' as verbal accounts negotiated and remade again and again.

However, most social science research *is* representational in its assumptions and claims, rather than taking as its task *the study of* representations, whether in the form of written or visual or verbal or any other kinds of accounts of (aspects of) social life. Typically,

research is treated as a means of uncovering and describing reality
for all practical purposes, and the 'data' that it collects and analyses
are assumed to exist in an effectively one-to-one relationship with
a social reality they supposedly provide description of.

This is particularly clearly seen in relation to history construed
in representational terms as the 'recovery' of past events, persons
or 'mentalités'. Some varieties of oral history, for example, treat
collections of or even individual oral histories as unproblematically factual 'histories from below' to stand alongside more conventional histories, rather than accounts which should be treated
as topics for investigation in their own right and not data to
investigate something lying outside the account itself. Histories
are, in our view, better seen as *historiographies*: accounts of particular aspects of the past in competition with each other.[6] This
doesn't mean that histories are *only* representational, that they
have no factual basis at all; but it does mean that their facts are
those that survive (a tiny proportion of the whole) and are dependent on a researcher/historian for their interpretation, rather than
having a meaning somehow 'there' within what can unproblematically be seen as past realities. Plausible counter-factual claims
are always possible, and generally there are no incontrovertible *a
priori* grounds for assuming one historiography only is the 'true
history' – 'the facts' are highly partial and constitute elements of
a framework stitched together by the preoccupations and intellectual concerns of the historian, not of 'the past' itself.

Debates about the representational nature of history have an
especial, although as yet largely unassimilated, importance for
feminist analysis, as Joan Scott's (1988) work and her debate
with Linda Gordon (Scott, 1990a; Scott, 1990b; Gordon, 1990a;
Gordon, 1990b) suggest. That is, if all historiography, including
feminist historiography, is a textual representation, then such
historiography is to be seen as a partial and motivated account
predicated upon a number of other highly partial, fragmentary
and motivated accounts, which have an unknowable but certainly
highly complex relationship to the underlying events that these
written accounts are treated as being 'of'. There are (at least)
four important aspects of feminist thought where a non-
representational understanding of historiography will have powerful reverberations.

First, the concept of 'patriarchy' has been criticized for its
'ahistoricity'. This criticism depends upon the assumption that

'the past' exists in a potentially (even if not actually, given the present state of knowledge) representational relationship to accounts of it. However, once it is accepted that 'the past' is actually unrecoverable and that analysis should be focused upon representations, upon accounts of the past, then what are revealed are two competing representations or knowledge-claims, not one (patriarchy) versus 'the truth' as enshrined in the critics' view. Second, claims for the historical materialist basis of socialist feminism, and indeed the highly representational claims made more generally by proponents of this variant of feminism, need to be looked at with a considerably more critical eye, especially by those who hold up this position as the 'superior' one among feminist theoretical accounts (e.g. Jaggar, 1983; Tong, 1989). Third, all feminists, both in and outside academic life, need to rethink feminist accounts of 'gender' in the past and the search for the 'origins' of the contemporary gender order, as do those concerned with investigating and theorizing the historical point/s of origin of 'the lesbian'/'the homosexual'. An almost unthinking assumption of the facticity and representationality of feminist historical accounts of the past must give way to an awareness that these are *accounts*, historiographies, present-day *constructions*, and not slices of the past itself.

However, as we have already suggested, it is not only historical research that needs to have its representational underpinnings analytically scrutinized. *All* research involves the production of the textual representation of a research reality, using whatever conventional stylistic and rhetorical devices are considered appropriate by the various theoretical and other allegiances a researcher locates themselves by. Within writing, researchers have the last – or rather the penultimate (for readers have the last)[7] – say about what 'the research' meant, found, concluded. Writing dispossesses the researched. Although the researched may exert a good deal of influence in the interaction that composes research, when it comes to *writing* researchers can – and indeed in a sense ultimately must – take responsibility for the research carried out, because it comes to bear their names as textual products of the academic labour process.

The written product of any research process is a construction, and not a representation, of the reality it is 'about'. However, foundationalist Cartesian precepts not only discourage but also proscribe the inscription of any other stance, for making representational claims about the relationship between 'research' and 'life' is the cornerstone of science's presumed authority as a source of authoritative knowledge about the world. Moreover, the specifically rhetorical means by which the complexities and confusions of research are brought to clear and definite conclusions and findings are a key element in how the 'authority' of researchers is signalled to others, both to outsiders and also to other members of the researcher's particular epistemic community. Within the writing process what are in fact situated knowledges (Haraway, 1988), produced both in and about particular contexts with marked indexical properties, are written about as something other than situated and indexical: as generalizable transferable 'knowledge' which is apparently not tied to the specifics of time, place and person, and which seems not to be a product of its own labour processes.

Useful reading

Abu-Lughod (1990); Alexander and Taylor (1981); Barwell (1990); Gordon (1990a; 1990b) Jaggar (1983, pp. 353–94); Rowbotham (1981); Scott (1988; 1990a; 1990b); Stacey (1988); Stanley (1992a); Tong (1989, pp. 235–8).

DIFFERENCE AND 'DIFFÉRANCE'

The debate on difference encompasses both *difference* as the multiple fragmentations and differences existing between women, between men, as well as between women and men; and also *différance* in the Derridarian sense. 'Différance' (an invented word) is the gap between objects of perception and the meanings these have as symbols or representations; and its theoretical importance in deconstructionism reveals the essentialist elements at its foundation, for it proposes that there are 'real' social objects outside or beneath the social construction of these.

A crucial formulation of 'différance' lies in Derrida's question 'what is woman?' (oddly echoing Freud's 'what do women want?') and his answer that 'woman' has the particular ontological quality of 'undecidability'. However, if 'différance' indeed stands for the 'switch points of meaning', the social junctures which reveal the moving discord of different voices and forces which invoke essentialist claims, then there is surely no need either to pose or to answer such a question at all, and certainly not to answer it by essentializing 'Woman'. Far preferable, and more consonant with the deconstructionist project, is the long-standing feminist insistence that 'Women' is a becoming: 'Women' is Other to 'Men'/men, and the category's 'O' of Otherness is precisely a cipher to be filled by those seeking, for varied and often competing purposes, to impose meanings on it, some of which are essentialist and others of which are not. This does *not* mean that it is an 'empty space' in the sense used by Wittig: it is rather – like 'the lesbian' – over-filled, with most of its naming being imposed and enforced on category members.

Essentialism is named and defined in opposition to 'différance', around the rejection of any claims for the existence of relatively stable sets of properties which systematically differentiate between types of persons. It leads to a thoroughgoing individualism of a kind rarely seen in modern intellectual life. That is, the logic of this approach insists not only upon 'différance' – competing constructions of meaning – but also upon 'difference' – the complete fragmentation of experience between people conventionally seen as sharing the 'same' social structural attributes, such as gender, class, sexuality and race/ethnicity. It denies such unities of experience.

Focusing here on 'race' (although the same arguments apply elsewhere), there is no reason why the concept of 'race' needs to be assigned any essentialist meaning or characteristic derived from biology or physiology or any other supposedly fixed physical or psychological characteristic. That is, we can – and should – see 'race' as a label which both reflects and helps construct the discourses of oppression; and there is consequently no reason to travel the deconstructionist road in rejecting 'race' (and gender and so on) as an allowable category. There is, however, *every* reason to recognize that, for instance, broad shared differences in skin colour – those known as black, brown, yellow, white – are categories with immensely consequential political and social implications which need to be attended to, both intellectually and politically, rather than argued away as humanist naiveties. And similarly feminists should continue to insist that the categories 'Women'/'Men', and 'the lesbian' and 'the homosexual'/'the heterosexual', remain central to a feminist ethic as well as epistemology, for these sociopolitical constructions are fundamental to the systematic assignment of positions of super- and subordination in their composing binaries and the underlying evaluation of their relative social, moral, economic and other worth.

Until recently, feminist discussion has been concerned with difference rather than 'différance', and in particular with those differences which cohere around recognition of oppressions of race/ethnicity, specifically the subordinate position of black feminism within supposedly generic but actually white feminist theory. Increasingly white feminist theorists genuflect in the direction of questions of 'race', but little has changed in terms of the organizational structure of feminist theorizing except the admittance of a few black feminist writers to a still hegemonic feminist theoretical canon. These feminists – largely white, heterosexual, middle-class academics – retain hegemonic control of the knowledge-producing process and the epistemic basis of this, but fail to make apparent the highly particular subject-position from which they speak.

Another example of this process: criticisms of radical feminism underpin attempts to retain epistemic privilege by a hegemonic group within academic feminism, for it is repeatedly marked out as offending against the standards and procedures of 'proper' feminist science. Indeed the recent flood of deconstructionist writings by feminist theorists can be seen as a means of retaining their control of 'feminist theory' in the face of the entrance of the dispossessed to the theoretical arena of feminism. Because of its 'wildness', lack of systematic theory, emphasis on practice, naming of an 'enemy' in the form of men and patriarchy, its internal fragmentation, and its failure to come up with the theoretical goods in the form of 'a theory' comparable to other grand theory accounts such as those of socialist feminism, radical feminism is damned as a failed conventional theoretical account. In contrast, as already noted, we see it as *different in kind* from the other approaches, as fragmentary, internally highly diverse, containing no theoretical or any other centre, rejecting the grand narrative of 'theory', and unconcerned with seeking or claiming academic respectability for its own sake.

Difference needs to encompass more than 'race' and ethnicity. As we argued in *Breaking Out*, a feminist concern with theorizing women's experience needs to embrace difference in a more thorough-going way, to take on board the multiple fragmentations of the experiences of oppression by 'Women'/women of different ages, sexualities, classes, political persuasions, interests and com-

petences, religions and beliefs, education or its lack, country and
continent, health or illness, able-bodiedness or disability, feminism or its lack. Ten years on it still needs to do so. It also still
needs to accept, for once and for all, that if feminism is to
survive as a political force for change, then it must recognize that
difference is fundamental to feminism, which must necessarily
revolve around fragmentations and differences of thought and
practice. However, to date its theory has largely denied or ignored
this by attempts to define theory as the preserve of a specialist
group with a hegemonic position over contrary feminist voices.

Useful reading

Dill (1983); Grosz (1990a; 1990b); Lather (1991); Muraro (1987); Ramazonaglu (1986); Rich (1980a, pp. 275–310); Rothenberg (1990); Sawicki
(1986).

EPISTEMOLOGIES OF THE OPPRESSED

The ontologies of the oppressed rest on forbidden emotions and
forbidden thoughts – such as loves which are supposed not to
dare to speak their name but do; and white masks of apparent
acquiescence on actually rebellious black faces. That is, fundamental here are actual or suspected subversions, as subversion is
named and categorized within dominant ideological practices. But
the ontologies of the oppressed are not merely negatively
inscribed as Other, a counterpoint to dominant group ontologies
and experiences. Central to the political projects of oppressed
groups is the construction of an everyday life, a mundane reality,
no matter how hidden from or denied to oppressors, and with it
an ontological system for explaining and thus also defining and
constructing the very being of members of such groups. But of
course there are internal ontological fragmentations and differences, and also points of 'différance'. In relation to black and
lesbian feminist epistemologies, and recognizing the complex
overlaps between category members of these 'different' groups,
these fracture-points include the commonalities but also the differences of a black womanist in comparison with a black feminist
epistemology, and the differences between a lesbian feminist in
comparison with a lesbian epistemology. But there are also

important commonalities between the constitution of the two categories.

'The black community', 'the gay community': to be a woman here is to be Other, a stranger within these supposedly generic outsider communities. To be a feminist within them is to be doubly Other, doubly a stranger – an outcast of outcasts. And to be a black lesbian feminist is to be positioned on the periphery of these ontologies rather than being seen as the possessor of a being, an ontology, unique in its own terms: not deviant from others but its own self and being.

A black feminist epistemology has been described by Patricia Hill Collins (1990) as encompassing four defining attributes: it uses concrete experience as a criterion of meaning and is predicated upon an assumption of the ontological basis of knowledge; it uses dialogic means of assessing knowledge-claims; it has an ethic of caring as the basis of relationships between people; and it positions an ethic of accountability as central to this epistemic community. We see these attributes as the basis of all feminist epistemology, rather than being specific to black feminism; there are, however, experiential aspects of being that have been described by other black feminist writers, such as Audre Lorde (1982; 1984; 1985), bell hooks (1981; 1984; 1989), Michelle Cliff (1980), Barbara Christian (1985; 1988) and Sondra O'Neale (1986), which are specific to a black feminist *ontology* which is then constructed as an epistemological position. Given our conviction of the symbiotic relationship between epistemology and ontology, we find this approach particularly pertinent.

Black liberationists as well as black feminists have used a 'mask' metaphor to describe the black experience of being constrained to dissemble, to hide feelings and thoughts that may or may not be 'there', but which were/are feared to be so by white oppressors. For black feminists and especially black lesbian feminists, a 'mask' can characterize social relationships not only when among whites, but also when among black people: 'home', the 'black community', is another place where dissembling may be necessary. Difference, the awareness of the multiplicity and complexity of experience, is then a fundamental characteristic of black feminist ontology, as is 'passing' in ways other than appearing as white: appearing as a non-deviant black woman rather than as a feminist, for example.

A black feminist ontology also encompasses a sharp awareness of the ways that black women are sexualized – are treated as 'the body' incarnate. White heterosexual men's colonization of black women's sexuality and reproductive capacity in the service of slavery has been discussed by black feminists. However, it is equally important to note that white gay men have constructed images, representations and actualities around black men's bodies and sexualities in highly comparable ways, while black heterosexual men are often co-competitors with white for black women's bodies, and black lesbian feminists have often protested against white lesbian sexual predatoriness towards them. These complex processes of sexualization have come to be treated by outsiders as the defining representation of black women, but to which their actual experience of the social world bears a diverse and complex relationship.

Black feminists also frequently emphasize the colonizing role of much of 'feminist theory', actually white feminist theory of white feminist experience, in replicating the dynamics of exclusion on grounds of race. Barbara Christian, for example, has noted the white feminist preoccupation with totalizing generalizations and the related assumption that what she calls 'the race for theory' will also preoccupy black feminists. Similarly bell hooks has emphasized the epistemologically achieved marginalization of black feminists within an implicitly white but rhetorically open and generic 'feminism'. These differences are ontologically founded as part and parcel of more subtle variants of racism, but racism none the less.

For lesbian feminists, the wearing of masks takes the form of passing, a term adapted from black writing and experience to indicate, not black people passing as white (neither a matter of choice nor even a possibility for the vast majority of black people), but lesbian women (or gay men) passing as heterosexual. Passing here is a choice and a possibility available for all lesbians, a choice even the most thoroughly 'out' of lesbian women are often constrained to make, for there is the presumption of heterosexuality in all times, place and circumstances unless and until its falsity is made apparent (and sometimes even then).

Passing, being in 'the closet', has powerful metaphorical importance as well as providing a useful gloss for elements of lesbian women's experience, and in Britain it has had this importance since the early gay movement of the 1890s to the First World War. 'The closet' represents powerlessness – enforced silence; it also represents power – deliberately keeping secrets from people, secrets shared with like minds but denied to others; and is a profoundly janus-faced contradictory element in the lives of lesbian women. It is an emblem of *silence* but one which resounds, for it speaks of disavowal and denial but also of the claiming and making of an identity at least in part separate from its naming by 'oppressors', those other to the lesbian Other within. It is also a sign of *knowledge*, shared knowledge of the signs and symbols which reveal 'the lesbian beneath' the clothes, looks, demeanour and behaviour of the passing woman; and as such it has both an ontological basis (it takes one to know one) and epistemological implications (to know others as oneself is known). The ontology of the lesbian turns upon 'the closet' known and seen from within; and the relations of the closet turn on the liminality of shifts between guises: between the implicit and explicit, the hidden and open, the shamed and proud, and – crucially – on its liminality with its supposed binary, 'coming out'. These ontological shifts carry epistemological baggage: how and when to know not only which is which of these binaries (for telling them apart is not always as transparent as it might seem), but also when the explicit, open and proud will be safe or at least safe enough. And it also includes knowledge of how to tell apart what is lesbian and what is heterosexual, and what are the behaviours, emotions and persons that link these supposed binaries, for all is continuum and almost nothing composes the extremities of these categories (and perhaps this is the source of the attraction of the 'butch' in the commercial lesbian scene, one certainty in a world of ambiguities).

'Hetero-sexualization' occurs for lesbian women as a major way that many heterosexual men respond to knowledge of a woman's lesbianism. Conceptualizing heterosexuality as a weapon used to control deviant women who threaten these men's sense of themselves and their power is no abstract theoretical notion to be cavalierly dismissed by heterosexual feminist theorists. It is rather the common experience of women known to be lesbian; and knowledge of the likelihood and prevention of its occurrence forms an important part of the ontological basis of being a lesbian. Knowing and differentiating between 'types of men', and the circumstances that lesbian women find themselves in with men, has as many complexities as the Inuit relationship to snow, and as much importance. Moreover, gay men too have means of rendering lesbian and other women subordinate, some of which involve sexualization processes applied particularly to those heterosexual women who spend time with and emotional commitment on gay men, as discussed in *Breaking Out*. However, the sexualization activities of heterosexual men are typically far more intrusive, openly aggressive and potentially violent, and are therefore more crucially present in everyday analyses of experience and action: their ontological importance is far greater, and thus their centrality for lesbian feminist epistemology.

Marilyn Frye's (1983) view of this epistemology remains an evocative and powerful one. On the stage of life men play all the major parts and remain centre-stage and under the limelight. However, their performances depend upon the backstage activities of women, in directing them and lighting them well, and their audience is each other and the women. But there is another audience, of lesbian seers who watch the women and not the men; for them the play *is* the women, all the light is concentrated upon them. The performing men fear the lesbian seer, their particular terror the possibility that her watching will encourage the women to see themselves as she does, to remove their gaze from the men and become concerned with and focused upon their own activities. Of course this should not be taken as a literal account, but it does symbolically characterize how many lesbian feminists feel about their relationship to 'Women' and 'Men' and the implications of this for the ontology of all concerned.

The relationship between ontology, epistemology and ethics is no relationship at all in our view, for these are merely different terms for the same thing and are entirely substitutable for each other. Thus, although we have focused on the ontological specificities of black feminism and lesbian feminism, we have stressed that these have epistemological consequentiality, such that the one is mutually subsumed within the other: a perfect union. And each of these specificities has clear ethical dimensions and consequentiality for the social relationships of those involved – that is, everyone. We have assigned generalized attributes to 'a black feminist epistemology' and 'a lesbian feminist epistemology', but these broad unities – which *do* express common experiences and understandings, broadly speaking – also encompass internal fractures and fragmentations. It is also important to recognize that it is difficult not to gloss the relationship between what derives from *women's* experience and what from *feminist* understanding in discussing these ontologies/epistemologies; and a detailed analytic exploration of the ontological and epistemological separations, overlaps and specificities existing between them is long overdue.

Do feminists have epistemological privilege? That is, do oppressed people, by virtue of their knowledge of both oppressors' views of reality and that of their own subjugated group, have access to an *a priori* better or truer knowledge of reality? Key figures in present-day feminist theory such as Nancy Hartsock (1987), Alison Jaggar and Sandra Harding assume they do, and take the position that a feminist epistemology *is* a privileged one. However, while these ontologies/epistemologies certainly provide a *different* view on what passes for 'reality', a different interpretation of people and events, and one *preferable* to those who gain and hold it, we cannot accept that the existence of difference, of multiplicity, means that there must be a *hierarchical* relationship between these degrees of different vision. On the surface, assuming the epistemological privilege of the oppressed is both attractive and plausible. It is attractive because for once it positions the oppressed as superior; and it is plausible because the theoretical and epistemological writings of black people, black feminists, lesbians and lesbian feminists, as well as those about the generic 'Women', stress the 'double vision' of the particular oppressed group.

However, it is precisely this commonality that points up the fallaciousness of the assumption: what happens when such epistemologies are lined up and judged against *each other*, rather than against that of an oppressor group? How then are these '*a priori*' claims to superior knowledge to be adjudicated? Do we start measuring comparative suffering, judging the ontological situations of members of these groups against each other and finding the one which involves the greatest degree of suffering to be superordinate among the epistemologies of the oppressed? And just how should degrees of suffering be adjudicated? Some feminists already do this, surrendering any notion that 'Women' might be right in favour of 'blacks' or 'Jews' because of their perception of the relative degrees of oppression of members of these groups. However, measuring suffering seems to us much like calculating the number of angels on a pinhead, although considerably more ethically and politically objectionable.

Our view is that there are *no* foundational grounds for judging the *a priori* superiority of the epistemologies of the oppressed, nor of any one group of the oppressed, in relation to the production of 'knowledge' and the settling of its problematics, other than by comparing and judging the ontological bases of these epistemologies; and such a comparison and judgement is, as we have noted, ethically objectionable. There are however acceptable moral and political grounds for finding one of these *preferable*, a rather different claim than that which is concerned with staking claim to a 'truer, more real reality'. For us, the grounds of preference are *ontological*: that is, that it better fits with a proponent's experience of living or being or understanding. Knowledge, as we have argued, is situated, specific and local to the conditions of its production and thus to the social location and being of its producers.

Useful reading

Allen (1990); Card (1986); Collins (1990, pp. 201–20); Frye (1983, pp. 152–74); Hartsock (1987); Hoagland (1988a; 1988b); Narayan (1988); Sedgwick (1991, pp. 67–90); Trinh (1989, pp. 79–116).

SOME CONCLUDING THOUGHTS

Our insistence upon the ontological basis of knowledge, and thus of the valid existence of varieties of feminist epistemology, brings us full circle in our discussion of recent feminist debates concerning the kinds of issues and questions discussed in the first edition of *Breaking Out*. Here, as in *Breaking Out*, we have argued throughout for the symbiotic relationship between ontology and epistemology. Proclamation of the reflexivity of feminist research processes; acknowledgement of the contextual specificity of feminist as of all other knowledge; recognition that who a researcher is, in terms of their sex, race, class and sexuality, affects what they 'find' in research is as true for feminist as any other researchers: these and other components of feminist epistemology emphasize the *necessarily* ontological basis of knowledge-production. This is one of the most profoundly radical of feminist statements, for it mounts a fundamental challenge to the basic precepts of Cartesian epistemology. This is partly because it denies that the binaries of reason and emotion and subjectivity and objectivity are *binaries* at all, instead insisting that these are different names for *the same sets of activities enacted by persons deemed to be different on grounds of gender* (and race, and sexuality, and class, and so on). It is also because it emphasizes that 'scientists' necessarily produce context- and person-dependent, and thus 'subjective', knowledge; and it thereby refuses to accept the supposed subject/object divide that science enshrines. A feminism grounded in Cartesian presuppositions will produce no revolution in intellectual or any other aspect of social life, but merely admit feminist experts into the hierarchies of scientism. A feminist fractured foundationalism such as ours may or may not contribute to an epistemological revolution, but at least it will make a wholehearted attempt.

Readers will have noted that the recent debates within feminist social theory we have addressed here are, in their fundamentals, largely those that we identified at the beginning of this essay with the 'sociology of knowledge' concerns of feminist debates of the 1970s. That is, many of these debates are to be seen as old feminist wine in new deconstructionist bottles – the same ideas and issues but expressed in a more mystificatory and abstract way. It is difficult, for example, not to conclude that deconstruction of the presumed unitary and essentialist nature of the category 'Women' has proved attractive to erstwhile structuralists within feminism, now at last coming to terms with the kinds of issues that interactionists have always addressed, but doing so in ways which preserve 'theory' as the prerogative of an élite. In a similar way, the kind of feminism we have aligned ourselves with has always rejected Cartesian scientistic ideas and assumptions, has always eschewed 'grand narrative' approaches to feminist topics of inquiry, has always accepted the fragmentary and complex nature of reality. Is there, then, anything new that these debates add beyond an abstract and often forbidding theoretical language through which to express them? Our view is that no new ideas or approaches are contributed by them, but that they *have* significantly shifted epistemological concerns and debates from the margins to centre stage. This is of signal importance for academic feminism, for it opens up the possibility of far greater change in academic life than feminism has achieved thus far. This is not, however, to suggest this has happened in an unproblematic way. There are four issues in particular we want to raise here.

First, the role we ascribed to 'positivism' in the original *Breaking Out* – as an orthodoxy which prescribed 'scientific' research behaviour – has been taken over by foundationalism. The relationship between positivism and foundationalism, while close, is not one of complete overlap: most if by no means all varieties of positivism, for example, are concerned with quantification, while a foundationalist epistemology characterizes the large majority of qualitative as well as quantitative research. 'Foundationalism' is now used predominantly as a buzzword indicating simplicity and naivety: it has been essentialized in the same way that 'essentialism' has. However, as we hope readers will have noted, in the original *Breaking Out* we were careful not only to note the existence of varieties of positivism*S* but also the fact that positivism did not correspond to a quantitative/qualitative divide; and similarly in this second edition we have been careful to note not only the existence of foundationalism*S* but also the fact that foundationalist and anti-foundationalist impulses may coexist in the same epistemological position. The description of our own epistemological position as a *feminist fractured foundationalism* indicates our refusal to essentialize foundationalism and to erect it into a binary categorical relationship with anti-foundationalism.

Second, the recent feminist debates we have discussed in this afterword have been conducted in an increasingly specialized 'language' – or rather a 'language-game', using Wittgenstein's term – derived in part from feminist reworkings of philosophy and in part from the conjunction of postmodernism, deconstructionism and post-structuralism. Readers may feel partially or completely alienated from the ideas because of the often mystificatory way they are written about – after all, there is little or nothing in the debates we have reviewed here that could not be written about in more ordinary and accessible terms, as we did in *Breaking Out*.

Moreover, at basis these ideas are *not* specialist ones, but rather ones people grapple with all the time using everyday language and conceptual terms. However, it has become increasingly the case that unless this specialist language is used, then ideas are not taken seriously as a contribution to feminist social theory. This was, we think, a large element in negative responses to the original *Breaking Out*, and it underpins our use of a very different rhetorical style in what we have written for this second edition. That is, we wrote the original *Breaking Out* in such a way that highly complex epistemological ideas were dealt with in accessible everyday language – like Audre Lorde (1984), we felt that you cannot 'dismantle the master's house using the master's tools' – and for us, key among the master's tools is the mystification of 'science', so that not only do many people feel alienated from it, but they also fail to recognize their own behaviours as actually 'researching' and 'theorizing'.

While we are still convinced by this analysis, we also recognize that academic feminism is considerably more professionalized now than it was then, and that, in effect, it has become necessary to participate in its language-games in order to be taken seriously as a member of its epistemic community. Some readers may see this as a convenient selling-out on our part, others may think that at long last we have seen the light and are behaving as 'proper academics'. We see it as a case of 'beating them at their own game': if the debates of academic feminism are to be carried out in the medium of a language as complexly baroque as Old German (and sometimes as silly as Franglais), then we intend to help as many as possible to become proficient speakers of it, but not believers in it.

Third, the spread of this new theoretical meta-language into feminist debates brings with it not only the greater visibility of feminist philosophy, but also the proposal that feminist philosophy can provide foundational underpinnings to the existence and activities of a range of 'on the ground' feminisms (e.g. Sawicki, 1986). Although not necessarily a widely shared ambition, none the less such claims should alert us to the possibilities therein for the creation of new academic feminist élites and attendant hierarchies of knowledges and languages. We need to open up, as a preliminary to dismantling, such hierarchies, not construct new ones. Moreover, we need to proclaim as loudly as possible that no such foundational role is *possible*, for social life is such that no one feminist grounding for knowledge can or should exist.

And, fourth, we must beware of a fetishistic attachment (something common among academics) to such a specialized language and its accompanying language-games regardless of its practical 'in life' utility or lack of it. That is, feminist praxis should be the goal – an enhanced political engagement, rather than a preoccupation with textuality and intertextuality for its own sake. We also need to keep in mind that a part (but not the whole) of such a praxis is a feminist *political* engagement within *academic life itself*: we are here to change it.

In changing academic life, academic feminism must carve out a truly feminist approach to theorizing who produces knowledge, under what circumstances and in what ways, and by what means countervailing knowledge-claims are dealt with. Moreover, in doing this, it must do its utmost to ensure that this feminist epistemology, ontology and ethic becomes accepted as *the* epistemology that underpins *all* knowledge-production and no matter by whom produced. Consistently from the writing of *Breaking Out* to now, we have advanced the view that if academic feminism is to have a radical and permanent impact on academia then it must make its intervention at the most fundamental and centrally important level of academic life: that which is concerned with theorizing the nature of 'knowledge' itself. We see our feminist fractured foundationalist epistemology in such terms. Academic feminism must ensure, at long last, that knowledge has a human face and a feeling heart.

NOTES

1 To a considerable extent these changes in the discipline in Britain have been underpinned and supported by the British Sociological Association (BSA). Organizationally through its executive committee and sub-committees and also through its journals (but not necessarily its study groups), feminist involvement in the BSA has been central for around twenty years. Immense advantages have ensued for the discipline and generally for feminists within it; but sometimes with ironic consequences for those particular women involved in the BSA, for spending time on changing the professional association has meant time deducted from research and publication – and it remains these, rather than 'people work', that lead to public recognition and promotion.

2 We prefer to refer to this using the terminology of production rather than 'discovery': knowledge about both the social and the 'natural' world does not exist independent of its construction and interpretation by human inquirers; there is nothing about social life to be 'discovered', only knowledges to be produced through the labour processes of particular epistemic communities.

3 As we argue later, we reject traditional foundationalist separations between mind and body.

4 Many feminists are equally concerned with spirit as part of ontology, and with providing the analytic grounds to a feminist ethic so positioned. We are aware of this work but have not included it here.

5 We have yet to find self-identified cultural feminists – the term has comparatively recently come into existence as a critics' term which gathers together people, work and ideas they wish to criticize, which they do by assigning shared characteristics to actually highly diverse practices.

6 And for us 'historiography' includes not only present-day writing about the past – 'history' – but also the various kinds of documents

that such histories work with and are predicated upon – those small shreds of some highly partial aspects of the past that remain.
7 The empowerment of readers is a central concern of Stanley (1992b).

References and further reading

Abu-Lughod, L. (1990), 'Can there be a feminist ethnography?', *Women & Performance*, 5: 7–27.

Alcoff, L. (1988), 'Cultural feminism versus post-structuralism: the identity crisis in feminist theory', *Signs*, 13: 405–36.

Alexander, S. and Taylor, B. (1981), 'In defence of "patriarchy" ', in R. Samuel (ed.) *People's History and Socialist Theory*, Routledge, London, pp. 370–3.

Allen, J. (ed.) (1990), *Lesbian Philosophies and Cultures*, State University of New York Press, New York (esp. chs by Ferguson, pp. 63–88; Penelope, pp. 89–108; Tallen, pp. 241–57; Zita, pp. 327–45).

Allen, S., Sanders, L. and Wallis, J. (eds) (1974), *Conditions of Illusion*, Feminist Books, Leeds.

Altman, D et al. (1989), *Which Homosexuality? Essays from the International Scientific Conference on Gay and Lesbian Studies*, Gay Men's Press, London.

Ardener, S. (ed) (1975), *Perceiving Women*, Dent, London.

A Woman's Place, Women's Research and Resource Centre and Women's Liberation Movement National Information Service (1976), *Women's Liberation: An Introduction*, AWP et al., London.

A Woman's Place, Women's Research and Resource Centre and Women's Liberation Movement National Information Service (1978), *Supplement to Women's Liberation: An Introduction*, AWP et al., London.

Bannister, D. (1966), 'Psychology as an exercise in paradox', *Bulletin of the British Psychological Society*, 19: 21–6, quoted in D. Bannister, and F. Fransella (1971), *Inquiring Man*, Penguin, Harmondsworth.

Barrett, M. (1979), 'The concept of ideology in contemporary feminist analysis' unpub. paper, BSA Theory Group, Manchester.

Barrett, M. (1980), *Women's Oppression Today: Problems in Marxist Feminist Analysis*, Verso, London.

Barrett, M. (1988), *Women's Oppression Today: The Marxist/Feminist Encounter* (revised edition), Verso, London.

Barrett, M. (1991), *The Politics of Truth: From Marx to Foucault*, Polity Press, Cambridge.

Bartky, S. (1977), 'Toward a phenomenology of feminist consciousness' in M. Vetterling-Braggin, F. Elliston and J. English (eds), *Feminism and Philosophy*, Littlefield, Adams, New Jersey, pp. 22–37.

Barwell, I. (1990), 'Feminine perspectives and narrative points of view', *Hypatia*, 5: 63–75.

de Beauvoir, S. (1949), *The Second Sex*, Penguin, Harmondsworth.

Bell, C. and Newby, H. (eds) (1977), *Doing Sociological Research*, Allen & Unwin, London.

Bell, N. K. (1989), 'Women and AIDS: too little, too late?' *Hypatia*, 4: 3–22.

Bernard, J. (1973), 'My four revolutions: an autobiographical history of the American Sociological Association', *American Journal of Sociology*, 78: 773–91.

Bierstedt, R. (1966), 'Sociology and general education', in C. Page (ed.) *Sociology and Contemporary Education*, Random House, New York, pp. 141–53.

Blumer, H. (1969), *Symbolic Interactionism*, Prentice-Hall, New Jersey.

Bordo, S. (1986), 'The Cartesian masculinization of thought', *Signs*, 11: 439–56.

Bordo, S. (1989), 'The body and the reproduction of femininity', in A. Jaggar and S. Bordo (eds) *Gender/Body/Knowledge: Feminist Reconstructions of Being and Knowing*, Rutgers University Press, New Brunswick, NJ, pp. 13–33.

Bowles, G. and Duelli-Klein, R. (eds) (1980), *Theories of Women's Studies*, Women's Studies, University of California, Berkeley.

Bowles, G. and Klein, R. D. (eds) (1983), *Theories of Women's Studies*, Routledge, London.

Briggs, J. (1970), *Never in Anger*, Harvard University Press.

Bristol Women's Studies Group (1979), *Half the Sky*, Virago, London.

Broverman, I., Broverman, D., Clarkson, F., Rosenkrantz, P. and Vogel, S. (1970), 'Sex role stereotypes and clinical judgements of mental health', *Journal of Consulting and Clinical Psychology*, 34: 1–7.

Brownmiller, S. (1975), *Against Our Will*, Secker & Warburg, London.

Bruley, S. (1976), *Women Awake: The Experience of Consciousness-Raising*, Bruley, London.

Brunsdon, C. (1978), 'It is well known that by nature women are inclined to be rather personal', in Women's Studies Group (eds), *Women Take Issue*, Hutchinson, London, pp. 18–34.

Bunch, C. (1989 [1975]), 'Not for lesbians only', in S. A. Gunew (ed.) *Reader in Feminist Knowledge*, Routledge, London, pp. 319–25.

Butler, J. (1988), 'The body politics of Julia Kristeva', *Hypatia*, 3: 104–18.

Butler, J. (1989), 'Gendering the body: de Beauvoir's philosophical contribution', in A. Garry and M. Pearsall (eds) *Women, Knowledge and Reality*, Allen & Unwin, London, pp. 253–62.

Butler, J. (1990), *Gender Trouble: Feminism and the Subversion of Identity*, Routledge, London.

Cain, M. (1990), 'Realist philosophies and standpoint epistemologies or feminist criminology as a successor science', in L. Gelsthorpe and A. Morris (eds) *Feminist Perspectives in Criminology*, Open University Press, Buckingham, pp. 124–40.

Caine, B., Grosz, E. and Lepervanche, M. de (1988), *Crossing Boundaries: Feminisms and the Critique of Knowledges*, Allen & Unwin, Sydney.

Campaign for Homosexual Equality (CHE) (1972), *Introducing CHE*, Campaign for Homosexual Equality, Manchester.

Card, C. (1986), 'Oppression and resistance: Frye's politics of reality', *Hypatia*, 1: 149–66.

Chester, G. (1979), 'I call myself a radical feminist', in Organising Collective (eds), *Feminist Practice: Notes From The Tenth Year*, In Theory Press, London, pp. 12–15.

Chetwynd, J. (1975), 'The effects of sex bias in psychological research', in J. Chetwynd (ed.), *The Role of Psychology in the Propagation of Female Stereotypes*, Proceedings of the British Psychological Society Symposium, Nottingham, pp. 3–5.

Chetwynd, J. and Hartnett, O. (eds) (1978), *The Sex Role System*, Routledge & Kegan Paul, London, pp. 1–3.

Chodorow, N. (1978), *The Reproduction of Mothering*, University of California Press, Berkeley.

Christian, B. (1985), *Black Feminist Criticism*, Pergamon Press, New York.

Christian, B. (1988), 'The race for theory', *Feminist Studies*, 14: 67–79.

Cixous, H. (1981a), 'Castration or decapitation?' *Signs*, 4: 843–54.

Cixous, H. (1981b), 'The laugh of the Medusa', in E. Marks, and I. de Courtivron (eds) *New French Feminisms*, Schocken Books, New York, pp. 245–64.

Cliff. M. (1980), *Claiming an Identity They Taught Me to Despise*, Persephone Press, Watertown, Massachusetts.

Code, L. (1989), 'Experience, knowledge and responsibility', in A. Garry and M. Pearsall (eds) *Women, Knowledge and Reality*, Allen & Unwin, London, pp. 157–72.

Cohen, C. (1986), 'The feminist sexuality debate: ethics and politics', *Hypatia*, 1: 71–86.

Collins, P. H. (1990), *Black Feminist Thought*, Harper Collins, London (esp. pp. 201–20).

Comer, L. (1974), *Wedlocked Women*, Feminist Press, Leeds.

Coulson, M. (1972), 'Role: a redundant concept in sociology?', in J. Jackson (ed.), *Role*, Cambridge University Press, pp. 107–28.

Coulter, J. (1975), 'Perceptual accounts and interpretive asymmetries', *Sociology*, 9: 385–96.

Coulter, J. (1977), 'Transparencies of mind', *Philosophy of the Social Sciences*, 7: 321–50.

Coward, R., Lipshitz, S. and Corrie, E. (1976), 'Psychoanalysis and patriarchal structures', in Women's Publishing Collective (eds), *Papers on Patriarchy*, WPC/PDC, London, pp. 6–20.

Currie, D. (1988), 'Re-thinking what we do and how we do it', *Canadian Review of Sociology and Anthropology*, 25: 231–53.

Curtin, D. (1991), 'Toward an ecological ethic of care', *Hypatia*, 6: 60–74.

Dalston Study Group (1976), 'Was the Patriarchy Conference "patriarchal"?', in Women's Publishing Collective (eds), *Papers on Patriarchy*, WPC/PDC, London, pp. 76–80.

Daly, M. (1973), *Beyond God The Father*, Beacon Press, Boston.

Daly, M. (1975), *The Church And the Second Sex*, Harper Colophon, New York.

Daly, M. (1978), *Gyn/Ecology*, Women's Press, London.

Daniels, A. (1975), 'Feminist perspectives in sociological research', in M. Millman and R. Kanter (eds), *Another Voice*, Anchor, New York, pp. 340–80.

Delmar, R. (1972), 'What is feminism?' in M. Wandor (ed.), *The Body Politic*, Stage 1, London, pp. 116–20.

Denzin, N. (1972), 'The research act', in J. Manis and B. Meltzer (eds), *Symbolic Interactionism*, Allyn & Bacon, Boston, pp. 340–80.

Dill, B. T. (1983), 'Race, class and gender: prospects for an all-inclusive sisterhood', *Feminist Studies*, 9: 131–50.

Duberman, M., Vicinus, M. and Chauncey, G. (eds) (1989), *Hidden From History: Reclaiming the Gay and Lesbian Past*, Penguin, Harmondsworth (esp. chs by Boswell, pp. 17–36; Halperin, pp. 37–53; Padgug, pp. 54–64).

Duelli-Klein, R. (1980), 'How to do what we want to do: thoughts about feminist methodology' in G. Bowles and R. Duelli-Klein (eds), *Theories of Women's Studies*, Women's Studies, University of California, Berkeley, pp. 48–64.

Ehrlich, C. (1976), *The Conditions of Feminist Research*, Research Group One, report no. 21, Baltimore.

Eichler, M. (1979), 'The origin of sex inequality', *Women's Studies International Quarterly*, 2: 329–46.

Eichler, M. (1980), *The Double Standard*, Croom Helm, London.

Engels, F. (1972), *The Origin of the Family, Private Property and the State*, Lawrence & Wishart, London.

Faderman, L. (1979), *Surpassing the Love of Men*, Junction Books, London.

Faderman, L. (1991), *Odd Girls and Twilight Lovers: A History of Lesbian Life in Twentieth Century America*, Columbia University Press, New York.

Firestone, S. (1970), *The Dialectic of Sex*, Paladin, St. Albans.

Firestone, S. (1971), 'On American feminism', in V. Gornick and B. Moran (eds), *Woman in Sexist Society*, Mentor, New York, pp. 665–86.

Fletcher, C. (1974), *Beneath The Surface*, Routledge & Kegan Paul, London.

Frankenberg, R. (1966), *Communities in Britain*, Penguin, Harmondsworth.

Freeman, C. (1974), 'Introduction to "domestic labour and wage labour" ' in *Women and Socialism Conference Paper 3*, pp. 1–6.

Freeman, J. (1970), *The Tyranny of Structurelessness*, Kingston Group of the Anarchist Workers Association, Hull.

Freeman, J. (1975), *The Politics of Women's Liberation*, Longmans, New York.

Friedan, B. (1963), *The Feminine Mystique*, Penguin, Harmondsworth.

Frye, M. (1983), *The Politics of Reality: Essays in Feminist Theory*, Crossing Press, New York, (esp. pp. 152–74).

Fuss, D. (1989), *Essentially Speaking: Feminism, Nature & Difference*, Routledge, London (esp. pp. 1–21, 97–112, 113–19).

Game, A. (1991), *Undoing the Social: Towards a Deconstructive Sociology*, Open University Press, Buckingham.

Gardiner, J. (1974), 'Women's domestic labour', in *Women and Socialism Conference Paper 3*, pp. 7–17.

Garfinkel, H. (1967), *Studies in Ethnomethodology*, Prentice-Hall, New Jersey.

Gatens, M. (1988), 'Towards a feminist theory of the body', in B. Caine, E. Grosz and M. de Lepervanche (eds) *Crossing Boundaries: Feminisms and the Critique of Knowledges*, Allen & Unwin, Wellington, pp. 59–70.

Gay Liberation Front (1971), *Manifesto*, GLF, London.

Gelsthorpe, L. (1990), 'Feminist methodology in criminology: a new approach or old wine in new bottles?', in L. Gelsthorpe and A. Morris (eds) *Feminist Perspectives in Criminology*, Open University Press, Buckingham, pp. 89–106.

Georges, R. and Jones, M. (1980), *People Studying People*, University of California Press.

Gilligan, C. (1982), *In a Different Voice*, Harvard University Press, Cambridge, Massachusetts.

Glaser, B. and Strauss, A. (1968), *The Discovery of Grounded Theory*, Weidenfeld & Nicolson, London.

Goffman, E. (1959), *The Presentation of Self in Everyday Life*, Penguin, Harmondsworth.

Goffman, E. (1976), *Gender Advertisements*, Macmillan, London.

Gordon, L. (1990a), 'Reply to Joan Scott's review', *Signs*, 15: 852–3.

Gordon, L. (1990b), 'Review of Joan Scott's Gender and the Politics of History', *Signs*, 15: 853–8.

Govier, T. (1992), 'Trust, distrust and feminist theory', *Hypatia*, 7: 16–33.

Greer, G. (1970), *The Female Eunuch*, Paladin, St Albans.

Grosz, E. (1986), 'Philosophy, subjectivity and the body: Kristeva and Irigaray', in C. Pateman and E. Grosz (eds) *Feminist Challenges: Social and Political Theory*, Allen & Unwin, Wellington, pp. 125–43.

Grosz, E. (1990a), 'A note on essentialism and difference', in S. Gunew (ed.) *Feminist Knowledge: Critique and Construct*, Routledge, London, pp. 332–44.

Grosz, E. (1990b), 'Contemporary theories of power and subjectivity', in S. Gunew (ed.) *Feminist Knowledge: Critique and Construct*, Routledge, London, pp. 59–120.

Halfpenny, P. (1979), 'Review of "Doing Sociological Research" edited by Bell and Newby', *Sociological Review*, 27: 382–3.

Haraway, D. (1988), 'Situated knowledges: the science question in feminism and the privilege of partial perspective', *Feminist Studies*, 14: 575–99.

Harding, S. (1986), *The Science Question in Feminism*, Open University Press, Milton Keynes.

Harding, S. (ed.) (1987), *Feminism and Methodology*, Open University Press, Milton Keynes (esp. pp. 1–14, 181–90).

Harding, S. (1991), *Whose Science, Whose Knowledge?*, Open University Press, Buckingham.

Hartley, R. (1966), 'A developmental view of female sex-role identification', in B. Biddle and E. Thomas (eds), *Role Theory*, John Wiley, New York, pp. 354–61.

Hartnett, O. *et al.* (eds) (1979), *Sex-Role Stereotyping*, Tavistock, London.

Hartsock, N. (1987), 'The feminist standpoint', in S. Harding (ed.) *Feminism and Methodology*, Open University Press, Milton Keynes, pp. 157–80.

Hekman, S. (1991), 'Reconstructing the subject: feminism, modernism, and postmodernism', *Hypatia*, 6: 44–63.

Heldke, L. (1988), 'Recipes for theory making', *Hypatia*, 3: 15–29.

Henley, N. (1977), *Body Politics*, Prentice-Hall, New Jersey.

Himmelweit, S., McKenzie, M. and Tomlin, A. (1976), 'Why Theory?', in Women's Publishing Collective (eds), *Papers on Patriarchy*, WPC/PDC London, pp. 1–5.

Hoagland, S. L. (1988a), 'Lesbian ethics; beginning remarks', *Women's Studies International Forum*, 11: 531–44.

Hoagland, S. L. (1988b), *Lesbian Ethics: Toward New Value*, Institute of Lesbian Studies, Palo Alto, California.

Hochschild, A. R. (1975), 'The sociology of feeling and emotions', in M. Millman and R. M. Kanter (eds) *Another Voice: Feminist Perspectives on Social Life and Social Science*, Anchor Books, New York, pp. 280–307.

Hollway, W. (1989), *Subjectivity and Method in Psychology: Gender, Meaning and Science*, Sage, London.

Holmes, H. B. (1989), 'A call to heal medicine', *Hypatia*, 4: 1–8.

hooks, b. (1981), *Ain't I a Woman: Black Women and Feminism*, South End Press, Boston, Massachusetts.

hooks, b. (1984), *Feminist Theory: From Margin to Center*, South End Press, Boston, Massachusetts.

hooks, b. (1989), *Talking Back: Thinking Feminist, Thinking Black*, Sheba Feminist Publishers, London.

Hypatia (1991), 6:3 special issue 'Feminism and the Body'.

Irigaray, L. (1980), 'When our lips speak together', *Signs*, 6: 4–28.

Irigaray, L. (1981), 'And the one doesn't stir without the other', *Signs*, 7: 60–7.

Irigaray, L. (1985), *This Sex Which Is Not One*, Cornell University Press, Ithaca, New York.

Jagger, A. (1977), 'Political philosophies of women's liberation', in M. Vetterling-Braggin, F. Elliston and J. English (eds), *Feminism and Philosophy*, Littlefield, Adams, New Jersey, pp. 5–21.

Jaggar, A. (1983), *Feminist Politics and Human Nature*, Rowman & Allanheld, Totowa (esp. 'Feminist politics and epistemology: justifying feminist theory', pp. 353–94).

Jaggar, A. (1989), 'Love and knowledge: emotion in feminist epistemology', in A. Jaggar and S. Bordo (eds) *Gender/Body/Knowledge:*

Feminist Reconstructions of Being and Knowing, Rutgers University Press, New Brunswick, pp. 145–71.

Jenkins, L. and Kramer, C. (1978), Small group process: learning from women', *Women's Studies International Quarterly*, 1:67–84.

Johnson, J. (1977), *Doing Field Research*, Free Press, New York.

Johnson, V. (1975), *Violence in Marriage*, unpub. MA thesis, University of New South Wales, quoted in C. Bell and H. Newby, *Doing Sociological Research*, Allen & Unwin, London, p. 9.

Kaplan, A. (1964), *The Conduct of Inquiry*, Intertext Books, Aylesbury.

Kelly, A. (1978), 'Feminism and research', *Women's Studies International Quarterly*, 1:225–32.

Kittay, E. F. (1988), 'Woman as metaphor', *Hypatia*, 3: 63–86.

Kleiber, N. and Light, L. (1978), *Caring For Ourselves*, University of British Columbia.

Kohlberg, L. (1966), 'A cognitive-developmental analysis of children's sex-role concepts and attitudes', in E. Maccoby (ed.), *The Development of Sex Differences*, Tavistock, London, pp. 82–173.

Komarovsky, M. (1973), 'Some problems of role analysis', *American Sociological Review*, 38: 649–62.

Kramarae, C. and Spender, D. (1992) *The Knowledge Explosion*, Teachers College Press, Columbia, New York.

Kristeva, J. (1981), 'Women's time', *Signs*, 7: 13–35.

Kristeva, J. (1982), *Desire in Language*, Columbia University Press, New York.

Kuhn, M. (1960), 'Self-attitudes by age, sex and professional training', *Sociological Quarterly*, 1: 39–55.

Kuhn, M. and McPartland, T. (1954), 'An empirical investigation of self-attitudes', *American Sociological Review*, 19: 68–76.

Kuhn, T. (1962), *The Structure of Scientific Revolutions*, University of Chicago Press.

Laing, R. (1960), *The Divided Self*, Penguin, Harmondsworth.

Laing, R. and Esterson, A. (1964), *Sanity, Madness and the Family*, Penguin, Harmondsworth.

Lather, P. (1991), *Getting Smart: Feminist Research and Pedagogy With/In the Postmodern*, Routledge, New York.

de Lauretis, T. (1986), 'Feminist studies/critical studies: issues, terms, and contexts', in T. de Lauretis (ed.) *Feminist Studies/Critical Studies*, Indiana University Press, Bloomington, p. 1–19.

Lee, J. (1984), 'Innocent victims and evil doers', *Women's Studies International Forum*, 7: 69–73.

Leeds Revolutionary Feminist Group (1979), 'Every single academic feminist owes her livelihood to the WLM', unpub. paper, WRRC Summer School, Bradford.

Levine, C. (1974), *Tyranny of Tyranny*, Rising Free, London.

Light, L. (1978), 'Powerlessness and power in the North American radical feminist movement', paper given at the IXth World Congress of Sociology, Uppsala.

Lofland, J. (1971), *Analyzing Social Settings*, Wadsworth, California.

Lorde, A. (1982), *Zami: A New Spelling of My Name*, Sheba Feminist Publishers, London.

Lorde, A. (1984), *Sister Outsider*, Crossing Press, New York.

Lorde, A. (1985), *The Cancer Journals*, Sheba Feminist Publishers, London.

Lugones, M. (1987), 'Playfulness, "world"-travelling, and loving perception', *Hypatia*, 2: 3–19.

Maccoby, E. and Jacklin, C. (1975), *The Psychology of Sex Differences*, Stamford University Press.

Magas, B. *et al.* (1974), 'Some critical notes on Wally Secombe's "The housewife and her labour under capitalism" ', in *Women and Socialism Conference Paper 3*, pp. 26–33.

Martin, E. (1987), *The Woman in the Body*, Open University Press, Milton Keynes.

Mead, G. (1934), *Mind, Self and Society*, University of Chicago.

Mies, M. (1978), 'Methodological postulates for women's studies, exemplified through a project dealing with violence against women', *Beitrage zur Feministischen Theorie und Praxis*, 1: 41–64.

Millett, K. (1969), *Sexual Politics*, Abacus, London.

Mitchell, J. (1971), *Women's Estate*, Penguin, Harmondsworth.

Mitchell, J. and Oakley, A. (eds) (1976), *The Rights and Wrongs of Women*, Penguin, Harmondsworth, pp. 7–15.

Morgan, D. (1981), 'Men, masculinity and the process of sociological enquiry', in H. Roberts (ed.), *Doing Feminist Research*, Routledge & Kegan Paul, London, pp. 83–113.

Morgan, R. (1977), *Going Too Far*, Vintage Books, New York.

Morris, M. (1988), 'Introduction: feminism, reading, postmodernism', in *The Pirate's Fiancée: Feminism, Reading, Postmodernism*, Verso, London, pp. 1–16.

Muraro, L. (1987), 'On conflicts and differences between women: a reply to Sawicki', *Hypatia*, 2: 139–42.

Mussen, P. (1971), 'Early sex-role development', in D. Goslin (ed.), *Handbook of Socialization Theory and Research*, Rand McNally, Chicago, pp. 707–31.

Narayan, U. (1988), 'Working together across difference', *Hypatia*, 3: 31–47.

Nye, A. (1986), 'Preparing the way for a feminist praxis', *Hypatia*, 1: 101–16.

Oakley, A. (1972), *Sex, Gender and Society*, Temple Smith, London.

Oakley, A. (1974), *The Sociology of Housework*, Martin Robertson, London.

O'Neale, S. (1986), 'Inhibiting midwives, usurping creators: the struggling emergeance of black women in American fiction', in T. de Lauretis (ed.) *Feminist Studies/Critical Studies*, Indiana University Press, Indianapolis, pp. 139–56.

Page, M. (1978), 'Socialist feminism – a political alternative?' *M/F*, 2: 32–42.

Parsons, T. (1956a), 'The American family: its relationship to personality and the social structure', in T. Parsons and R. Bales (eds), *Family:*

Socialization and Interaction Process, Routledge & Kegan Paul, London, pp. 3–33.

Parsons, T. (1965b), 'Family structure and the socialization of the child', in T. Parsons and R. Bales (eds), *Family: Socialization and Interaction Process*, Routledge & Kegan Paul, London, pp. 35–131.

Parsons, T. (1956c), 'The organization of personality as a system of action', in T. Parsons and R. Bales (eds), *Family: Socialization and Interaction Process*, Routledge & Kegan Paul, London, pp. 133–86.

Parsons, T. (1956d), 'The mechanisms of personality functioning with special reference to socialization' in T. Parsons and R. Bales (eds), *Family: Socialization and Interaction Process*, Routledge & Kegan Paul, London, pp. 187–257.

Parsons, T. and Bales, R. (eds) (1956), *Family: Socialization and Interaction Process*, Routledge & Kegan Paul, London.

Platt, J. (1976), *Realities of Social Research*, Sussex University Press.

Pollner, M. (1975), 'The very coinage of your brain: some features of reality disjunctures and their resolution', *Philosophy of the Social Sciences*, 5: 411–30.

Poovey, M. (1988), 'Feminism and deconstruction', *Feminist Studies*, 14: 51–65.

Popitz, H. (1972), 'The concept of social role as an element of sociological theory', in J. Jackson (ed.), *Role*, Cambridge University Press, pp. 11–39.

Popper, K. (1972), *Objective Knowledge*, Oxford University Press.

Purdy, L. (1986), 'Nature and nurture: a false dichotomy', *Hypatia*, 1: 167–74.

Ramazonaglu, C. (1986), 'Ethnocentrism and socialist-feminist theory: a response to Barrett & McIntosh', *Feminist Review*, 22: 83–6.

Reinharz, S. (1979), *On Becoming A Social Scientist*, Jossey-Bass, San Francisco.

Reinharz, S. (1983), 'Experiential research: a contribution to feminist theory', in G. Bowles and R. D. Klein (eds) *Theories of Women's Studies*, Routledge, London, pp. 162–91.

Rich, A. (1979), *On Lies, Secrets and Silence*, Virago, London.

Rich, A. (1980a), 'Disloyal to civilization: feminism, racism, gynophobia', in *On Lies, Secrets & Silence*, Virago, London, pp. 275–310.

Rich, A. (1980b), 'Compulsory heterosexuality and lesbian existence', *Signs*, 5: 631–60.

Riley, D. (1987), *'Am I That Name?' Feminism and the Category of 'Women' in History*, Macmillan, London.

Roberts, C. and Millar, E. (1978), 'Feminism, socialism and abortion', *Women's Studies International Quarterly*, 1: 3–14.

Roberts, H. (1978), 'Women and their doctors', unpub. paper, SSRC Workshop on Qualitative Methodology, Warwick.

Roberts, H. (ed.) (1981), *Doing Feminist Research*, Routledge, London.

Roberts, J. (ed.) (1976), *Beyond Intellectual Sexism*, David McKay, New York.

Rosaldo, M. and Lamphere, L. (eds) (1974), *Women, Culture and Society*, Stamford University Press.

Rose, H. (1983), 'Hand, brain and heart: a feminist epistemology for the natural sciences', *Signs*, 9: 73–90.

Rosenkrantz, P., Vogel, S., Bee, H., Broverman, I, and Broverman, D. (1968), 'Sex role stereotypes and self-concepts in college students', *Journal of Consulting and Clinical Psychology*, 32: 287–95.

Rothenberg, P. (1990), 'The construction, deconstruction, and reconstruction of difference', *Hypatia*, 5: 42–57.

Rowbotham, S. (1973), *Woman's Consciousness, Man's World*, Penguin, Harmondsworth.

Rowbotham, S. (1979), 'The women's movement and organising for socialism', in S. Rowbotham, L. Segal and H. Wainwright (eds), *Beyond The Fragments*, Newcastle Socialist Centre and Islington Community Press, London, pp. 9–87.

Rowbotham, S. (1981), 'The trouble with "patriarchy" ' in R. Samuel (ed.) *People's History and Socialist Theory*, Routledge, London, pp. 364–9.

Rowe, M. (1975), 'False consciousness coops people up', *Spare Rib*, 30: 6–9.

Rush, F. (1974), 'The sexual abuse of children', in N. Connell, and C. Wilson, (eds), *Rape: The First Sourcebook For Women*, Plume Books, New York, pp. 64–75.

Ruth, S. (1987), 'Bodies and souls/sex, sin and the senses in patriarchy', *Hypatia*, 2: 149–63.

Sawicki, J. (1986), 'Foucault and feminism: towards a politics of difference', *Hypatia*, 1: 23–36.

Schutz, A. (1962), 'Common-sense and scientific interpretations of human action', in *Collected Papers I: The Problem of Social Reality*, Martinus Nijhoff, The Hague, pp. 3–47.

Schutz, A. (1972), *The Phenomenology of the Social World*, Heinemann, London.

Scott, J. (1988), *Gender and the Politics of History*, Columbia University Press, New York.

Scott, J. (1990a), 'Review of Linda Gordon's Heroes of their own Lives', *Signs*, 15: pp. 848–52.

Scott, J. (1990b), 'Reply to Linda Gordon', *Signs*, 15: 859–60.

Sebestyen, A. (1979), 'Tendencies in the Movement: then and now', in Organizing Collective (eds), *Feminist Practice: Notes From The Tenth Year*, In Theory Press, London, pp. 16–23.

Sedgwick, E. K. (1991), *Epistemology of the Closet*, Harvester Wheatsheaf, New York (esp. pp. 67–90).

Sharpe, S. (1976), *Just Like A Girl*, Penguin, Harmondsworth.

Sherwin, S. (1989), 'Philosophical methodology and feminist methodology: are they compatible?', in A. Garry and M. Pearsall (eds) *Women, Knowledge and Reality*, Allen & Unwin, London, pp. 21–35.

Sherwin, S. (1989), 'Feminism and medical ethics: two different approaches to contextual ethics', *Hypatia*, 4: 57–72.

Smart, C. (1976), *Women, Crime and Criminology*, Routledge & Kegan Paul, London.

Smith, D. (1974), 'Women's perspective as a radical critique of sociology', *Sociological Quarterly*, 44: 7–13.

Smith, D. (1978), 'K is Mentally Ill', *Sociology*, 12: 23–53.

Spacks, P. (1976), *The Female Imagination*, Allen & Unwin, London.

Spare Rib (1978), 'Radical and socialist feminism – what's behind the labels?', *Spare Rib*, 82: 42–5.

Spelman, E. V. (1988), *Inessential Woman: Problems of Exclusion in Feminist Thought*, Routledge, London (esp. pp. 133–59, 160–87).

Spender, D. (1978), 'Educational research and the feminist perspective', unpub. paper, British Educational Research Association Conference on 'Women, Education and Research', University of Leicester.

Spender, D. (ed.) (1981), *Men's Studies Modified*, Pergamon, Oxford.

Stacey, J. (1988), 'Can there be a feminist ethnography?', *Women's Studies International Forum*, 11: 21–7.

Stanley, L. (1974), 'Sexual politics in sociology: a content analysis of three sociology journals', unpub. paper, University of Salford.

Stanley, L. (1976), *The Sociology of Gender*, unpub. PhD thesis, University of Salford.

Stanley, L. (1981), ' "The problem of women and leisure" – an ideological construct and a radical feminist alternative', in Centre for Leisure Studies (ed.), *Leisure in the 1980s*, University of Salford.

Stanley, L. (1982), ' "Male needs": the problems and problems of working with gay men', in S. Friedman and E. Sarah (eds), *On The Problem of Men*, Women's Press, London, pp. 190–203.

Stanley, L. (1988), 'Rescuing "women" in history from feminist deconstructionism', *Women's Studies International Forum*, 11: 151–7.

Stanley, L. (ed.) (1990a), *Feminist Praxis: Research, Theory and Epistemology in Feminist Sociology*, Routledge, London.

Stanley, L. (1990b), 'Feminist praxis and the academic mode of production', in L. Stanley (ed.) *Feminist Praxis: Research, Theory and Epistemology in Feminist Sociology*, Routledge, London, pp. 3–19.

Stanley, L. (1992a), *The Auto/Biographical I: The Theory and Practice of Feminist Auto/Biography*, Manchester University Press, Manchester.

Stanley, L, (1992b), 'Romantic friendship? Some issues in researching lesbian history and biography', *Women's History Review*, 1, 2, pp. 193–216.

Stanley, L. (1992c), 'Epistemological issues in researching lesbian history: the case of romantic friendship' in H. Hinds, A. Phoenix and J. Stacey (eds) *Working Out: New Directions for Women's Studies*, Falmer Press, Brighton, pp. 161–72.

Stanley, L. (1992d), 'The impact of feminism in sociology' in C. Kramarae and D. Spender (eds) *The Knowledge Explosion*, Teachers College Press, Columbia, New York, pp. 254–69.

Stanley, L. and Wise, S. (1979), Feminist research, feminist consciousness and experiences of sexism', *Women's Studies International Quarterly*, 2: 359–74.

Stanley, L. and Wise, S. (1980), ' "Societal reactions" and the "lesbian threat" ', unpub. paper, University of Manchester.

Stanley, L. and Wise, S. (1983), 'Back into the personal, or our attempt to construct "feminist research" ', in G. Bowles and R. D. Klein (eds) *Theories of Women's Studies*, Routledge, London, pp. 192–209.

Stanley, L. and Wise, S. (1990), 'Method, methodology and epistemology in feminist research processes', in L. Stanley (ed.) *Feminist Praxis: Research, Theory and Epistemology in Feminist Sociology*, Routledge, London, pp. 20–60.

Strathern, M. (1987), 'The limits of auto-ethnography', in A. Jackson (ed.) *Anthropology at Home*, Tavistock, London, pp. 16–37.

Thompson, E. (1978), *The Poverty of Theory*, Merlin Press, London.

Tobias, S. (1978), 'Women's studies: its origins, its organization and its prospects', *Women's Studies International Quarterly*, 1: 85–97.

Tong, R. (1989), 'Conclusion: standpoints and differences', in her *Feminist Thought: A Comprehensive Introduction*, Unwin, London, pp. 235–8.

Trinh, M. (1989), *Woman Native Other: Writing Postcoloniality and Feminism*, Indiana University Press, Bloomington (esp. pp. 79–116).

Tuana, N. (1983), 'Re-fusing nature/nurture', *Women's Studies International Forum*, 6: 621–32.

Tuana, N. (1986), 'A response to Purdy', *Hypatia*, 1: 175–8.

Tufnell Park Group (1972), 'Organizing ourselves', in M. Wandor (ed.), *The Body Politic*, Stage 1, London, pp. 103–6.

Vicinus, M. (1989), ' "They wonder to which sex I belong" ': the historical roots of the modern lesbian identity', in D. Altman *et al. Which Homosexuality? Essays from the International Scientific Conference on Gay and Lesbian Studies*, Gay Men's Press, London, pp. 171–98.

Walker, M. U. (1989), 'Moral understandings: alternative "epistemology" for a feminist ethics', *Hypatia*, 4: 15–28.

Wandor, M. (ed.) (1972), *The Body Politic*, Stage 1, London.

Weedon, C. (1987), *Feminist Practice and Poststructuralist Theory*, Blackwell, Oxford.

Weinreich, H. (1978), 'Sex-role socialization', in J. Chetwynd and O. Hartnett (eds), *The Sex-Role System*, Routledge & Kegan Paul, London, pp. 18–27.

Weitzman, L. (1979), *Sex Role Socialization*, Mayfield Publishing Company, California.

Whitbeck, C. (1989), 'A different reality: feminist ontology', in A. Garry and M. Pearsall (eds) *Women, Knowledge and Reality*, Allen & Unwin, London, pp. 51–76.

Whyte, W. (1955), *Street Corner Society*, University of Chicago Press.

Wilson, E. (1977), *Women and the Welfare State*, Tavistock, London.

Wilson, E. (1982), *Mirror Writing*, Virago Press, London.

Winnant, T. (1987), 'The feminist standpoint: a matter of language', *Hypatia*, 2: 123–48.

Wise, S. and Stanley, L. (1987), *Georgie Porgie: Sexual Harassment in Everyday Life*, Pandora Press, London.

Wittig, M. (1980a), 'The straight mind', *Feminist Issues*, 1(1): 103–11.

Wittig, M. (1980b), 'One is not born a woman', *Feminist Issues*, 1(2): 47–54.

Wittig, M. (1992), *The Straight Mind And Other Essays*, Harvester Wheatsheaf, Hemel Hempstead.

Wolff, J. (1990), *Feminine Sentences*, Polity Press, Cambridge.
Women's Campaign Committee (1974), *Women Together*, WCC, Manchester.
Woolf, V. (1931), 'Introductory letter' in A. Davin (ed.) (1977), *Life As We Have Known It,*, Virago, London, pp. xvii-xxxxi.
Worsley, P. (1980), *Marxism and Culture*, Occasional Paper no. 4, University of Manchester.
Wrong, D. (1961), 'The oversocialized conception of man in modern sociology', *American Sociological Review*, 26: 183-93.
Zita, J. (1988), 'Review essay: a critical analysis of Sandra Harding's The Science Question in Feminism', *Hypatia*, 3: 157-68.

Name index

Subject index